AF622009

BHARATIYA JANATA PARTY AND INDIA'S FOREIGN POLICY

BHARATIYA JANATA PARTY AND INDIA'S FOREIGN POLICY

DR. MADHUSUDAN MISHRA

UPPAL PUBLISHING HOUSE
NEW DELHI-110 002 (INDIA)

UPPAL PUBLISHING HOUSE
3, Ansari Road, Daryaganj, New Delhi - 110002
Phones: Off. 3273756, 3286571, Res. 2242884

© Dr. Madhusudan Mishra
First Published 1997
ISBN 81-85565-79-1

Printed in India

Published by : B.S. Uppal for Uppal Publishing House 3, Ansari Road, Daryaganj, New Delhi
Lasertypesetting by : DV Graphic Prints Pvt. Ltd., Karol Bagh, New Delhi - 110005 Phone : 5749531
Printed at : Arora Offset Press, 817, Guru Ram Das Nagar, Delhi-110092

PREFACE

The area of foreign policy constitutes the base of international politics. It is this area which reflects the internal stability of a country, conditioned by the fixed facts of geography and the fluid fact of economic interest. Because of this importance, it has been the area of writers' thrust. The present study is also a move in that direction but simultaneously it precludes the influence of other writers because of its particular theme thrust upon a broad spectrum. Moreover, it is distinctly different from the earlier works due to its scope and analysis. Though it is not claimed that it is unique, it is still a humble attempt in making an analysis of a specefic policy followed by a particular ruling elite in a particular period towards a particular country and the specefic response of a party thereafter.

While talking of international politics one should consider the foreign policies of other countries also. Dealing with India's foreign policy one cannot ignore the foreign policies of the United States, Russia and many other countries involved in a particular event. So, the foreign policies of all countries are intrisically related. So this work attempts to study the foreign policy of India in the nineties linking it with the foreign policies of the Super Powers. This work has been divided into five chapters keeping in view the special ramifications in national as well as international politics.

The first chapter deals with the policy of non-alignment. The policy of non-alignment is considered an elementary instrument in bringing peace in the world. Though at times imperialist forces attempted to disrupt it, the Non-Aligned Movement gained more popularity. It is argued that after the end of the Cold War the is no relevance of the movement has lost its relevance Moreover, by pursuing this policy, India did not join any bloc, East or West. There were many questions relating to the policy of non-alignment. So this study makes an attempt to study all these questions, the problems government faced and the stands taken by the government. The response the BJP, being a major opposition political party, has been taken into consideration.

The second chapter is an attempt to study the nuclear policy of India in the nineties. The nuclear issue has occupied a pre-eminent position both in national as well as international fields in the eighties. In the international field both the Super Powers were moving towards denuclearisation. In contrast, Third World countries were acquiring nuclear arms from the nuclear powers. So the danger of nuclear annihilation was very much there in the developing world. At this crucial juncture a study of India's nuclear policy is important. In this chapter an attempt has been made to study India's role in the process of disarmament, and how far India's peaceful nuclear option influenced others. This chapter also covers the role of the Bhartiya Janata Party, its approach and stand taken towards the nuclear policy pursued by the Indian government and suggestions to the government.

The third chapter of this work touches upon the arms trade and security. The causes that prompted India and its neighbouring countries to acquire arms, and the reasons of supplying arms to the Indian sub-continent by the Super Powers have been discussed. The crux of this chapter is based on what should be the remedies to deter all countries from conveying arms, what role the Indian government should play in these days of danger, what should be the role of the regional organisations like SAARC and what the NAM can do in this regard. The response of the BJP to the nuclear policy of India has also been reflected with its suggestions and criticisms and how far these suggestions are feasdele.

The fourth chapter highlights the problems of the Indian Ocean. This chapter postulates various possible reasons of the Super Powers and other big powers involvement in the Indian Ocean; political, economic, geographical and strategic. To what extent indulgence of Super Powers in the Indian Ocean brought danger to the littoral countries have also been dealt. Facing imminent dangers, the adjacent countries struggled for declaring it a Zone of Peace. This section descesse the attempts of the affected nations to make the Indian Ocean a peace zone in various seminars, conferences and in the UN and how far their interests have been fulfilled. The reactions of other powers not involved in the Indian Ocean have been discussed as well. As the process of stockpiling arms and ammunitions in the Ocean is still going on what policy the Indian government is following and should follow has been touched upon. The reaction of the BJP to the Indian Ocean policy of the government has been taken into account. The stand the BJP has taken on various occasions has also been on focussed.

The fifth chapter of this work looks at the foreign economic policy of India in the eighties. The trade relations with the Super Powers have been elaborated in this chapter. This section of the study deliberates the two-way bilateral economic relations between India and the Super Powers. This chapter indicates what were the benefits India received and also some difficulties it faced in the nineties. The response of the BJP, here too has also been analytically presented.

Thus, the present work seeks to discuss and analyse India's foreign relations with the Super Powers and critical assessment of its success and failures during the nineties. These years are also important with events such as the New Delhi Conference, Harare Conference, INF Talks, Geneva Talks, Reykjavik Meeting and many others which influenced India's foreign relations. So this study makes attempt to include all eventful issues those were important in this period. Nevertheless, this work is not confined only to political relations. Economic and Cultural relations between India and the Super Powers are also widely covered.

Madhusudan Mishra

ACKNOWLEDGEMENTS

I was sailing... sailing on the waters... I was tired... tired for months together. I was anxious to anchor earlier. He guided me through the vapor, encouraged me to zoom all the bothers. I cruised the boat to the harbour. I am indebted to my commodore... Prof. C.P. Bhambhri.

I was missing... mislaying my destination. He rectified me on the briny deep as a master. He showed me the Pole Star. I navigated without slightest puzzle. I am thankful to him... to my teacher Prof. A.P. Padhi.

I was moving in hot waters... floundering to see the creatures. They lessened my burden... sat with me, with the campas to trace out the tenor. I looked for them and they undermined the sandpaper. I came out of all perplexities. I am thankful to them for their kind contributions... to the librarians and staffs of JNU, NMML, ICWA, American library and Indian Investment Centre.

I was in deep waters. Nobody was there to share my moments... he whispered me... I entered into the cabin and took up the task. I am grateful to him... to Mr. K.N. Rao.

I was alone... sailing indefatigably days and night. They stretched their warmth hands... piloted me to overcome all Daltonisms. They inferred me... I am appreciative for their invaluable help and assistance... to my friends and elders.

I heard their words to anchor by all means. I was bemoaning and they consoled me. My exploration would have been out of grain but their generosity, gracious cooperation and encouragement. I preserve with special care the love I received from them. I am grateful to them... to my parents.

26th January, 1997
New Delhi

Madhusudan Mishra

CONTENTS

CHAPTER I

Policy of Non–Alignment

The national liberation movement in Asia and Africa, growing strength of Socialist countries, the disarray of world economic system, all together brought a new turn in India's foreign Policy. Soon after independence India found many Asian and African countries trying to follow the path of peaceful co-existence. From the beginning, India had played an active and constructive role in various international fora. "In fact India's growing participation in international fora has reflected two principles. First, the United Nations and subsequently the non-aligned movement gave impression to fundamental Indian beliefs in peaceful cooperation between nations, to decolonisation and to the achievement of full independence through economic development as well as political freedom".[1] Though non-alignment as a movement started in 1961, it was a national impulse much earlier. It had been a prominent feature of Indian foreign policy since independence. " Non-Alignment is not a value, non-alignment in not a goal, non-alignment is a policy instrument.[2]'' A foreign policy of Non-alignment means an "anti-imperialism, anti-colonial policy for the strengthening of colonial liberation movement, world peace, mutual cooperation among the equal entities"[3]. It symbolises mankind's search for peace and security among nations and determination to establish a new and equitable international economic, social and political order. It is a vital force for struggle against imperialism in all its forms and manifestations, and all other forms of foreign domination. Non-alignment inspires independent strategy for development and participation in international forums. The basic postulates of non-alignment are freedom, peace and economic prosperity and following these principles the non-aligned states are trying to stand on their own feet.

1. Bradnock, Robert W., *India's Foreign Policy* (London: Royal Institute of International Affairs, Routledge, 1990), p.86.
2. *Rajya Sabha Debates*, 7 December, 1983, col. 337.
3. Sardesai, S.G., *Why Communists* (Bombay : Popular Prakashan, 1966), pp. 87-88

As a concept, non-alignment does not mean neutrality in the classical sense. Nor does it simply imply equi-distance between two rival power blocs. It does not even imply equi-distance between two friendly nations when they are engaged in a dispute. It has never tried to create a third bloc. Apparently, it reconciles with world peace as peace is vital for the progress of mankind in this overarmed and turbulent world. It is an important point to note that there are several reasons which prompted the non-aligned states to work in cooperation. Historical, political and economic factors are responsible for forming a concrete bond among the newly liberated countries. In the past they were suffering from exploitation of the colonial powers, politically and economically. They were not prepared to sacrifice their hard-owned independence. So they wanted to keep themselves aloof from big power conflict without joining or supporting their war-drive aims. They, therefore, became "keen to develop their economies and become self-reliant in the shortest possible time and importantly, they needed peace inside their own countries and in the world outside"[4].

The idea relating to non-alignment first was conceived in 1947. Jawaharlal Nehru, vice-president of the interim government of India, made a radio broadcast on 7th September, 1946 which the provided basic framework to our policy of non-alignment. He said:

> "We propose as far as possible, to keep away from the power politics of groups, aligned against one another, which have led in the past to world wars and which may again lead to disasters of even vaster scales."[5]

But the NAM did not originate only to avoid wars. ''NAM is neither in the image of inter-imperialist rivalries of the west nor is it the example of proletarian internationalism. It is a mosaic of different social systems, of different cultures but united in their desire to survive and progress...... NAM represents a multilateral process of discussion and decision as different from the one seen in negotiations on issues of security, arms limitation and reduction....It is a process that extends its hands of cooperation to those who plead for a restructuring of international relations on the basis of equality, justice, cooperation, development and peace".[6] Thus, non-alignment, in substance, is an

4. Srivastava, Govind Narain (ed.), *Commemoration Volume*, New Delhi, Indian Institute for Non-aligned Studies, 1983, vol. I, Seventh Non-aligned Summit, New Delhi,p. 64

5. Misra, K.P., "India and Non-alignment", in G.N.Srivastava (ed.), n.4, p.73.

6. Gupta, Rakesh, "NAM and Disarmament", in V.D.Chopra (ed.), *NAM Summit: New Delhi to Harare* (New Delhi : Patriot, 1986), pp.87-88.

affirmation of independence. But at the same time, to assert independence other things are taken into consideration. For example, if national interest is undermined, if it is threatened by pursuing the policy of non-alignment, then primary consideration is given to national interest and policies are moulded, diluted or manipulated accordingly. Moreover, a country cannot be non-aligned ignoring other societies. Every nation has to depend on others, because a country is not self-sufficient in all respects. So co-existence and cooperation is as vital as pursuing national interests. It is true that the newly liberated developing countries should not move into military alliances and should opt for their own course of action. Their primary task is to work for the betterment and upliftment of their societies. This, however, does not mean that a non-aligned country should not be active in international developments. India, for example, had been active in international issues, starting from the Korean War to War, where the imperialist powers were engaged in fighting to strengethen their hold. The liberated countries extended their full support in all times. India also took part in resolving confrontation and was restoring peace and was thus involved in almost every major issue the world faced now and then. The non-aligned countries refused to accept the destabilising attempts of the imperialist powers. They strived for sub-reliance in their economic, industrial and technical development, without coming under the grip of imperialist powers. "The major formulation in the Congress (I) was a reiteration of the party's faith in the foreign policy of non-alignment. The Congress (I) identified itself with the Third World and asserted the country's right to develop nuclear technology irrespective of the attitudes of the superpowers."[7] To the contrary, the United States had always sought to influence the decision-making process of developing countries by its massive economic and military package. "The recipient countries this way found themselves under control once more and the United States always sought to convince the developing third world countries to adopt American concept of development".[8]

In Afghanistan, the results were not so good. The Democratic

7. Bhambhri, C.P., "Lok Sabha Elections, 1980: Ideas on Foreign Policy in the Election Manifestoes", *International Studies,* vol.19 (2), April-June 1980,pp. 243-52.

8. Stauffer, Robert B., "The American Development Model: Hidden Agenda for Third World", *Phippine Journal of Public Administration,* vol. XXI, No. 2, April 1977,pp.123-25.

Republic of Afghanistan had proposed an early political settlement and it was ready for direct negotiation with Pakistan and Iran. In Pakistan and Iran all the political parties urged their governments to move towards a political settlement, but the Zia regime, at the behest of the US imperialists, did not hesitate to aggravate the conflict and thereby threatened the territorial integrity of Afghanistan. India called on the concerned parties to hold discussions for withdrawal of foreign troops from Afghanistan. But the US imperialists and its allies refused to hold any talk with Karmal Government. This way imperialist forces had been working to disrupt the non-aligned movement. The imperialists by arming their client states were openly abetting aggressions. The non-aligned countries with the support of India were determined to frustrate impact of western capitalist countries. V. Shirokov writing in Pravda "accentuated India's steps towards the Afghanistan problem and applauded India's stand in which she criticised the US position and asked it to stop military aid to the Mujaheeds."[9] "The BJP opposed all kinds of racism, colonialism in all their manifestations and urged the government to defend human rights whenever threatened. The party sought to build an international environment conducive to the free flow of knowledge and information and to cultural exchanges among nations. In its view, the government should make efforts to improve relations with the immediate neighbours. The BJP stood for genuine non-alignment adopted during the Janata regime and strove to pursue independent foreign policy aimed at preserving world peace and promoting and safeguarding the enlightened self-interests of the nation."[10] To quote A.B. Vajpayee, where stated in the Lok Sabha :

> "To abide by the principles of policy of non-alignment is not enough, rather we shall have to demonstrate that we are following and acting on those principles. In that account the government should outrightly condemn the Soviet invasion of Afghanistan which is against all canons and principles of non-alignment as well the United Nations Organisation. To keep themselves aloof from imperialist intervention and superpow-

9. *Pravda* (Moscow), 29 January 1980.
10. *Organiser*, May 25, 1980, p.10.

> ers hegemony, the newly independent nations have opted for non-alignment and if they are not protected against the super-powers intervention, not get the support of the NAM, then it is rather the NAM is irrelevant."[11]

It would be wrong to say that we had lost flexibility as far as non-alignment was concerned. The outstanding achievement of India was that it could bring all non-aligned countries to common table and could pursue to act together. Had non-alignment lost its flexibility, it would not have been possible to achieve consensus in the non-aligned ministers' conference held in New Delhi in 1981. Now that India is pursuing its policy of non-alignment, it would help many Third World countries to meet their needs. "Our movement has consistently worked for the eradication of colonialism, racism and imperialist domination. We have supported liberation struggles all over the world. Peaceful co-existence is one of the first articles of the credo of non-alignment. The elimination of nuclear weapons and of war is imperative if the people of the world can grow to their fullest stature. Big power presence have increased in various parts of the world. Armed conflicts have increased. These developments give special urgency to efforts to find peaceful resolution of tensions. Non-alignment thus assumes added relevance".[12] "In a gathering of independent sovereign countries, practicing their own forms of self-governance, differences of approach, and emphasis are bound to exist. Such differences testify to the health of the movement rather than to its weakness. Resilience is a greater sign of strength than rigidity. What is significant is the harmonious manner in which we resolve differences. So long as we continue to be motivated by a spirit of conciliation, non-alignment will continue to be a source of strength to us and a benign influence in the world."[13] It is true that the performance of non-aligned movement have not come upto expectations and some major problems continue to persist in the world. There is mounting pressure on the non-aligned countries to bring them under the influences of imperialist countries, the outside powers intervene in the internal affairs of non-aligned countries. These

11. *Lok Sabha Debates*, Sixth Series, Third Session, vol. VI (23), July 9, 1980, cols. 285-89.
12. *Selected Speeches and Writings of Indira Gandhi*, vol. V (New Delhi : Publication Division, Ministry of Information and Broadcasting, Government of India, November 1986),pp. 503-04.
13. *Ibid.*, p. 511. (Address at the opening session of the CHOGM, New Delhi, September 4, 1980).

countries have turned to be battle grounds for bloc rivalries, but it must be noted that those nations rejected out Western countries and struggled to achieve their target of self-reliance and all round development.

It was a fact that increasing foreign intervention in the affairs of non-aligned countries was a grave danger to their security and integrity. Most Third World countries were economically and militarily weak and so they thought it proper to get themselves associated with the non-aligned movement to concentrate on their developmental efforts. The BJP party resolution remarked that "the Soviet military intervention in Afghanistan was a violation of U.N. Charter and a blow to aspirations and ideals of the non-aligned movement."[14] "Decolonisation, Detente, disarmament and development are intertwined with each other and only by adhering to the principle of genuine non-alignment, India would be able to contribute its mite towards freedom, peace and progress in the world."[15]

The Indira Gandhi regime suffered criticism from many quarters with regard to its Afghan policy. It was pointed out that Mrs Gandhi was wavering her stand on Soviet intervention in Afghanistan. The Indian government justified Soviet intervention as a bilateral problem between the USSR and Afghanistan and at the same time it opposed the presence of foreign troops in Afghanistan in corroboration with the policy of non-alignment. "It was clear that India could not go the whole hog with the Soviet Union on Afghanistan, nor it could support Soviet moves in the Gulf region where super power intervention was fraught with grave consequences."[16] According to the BJP, "India is the only country in South Asia which is left to Soviet Union to rely on and so Soviet Union could not afford to lose India or even a little bit of its support particularly with regard to Afghanistan''.[17] In the view of the BJP, "by acquiescing in USSR's military intervention in Afghanistan the Government of India tarnished the country's image in the world, and isolated India completely from the neighbouring countries,

14. *Miscellaneous Party Resolutions of the BJP*, 1980, pp. 1-2.
15. *Resolution of the National Executive of the BJP*, *vide* A.M. Zaidi, *Annual Register of Indian Political Parties*, 1980 (New Delhi : S. Chand & Co., 1981), p.652.
16. *Organiser*, October 19, 1980, p.1.
17. *Ibid.*, November 23, 1980, p.1.

the non-aligned nations and the Islamic world."[18] Replying in a debate in Rajya Sabha, Jaswant Singh said, "We have no flexibility of response. We seem to have tied our option to a single thread. There is an absence of alternative policy postures."[19] The BJP was dissatisfied with the working of the Congress government under Indira Gandhi. In its view the original principle of non-alignment had been sacrificed. India's stand on Afghanistan and Kampuchea could not improve India's image abroad. The party noted that to ensure a positive thrust to our principles and policies of non-alignment the government should see the world with open eyes. Both the Super Powers should be unequivocally condemned, may it be Vietnam, El Salvador or Afghanistan problem. The BJP strongly rejected that "there was any superpower exclusivity in giving directions to world events, nor the party recognised the right of nations to intervene in the affairs of others on the basis of the imperial concept of sphere of influence."[20] "The BJP was opposed to racism, colonialism in all their manifestations and vowed to protect human rights wherever threatened. The party stressed that it would seek to build an international environment conducive to the free flow of knowledge and information and to cultural exchanges among nations. It adhered to the path of non-alignment adopted during the Janata period and advocated an independent foreign policy aimed at preserving world peace and promoting and safeguarding the enlightened self-interests of the nation."[21] However, Government of India, under the leadership of Indira Gandhi, took a realistic stand on Soviet action in Afghanistan. As Mrs Gandhi said, "The non-aligned movement is not a mere or casual collection of individual states. It is a vital historical process. It is an assertion of mankind's will to survive despite oppression, despite the growing arms-race and ideological divisions. We challenge the doctrine and practice of racism. We now strive to enforce the right to economic self-reliance. Alignment denotes dependence. That is why something akin to the non-aligned outlook is spreading noticeably even among people of aligned coun-

18. *Text of Presidential Address by Shri A.B. Vajpayee* delivered at the First National Convention of the BJP held in Bombay on 28th to 30th December, 1980, p. 18.

19. *Rajya Sabha Debates,* 11 March 1981, vol. CXVII (18), cols. 301-03.

20. *Resolutions as adopted by National Executive,* National Council Session, Cochin (Kerala), 25th to 27th April, 1981, pp.19-20.

21. *Our Five Commitments,* BJP Publication, pp.19-20.

tries."[22] Brajesh C. Mishra, India's permanent representative in the UNO, expressed India's stand on the Afghanistan issue in these words:

> "India was deeply concerned and vitally interested in the peace, security, independence and non-alignment of this traditionally friendly neighbour. India cannot look with equanimity on the attempts by some outside powers to interfere in the internal affairs of Afghanistan and encouraging subversive elements to create disturbances inside Afghanistan. We hope that the people of Afghanistan will be able to resolve their internal problems themselves without any interference from outside. India hopes that Soviet Union will not remain a day longer than necessary."[23]

The non-aligned countries viewed NAM as a movement to support anti-colonialism, racism and to secure economic and social development, and for better cooperation among nations throughout the world. Whenever any conflict arose, it was assessed on its merits, as for example during the Afghan crisis. India being a firm follower of the movement opposed any type of intervention in the foreign soil by any power and so it condemned Soviet aggressive design. The Indian government asked for withdrawal of Soviet troops with immediate effect, but it could not rule out military aid to the Mujahideens by the US satellites. India upheld her principled stand when she condemned US military interference and insisted on an end to US action before the withdrawal of Soviet forces.

In the same period, India's relations with the US had been marked by more divergences than convergences. It has been seen that the US was not courteous to all that India had been doing in the diplomatic field. "The two specific events – the Korean war and the Japanese treaty – that took place in the early fifties were a bad start in our relations with America."[24] There were many reasons for US antipathy towards India. "America's support to any country was conditioned to its policies of global domination which India had been unable to give because by and large the US policy had been to support the status quo

22. *Selected Speeches and Writings of Indira Gandhi*, vol. V, op.cit, pp. 393-95.
23. GAOR, 1980, p.34.
24. Suri, Surinder, "Foreign Policy Dilemma", *Tribune*, 25 December 1981.

in a rapidly changing world and so the US had generally tended to support decrepit dictatorships rather than incipient democracies."[25] But it would be improper to say that United States and India were at loggerhead without any sign of improvement of their bilateral relations. The United States had always attached great importance for developing cordial relations with India. President Reagan observed the invaluable contribution India contributed for maintaining international peace and disarmament. The American policy makers acknowledged the leading role India played in world affairs as the leader of non-aligned movement.

The Iran-Iraq War had been escalated and it was not conducive for world peace. In this situation, the Non-aligned Foreign Ministers Conference opened in New Delhi in 1981. But the meeting was overshadowed by bitter dissensions and bickerings revealing contradictory and hostile stands on many problems. In this situation the critics remarked that the non-aligned movement was by virtual collapsing. However, the BJP remarked, "such divisive trends did not imply any danger to the break up of the movement in near future because both the superpowers were interested in its continuance."[26] Reacting to the suspicion of the critics on the role of the NAM, Indira Gandhi, the then Prime Minister of India, expressed and stated India's approach in these lines:

> "We express our profound regret at the Iran-Iraq conflict and the grievous loss of life and destruction of property which it has caused to the two nations and their peoples.... The non-aligned movement should exert every effort to bring about a speedy and peaceful termination of this tragic conflict.... I shall continue consultations and take all possible and appropriate measures towards this objective."[27]

Human civilisation confronts a big challenge of annihilation in a nuclear disaster. Hiroshima disaster is not forgotten and mankind faces danger with the production of nuclear arsenals. It is estimated that there are more than 60,000 nuclear weapons all over world which can destroy the world hundred times. To add fuel to flame, non-nuclear countries are importing destructive nuclear weapons and this way

25. Menon, K.P.S., "International Standing", *Tribune*, 25 January 1981.
26. *Organiser*, February 15, 1981, p.2.
27. *Selected Speeches and Writings of Indira Gandhi*, vol.V, op.cit., p.396.

inviting nuclear war to their doorsteps. Thus, it is time to think of disarmament. The Indian government also supported disarmament efforts. But the BJP had some differences with the Congress government's foreign policy. A.B. Vajpaee in the Lok Sabha remarked that "the Indian government should formulate such policy which would keep India aloof from superpowers game, to halt arms race and nuclear weapons programme. This would enable to preserve world peace. The party added, we should condemn the racist regime, should give support to the Namibian people who were struggling for their natural rights."[28] In the view of the BJP, "non-alignment is not equi-distance, not neutrality and certainly not leverage to be used for politicking between superpowers. The BJP unequivocally rejected all theories which confer any exclusivity of superpowers interests in the comity of nations. The BJP wished to reiterate that in its perceptions, the basic postulates of India's foreign policy, providing the needed anchor of continuity, along with the ability to cope with change, lie in the three precepts of (a) genuine non-alignment, (b) peace and cooperation with neighbours, (c) beneficial bilateralism."[29]

The arms race, production of nuclear weapons and their deployment, spending money for military purposes enforced the leader of the NAM to accelerate the process of nuclear disarmament. Many questions arose before them: would we able to save mankind from annihilation ? Would the world drift away from nuclear arms race? To complete this herculean task the NAM had always strived for peace and disarmament. It is really strange then that the small countries were so keen to stockpile arms, frittering away their scarce resources and why the developed nations wanted to spread their nuclear tentacles. Therefore the Heads of states of non-aligned countries "appealed to the great powers to halt the arms race which was consuming at an ever increasing rate, the scarce natural resources of our planet, destroying the ecological balance and wasting much of our scientific talent in sterile and destructive pursuits. This should be used to revitalise and restructure the world economy. The resources released by measures of

28. *Lok Sabha Debates*, Seventh Series, Eighth Session, vol. XXVI (29), March 30, 1982, cols. 379-383.

29. *Resolution of the BJP*, National Executive Meeting, August 28 to 30, 1982, Bangalore, p.16.

disarmament should be diverted to promote the development of developing countries."[30] "Just as growing confrontation and armament race was dangerous to world peace, so also the gap between the rich and the poor. So the NAM had a double role to perform – first, to focus on the more basic problems, and second, not to get involved in bilateral issues. The basic problems were of peace and war and the economic development of third world countries. So to have greater cooperation among the developing countries was the major task of the time."[31] It may be correct to say that by possessing nuclear weapons Third World countries would be in a position in influencing international relations. But it can be said at the same time that not only do nuclear weapons provide an opportunity to play a dominant role but through arbitration and mediation too they can influence events.

So India took the initiative for world disarmament. She had always advocated against flow of arms and defence spending in the sensitive parts of the world. India had stood for peaceful relations with all countries including the Super Powers. On this basis Indo-Soviet relations flourised. The visit of Soviet defence minister Dimitri Ustinov to New Delhi in 1982 and the return visit of Indira Gandhi to Moscow in 1983, their meetings and talks testified to strong bond between India and the USSR. Mrs Gandhi passed her message to the world that friendship between the two nations were not based either on ideology or on sentiment. She said that the bilateral relation between India and the USSR was based entirely on the compatibility of national interests. President Brezhnev of the Soviet Union in his talk with Mrs Gandhi said, "The USSR would like to see greater unity among the non-aligned nations. The USSR would continue to make every effort to strengthen India and the movement."[32]

Initially the non-aligned movement did not get sufficient support from other countries but gradually its policies and programmes attracted many Afro-Asian countries and drew sympathy from the Super Powers. "At one time India was virtually alone and many critics

30. Satish Kumar (ed.), *Yearbook on India's Foreign Policy*, 1982-83 (New Delhi: Sage, 1985), pp. 251-52.

31. *Selected Speeches and Writings of Indira Gandhi*, vol. V, op. cit., pp. 471-73.

32. *The Statesman* (New Delhi), 22 September 1982.

decried India's isolation. Gradually, the movement encouraged scores of other countries to join hands. Mrs Gandhi, too, pushed the movement forward and gradually hundreds of members joined in the movement."[33] By attaining such a wide recognition and popularity the first and foremost task ahead was to attain self-reliance in economy, science, agriculture; to find problems and solve them according to their own genius by dissociating themselves from the bloc approach. The non-aligned countries were worried abount to their problems pertaining to their economic conditions. Without imitating for their economics they were thinking of spending money for lifting the poor and ameliorating the deplorable conditions of the depressed class. Even if they denounced political alignment, the invisible economic alignment spread its tentacles. The strings attached to economic package they received from capitalist countries made the matter worse. "The experience of India shows that the design of the neo-colonialists can succeed only if they penetrate the political process.... The basic interests of world capitalist countries in the newly liberated countries are economic but they are pushed through politics in which the local groups play an active role. The non-aligned countries cannot meet the challenge of neo-colonialism without insulating their politics from external interventions. Unless the governments of non-aligned countries attach great importance to social justice, imperialists cannot be kept at bay."[34]

The problems being complex and difficult, the call of the hour was to strive for individual as well as collective self-reliance, to have a fair and equitable terms for transfer of technical know-how or resources from the Western industrialised countries. Therefore, India endeavoured to consolidate on her national identity. "Alignments might bring more aid but it does not strengthen the self-reliant foundations of freedom. It inhibits people from making their own economic conditions. Hence, non-alignment helped us to become more technologically self-reliant."[35] Thus, NAM persists for a new economic order and as a challenge to Western capitalist countries

33. Bhatia, V. (ed.), *The October Revolution and 70 years of Indo-Soviet Relations* (New Delhi: Panchasheel, 1987), pp.91-92.

34. Bhambhri, C.P., "Non-alignment: Challenge and Response", in V.D.Chopra (ed.), *NAM Summit: New Delhi to Harare* (New Delhi: *Patriot*, 1986), p.23.

35. Speech of Indira Gandhi at the Silver Jubilee Celebration of SIS, JNU, on October 10,1981, vide *Selected Speeches and Writings of Indira Gandhi*, vol. V, op.cit., p.499.

sticked to this demand. It was also realised that unless there is a sense of mutual cooperation, efforts to pool their resources, skills and talents together, unless they explore their complimentraries in their economies, sordid stage of the developing world would further deteriorate. They will have to battle all attempts of imperialists to divide the non-aligned world. If a problem crops up, it needs to be solved bilaterally instead of looking to other powers. Instead of pre-judging any problem and without showing any room to the access of imperialists, attempts should be made for independence of judgements deciding all issues on their own merit. So long the outside powers stick to their lines and become reluctant to think for newly born states, policy of non-alignment will remain as a foreign policy option to get the demands implemented, to see a world free from hunger and poverty.

The economic problem occupied a major item on the agenda of the Seventh Non-Aligned Conferrence in 1983. The worldwide economic recession and mainly Soviet Union's economic crisis brought attention of the non-aligned countries. There was a strong feeling that unless there is an economic regeneration and unless a NIEO is established the economic prospects and progress of developing countries seemed bleak. The most significant contribution of the Seventh Non-Aligned Summit was that it opted two phased global negotiation strategies. Those included North-South dialogue on economic aid, trade, food and energy. It called for changes in the existing system of monetary help from World Bank and IMF, so that the hardship the non-aligned and developing countries were facing would be reduced. Besides these, the summit had wide range discussion on South-South cooperation. A substantial economic cooperation among the member states taking into account their potential and credibility in the movement has been rehabiliated."[36] The Soviet Union expressed satisfaction on the non-aligned movement. Precisely speaking, "the decisions of the Summit were aimed at consolidating detente and spreading it to all the regions of the world and restructuring international economic relations on a just and democratic foundation."[37] "The Chinese government also deeply appreciated and supported independent, sovereign and non-bloc principles followed by this movement."[38] The American reaction was that, "on balance, many of the radical imprints

36. *The Times* (London), 14 March 1983.

37. *The Soviet Land* (New Delhi), April 1983, p.39.

38. *The Hindustan Times* (New Delhi), 15 March 1983.

that had characterized previous Summits was excised."[39] India, the pioneer of the movement, leaving aside the criticism of the conservative sections, was successful in bridging the misunderstanding of the member and non-member states of the NAM with full-hearted cooperation of many like-minded parties. Her dynamic and peaceful approach to the conflicts, that cast a shadow in the eighties, boosted the working of the movement. Initiatives were taken at different phases of the movement and continuous endeavour of the Socialist countries, took the non-aligned approach to such a height that now about two-third countries all over the world express their strong faith in this movement. In subsequent years, leaders of the NAM extended their support to strengthen the movement. But the BJP was not satisfied with the achievement of the NAM. The BJP's criticism was that "though India is committed to the non-aligned movement or its concept, we are committed to the concept of the movement as it was originally conceived of by the founding fathers of the movement, yet the movement has got totally derailed from its track and has gone into wrong direction and has acquired principles and purposes which would shock the founding fathers. If the movement has failed in its purpose because the movement is not able to clean its own Augean stables, it cannot clean that filth from its own stables, it will be in no position to make any serious moral impact on others. We have not able to bring the movement in harmony with this accepted new notion of International Law."[40] The Bharatiya Janata Party did not approve the policy of non-alignment of the Congress government. The party alleged that "it has been dominated and overtaken by the forces of religious fanaticism. We are in a bad company, in the company of people who do not share the internal values of our democratic politics and our effort should be to stay in that company knowing the dangers of it. The Soviets and their supporters support this movement because it happens to further their purposes and because it is dominated by them. Soon the movement goes contrary to their purposes, they will go against it".[41]

Relations with the Super Powers has been a major concern of India's foreign policy since independence. Being a champion of the policy of non-alignment India has always been seeking to maintain

39. *International Herald Tribune* (Paris), 16 March 1983.

40. Jethmalani, Ram, *Lok Sabha Debates*, vol.XXXV (19), Seventh Series, Eleventh Session, 22 March 1983, cols. 459-63.

41. *Ibid.*, vol. XXXVI (21), Seventh Series, Eleventh Session, 24 March 1983, cols. 393-94.

equidistance from the Super Powers. No doubt the 1971 treaty of peace and friendship brought criticisms to India's foreign policy that it had aligned with Soviet Union. But the Indian Prime Minister Indira Gandhi had always opted independent course of action in international relations. In the words of Indira Gandhi, "Non-alignment is neither neutrality nor indifference. It involves active and free exercise of judgement on certain principles. Peace is not passive... Today, let us concern ourselves with future, mobilising all our resources, material and moral, in our cooperative quest for such a peace."[42] So India started deepening bilateral relations with the Soviet Union not because it is anti-American but Soviet Union had shown ample eagerness to give India an important place in her global role. "It is unambiguously clear that India's relations with the Soviet Union in political, economic and security fields are based on mutuality of interests. In a sense closeness of relationship is inherent in their geopolitical and geostrategic locii."[43] "Gorbachev was forthright in recognising India's political and military status in South Asia specifically, and also in the larger sphere keeping in view its eminent position in the non-aligned movement. The Soviets have fully understood the parameters of Indian diplomacy. They have been assiduous in consolidating the Indo-Soviet friendship but have never tried to entice India into a closer embrace."[44] The Indo-Soviet relations had been extended on political, economic and security aspects. But the security requirements had been dominated over all other fields due to America's military and economic aid to Pakistan. Both the countries had their own perceptions to extend friendship. It revealed that their interests cover the same in the region. Soviet Union had accepted India as a major partner in South Asia. India wanted to check Pakistan's dominance in South Asia and on the other hand the Soviet Union could not allow US to expand her influence and the US-Pakistan axis was one among many reasons why India and the Soviet Union came closer to each other. Inspite of being a member of the non-aligned movement Pakistan allowed its territory to be used for the interests of US. The Bharatiya Janata Party warned the Indian government to be vigilant infront of US-Pakistan military alliance. The party remarked that "the possibility

42. *Selected Speeches and Writings of Indira Gandhi*, vol. V, op.cit., p.509.

43. Misra, K.P., "India's Non-alignment and the Indo-Soviet Treaty", *Biiss Journal*, vol.4, No.2, April 1983, pp. 39-47.

44. Satish Kumar (ed.), *Yearbook on India's Foreign Policy, 1983-84* (New Delhi: Sage, 1986), pp.157-65.

of such a military alliance was pregnant with serious potents for the South-Asian region, which would bring a series of geo-strategic changes and would push the region closer to a superpowers confrontation."[45] The BJP viewed that "the NAM could be a serious movement only if the military and dictatorial regimes were kept firmly out of it."[46]

The policy of non-alignment upholds the equality of men and equality of nations. So when the people of South Africa were fighting for their rights and liberties, the non-aligned countries played a crucial role and extended their support to the people of South Africa. Similarly, the non-aligned movement expressed its support to the people of Namibia and Palestine to restore their rights and liberties. The non-aligned countries led by India committed to their cherished principles, inspered the people struggling against imperialistic forces, and mobilised world public opinion to give their support for reasserting inalienable rights of those countries. They thought that unless the imperialist forces were withdrawn and exterminated, the struggle is incomplete. The germinated principles of the NAM inspired the countries of Asia and Africa to work together, to look after one another. Anti-imperialism being the bedrock of the policy of non-alignment, Third World countries consistently pursued and worked for it, which testified their independent and dynamic action. India's Chairmanship witnessed many hurdles in its way. The Namibians were fighting to inherit their natural rights. The non-aligned countries under the chairmanship of India put continuous pressure on the South African government. Several meetings were organised to draw the attention of other countries who were not parties to the movement. Apartheid was severely condemned and the non-aligned movement at that moment evolved the way for Namibians to enjoy justice and human rights. A UN resolution was passed condemning the South African racist regime. extraordinary ministerial meeting was organised to put the resolution into effect. The NAM supporting the rights of the people of Namibia to self-determination was determined for liberation by all available means, and worked for an end of apartheid. "The AICC(I) strongly deplored the persistence of racist regimes and extended its whole hearted support to the brave struggles of the people of South Africa and Namibia. The AICC(I) wished to pledge the services and support

45. *Organiser*, December 25-31, 1983, p.1.

46. *Organiser*, April 3, 1983, p.2.

of the Congress Organisation in India's endeavour in the International sphere. Reiterating the faith in the principles of non-alignment, the AICC(I) expressed the confidence that the movement would continue to grow, both in number and in effectiveness and serve as a beacon of hope in the encircling gloom the world over."[47] "Articulating the protest of the erstwhile colonial countries against economic inequality, socio-political injustice, and discriminatory treatment based on colour, race and creed meted out by major industrial and ex-colonial powers, it represents a protest movement against multiple patterns of domination and hegemony, dependence, 'Satelitism', and neo-colonialism. In its main focus, non-alignment is a movement of solidarity of the newly liberated countries aspiring to a position of independence and equality in a highly interdependent world."[48]

Apart from these problems, the NAM had another task before it. The growing militarisation of the Indian Ocean was a challenge before the non-aligned movement. So, the non-aligned countries took initiatives in the development of the Indian Ocean. The escalation of military distributed in the Indian Ocean region thwarted the congenial atmosphere of the adjacent countries. Several meetings were organized to declare Indian Ocean as a zone of peace. The imperialists exercised their influence not only in Indian Ocean but other parts of world were also equally suppressed. Central America was facing a serious political, social and economic crisis and Nicaragua was being suppressed by the United States where the people suffered from poverty, inequality and misery. The urgent task before the NAM was to find out a non-violent solution to the grave volume The NAM during India's chairmanship held several meetings which formulated different policies to resist imperialists' pressures and at the same time the US was pressurised to withdraw from her imperialistic design. Iran-Iraq war and the Palestine problem were other problems which required speedy and peaceful solution and the non-aligned movement provided necessary skills and a way out to these problems. The NAM supported the Palestinians with the help of Arab frontline states to ease the tension. Israel was motivated to desist from its hostile actions. Thus the steps taken by the non-aligned countries were constructive and non-

47. *Resolutions Passed in the AICC (I) meeting* held in Bombay on 20th and 21st October, 1983, pp.20-23.

48. Khan, R., "India and the non-aligned movement", in Satish Kumar (ed.), *Yearbook on India's Foreign Policy*, 1984-85 (New Delhi: Sage, 1987), p.88.

confrontationist. In a nutshell, the movement during India's chairmanship and mostly under Mrs. Gandhi's auspices had strived hard to solve the problem of the Afro-Asian countries. But the BJP viewed the achievements of NAM from a different angle. The main criticism of the BJP was that India could not persuade the big powers to stop their arms aid and that was the main drawback of the Indira Gandhi government. Taking part in the discussion in Rajya Sabha, Jaswant Singh, the BJP member of Parliament, "urged the government to move away from global aspirations to our Asian realities."[49] Further, the party added, "the Indian government was not able to make any purposeful move for the cessation of Iran-Iraq war and for resolving the mutual conflict between Palestinians. The aims and objectives of our foreign policy, the BJP emphasised, should not be to promote the image of an individual but to preserve and protect the interest of the nation. The party did not deny the usefulness and relevance of the non-alignment policy, but they differed in the manner of its implementation."[50]

In a nuclear age when the nuclear powers are competing among themselves, non-alignment works as a balance of power getting support of two-third nations of the world. At the same time it provides necessary pliability to negotiate with the nuclear powers and contributes a lot to desist themselves from any sort of nuclear catastrophe. It is a positive direction to step up detente and reduce tensions. It is thus imperative that the non-aligned movement should be strengthened to forge greater unity, to eliminate wars and destructions, to end the East-West divide. If there is a nuclear war any where in the world it would destroy mankind. The only way to over come this major crisis of the world is to stick to the strict principles of non-alignment or else the globe would be divided into camps and their followers where the prevalence of peace would be outspoken. In this context as Arnold Rutel rightly remarked that "the 1971 peace and friendship treaty between India and the Soviet Union was a treaty of cooperation for peace in Asia and the world and the progress of the two countries. It was not a treaty to preserve peace in the continent alone, but all over the world. He said that both the countries would work for peace in times of peace and war."[51] And the Indo-Soviet treaty should not be

49. *Rajya Sabha Debates*, 7 December 1983, col. 337.

50. Presidential address; A.B.Vajpayee, *Fifth National Council Session* in Indore (M.P), 6th to 8th January, 1984, pp. 9-10.

51. *The Hindustan Times* (New Delhi), 23rd August 1984.

viewed as a breach of the policy of non-alignment. It still provides an opportunity to both India and the Soviet Union to continue their struggle for peace and security.On the occasion of the 37th year of independence of India, the Soviet Union noted that it was because of the policy of non-alignment that India had been able to achieve the success in economic and cultural field and could preserve country's unity and integrity. The USSR hailed India's stand on many occasions, as for example in halting arms race and preserving peace by eliminating nuclear race. The Soviet Russia willingly extended her cooperation and supported the policy of non-alignment. Significantly, Soviet recognition of India's role in the NAM came from the highest level like Gorbachev's Vladivostok speech when he said,"the recognised leader of this movement is great India, with it moral authority and traditional wisdom, with its unique political experience and huge economic possibilities."[52] The Bharatiya Janata Party advocated also to follow an "independent foreign policy committed to world peace, disarmament and a new international economic order. The party believed in the task of freeing the world from economic exploitation, external influences, domination and colonialism in all its new forms. For this a continued strengthening of the non-aligned movement was the policy plank of the BJP which would work towards re-imparting dynamism to the non-aligned movement."[53] The party also reiterated that "fresh endeavours should be taken for withdrawal of foreign troops from Afghanistan, a political solution of the Afghan problem, free from outside intervention should be made so that Afghanistan and its identity as an independent, non-aligned nation could be re-established."[54]

In 1984, India and five other countries made an appeal to the nuclear powers to halt nuclear race and particularly its deployment in Third World countries to avoid the possibility of nuclear war. They attempted to launch a world wide campaign through the auspices of the UN and countries who were not non-aligned also were welcome to join in the struggle. The Delhi Declaration and the Mexico Declaration were other important steps in favour of nuclear disarmament. The initiative of the six nations were widely acclaimed by the Socialist countries like the Soviet Union and China. Apart from this, the movement was highly concerned about global economic situation.

52. Duncan, Peter J.S., *The Soviet Union and India* (London: Routledge, 1989), p.64.

53. *Election Manifesto of the BJP,* 1984, pp.20-21.

54. Ibid., p. 21.

Mrs. Gandhi appointed a group of experts from five countries to make necessary recommendations on the improvement of economic situation. The group worked for and produced a report for a more stable and equitable global economy. What disturbed the movement throughout the years was the worsening economic conditions of the African countries. Subsequently, the group battled to do something concrete for bettering the economy of the African nations. Several meetings were held and monetary packages extended to the African countries for quick economic recovery and to emerge out of the unprecedented drought. The developed countries were also urged to raise the level of their aid.

Like the Indo-Soviet ties, the Indo-American relations developed without any harm to non-alignment. A critical analysis of Indo-American relations reveals that despite India's inclination towards the West for financial aid and training for its scientists and technicians, yet the Indian attitude signifies that Indian classes were pursuing a policy of anti-imperialism. "There is no doubt that on a range of issues, the Indian government had found itself in contradiction with world monopoly capitalism. Thus, India's foreign policy of non-alignment had some anti-imperialist features which revealed the confrontational character of the Indian bourgeoisie."[55]

On almost all issues alliance between Soviet Union and developing countries had been opposed by the Western capitalist countries. Inspite of that the non-aligned countries worked together inside and outside the UN. They drew moral support from the Socialist countries. The assistance from the Soviet Union and other Socialist countries could help the non-aligned countries to build their infrastructure and self-reliant economy. Moreover, the Socialist countries extended their full support to the non-aligned movement, as a result of which the movement had been able to prove itself a movement standing for the causes of the developing world. In an interview with the PTI, Gorbachev firmly stated that "Soviet Union greatly appreciated India's contribution to the collective effort to preserve peace and remove the nuclear threat. India was doing much for the developing countries against imperialist oppression, for strengthening non-aligned movement."[56]

55. Bhambhri, C.P., "India's Foreign Policy", *Social Scientist*, No. 113, October 1982, pp.51-55.

56. Singh, Darshan, *Soviet Foreign Policy Documents, 1985* (New Delhi: Sterling, 1986), pp. 122-23.

"They had done much for the rise and development of the non-aligned movement as an important positive factor in the present-day world."[57] "To a significant extent, India's non-alignment gave greater bargaining leverage to this countries than its alignments to either superpower."[58]

Despite India's denial of any fundamental shift in its non-aligned foreign policy approach, some observers viewed India as a betrayer of the policy of non-alignment, particularly when India under Rajiv Gandhi had accepted the conditions suggested by the West as a prelude to transfer of hi-tech, which Indira Gandhi had rejected with contempt. The Bharatiya Janata Party viewed this alliance and the on-site inspection by the US against India's interests as it would mean breach of India's sovereignty. The party condemned the Congress government's preference to the US "when other countries were willing to meet our requirements at less severe terms than those of Washington."[59] The Bharatiya Janata Party recalled the rule of the Janata government when India's warm relations with the USSR continued and also good rapport was built up with the US. The resolution of the BJP observed that "during Rajiv Gandhi's days India's friendship with the USSR is viewed with suspicion by the Western bloc, the policy of non-alignment is distrusted particularly with the Libyan incident."[60]

But it was the even pitched Indo-American relations that never undermined the non-aligned policy of India. It is seen that there are several criticisms about the role of the non-aligned movement, its performances on different occasions. But we can well note that after 25 years of its existence, "the movement had shown its capacity to act in a meaningful and principled way and contributed significantly to lowering of tensions globally. We have not been neutral or fence-sitters when our principles have been challenged or violated."[61] So the task before them was to strengthen NAM, to restore its credibility and to do it the summit urged to work with unified mind and spirit. Most of the member states were over burdened with foreign debt. Having limited resources and potentialities they were afraid of huge debt

57. *Ibid.*, p. 134 (Gorbachev's Speech at a dinner in honour of Rajiv Gandhi).
58. Subramaniam, K., "Strategic Reality", *World Focus*, vol. 6, No.7, July 1985, p.12.
59. Agrawal, A.K., "Rajiv's U-turn towards USA", *Organiser*, vol. 37, No. 43, March 9, 1986, p.1.
60. *Presidential Address* by L.K.Advani, Plenary Session, Ekatmata Nagar (Indraprastha Stadium), New Delhi, 9 May 1986, p.18.
61. *Foreign Affairs Record*, vol. XXXII (3), March 1986, pp.81-82.(Speech of Shri B.R. Bhagat on India's Foreign Policy on March 15, 1986).

burden. Therefore they gave primacy to the financial and monetary issues. So they unanimously recommended an international debt restructuring facility to avoid the emergence of a serious debt crisis. And, it was believed, all these can be attained if there is universalisation of decision making process of the international financial institutions.

After the Seventh Summit it is clearly evident that the contribution of non-aligned movement has been widely recognised. It is because "by skilful management of conflicts within the movement, a sense of unity has been restored; by choosing the right kind of priorities, giving more importance to economic matters, and atmosphere of greater faith recognition was taking place in the world. At one time it was called immoral. Subsequently it was accepted by all nations. The principles and practices of non-alignment were seen as the only path for assured peace, stability and prosperity in the world."[62] Gorbachev spoke highly of the role of the non-aligned movement. He remarked "Great India, with its moral authority and traditional wisdom, with its specific political experience and huge economic potentialities, is the recognised leader of this movement. It has played a remarkable role in looking for ways to diminish the nuclear threat, in rejecting and condemning exploitation as well as the policy of aggression and neocolonialism."[63] The Indian Prime Minister also equally appraised of the Soviet assistance to the non-aligned movement. Moreover, he reiterated that "with the support of the non-aligned countries India had been in the forefront of the non-aligned movement for abolition of the nuclear arsenals."[64]

The Harare Summit once again drew the attention of the Super Powers regarding disarmament issue. The non-aligned countries tried to create awareness among the people through seminars, meetings and the media. Delegates were sent to foreign countries to halt the arms race. But the Super Powers were not much influenced by the appeal of the non-aligned countries. Though the desired result could not achieve, the summit worked with remarkable unity and speed for an early end to testing, using and deploying nuclear arms. A commission was set up to coordinate the work of the NAM. This way the NAM

62. *Statements on Foreign Policy, Prime Minister Rajiv Gandhi* (New Delhi: Publication Division, Ministry of External Affairs, Government of India, September 1988), p.12.

63. *Pravda* (Moscow), 29 July 1986.

64. *Dialogue Between Trusted Friends,* a Publication of the Information Department of the USSR Embassy in India, New Delhi, 1986, p.8.

demonstrated that it was not only a moral force but also on many occasions proposed concrete plan of action. "Non-Alignment was no longer looked upon as a means of protecting one's own interests and a way to overcome bloc divisions but rather as a policy which advocated democratisation of international Pls rechele somethy many here in general. It had become a dynamic factor which was mobilising increasingly broad forces and inspiring them to action and struggle for independence and equality against every form of domination and interference in the internal affairs of other countries, a struggle for the settlement of acute international problems, for the promotion of international cooperation and for peace and progress in the world."[65] The achievement of the NAM can be best seen in the statement of Rajiv Gandhi. He stated, "We have moderated areas of conflict and forestalled a scramble for allies. Without non-alignment, disaster might well have overcome the world."[66] Whatever wrong doors that may be laid on its way, whatever the criticisms may be, it cannot be denied that the task before the NAM was uphill. "The outside powers always tried to influence the non-alignment summits and to twist the deliberations in their favour."[67] The great powers were not quite responsive to the non-aligned approach. In order to achieve their goal the members of the NAM will have to acquire a better understanding of each other's problems and work with one mind and spirit. They will have to demonstrate that in an explosive international market where the world has been dominated by the great powers, it is the non-aligned which can supply independence to them, in their judgement and action, and above all can forge strong domestic ties. It has been rightly pointed out that it will be wrong "to deny that the Eighth Summit of the non-aligned movement at Harare had proved purposive and successful within the parameters that define the 25 years old initiative."[68]

One among many problems which concerned the non-aligned countries was the naked act of aggression and illegal occupation of Namibia by the racist regime of South Africa. The frontline states who supported the NAM were afraid of the consequences. They were facing acute problems not only on economic aspect but also political and social. Robert Mugabe, the Prime Minister of Zimbabwe proposed a

65. *Foreign Affairs Record*, vol. XXXII (8), August 1986, pp.234-35.
66. *The Hindustan Times* (New Delhi), 26 August 1986.
67. *The Hindu* (Madras), 31 August 1986.
68. *The Times of India* (New Delhi), 9 September 1986.

Security Force to guard the frontline states. But India was not in favour of creating a military force, not in favour of sending military help to tackle the aggressive designs of South Africa. Rather it offered agricultural cooperation if the frontline states meet drought conditions. Thus, the only way to supplant South Africa's firm position was mandatory sanctions. Apart from immediate sanctions the important task before the summit was to make the frontline states self-reliant, so that it would reduce their dependence on South Africa. So the members of the NAM agreed to create African Fund to assist them and India was chosen as chairperson of the fund. Moreover, the apartheid policy being pursued by the South African government resulted in a confrontation between the people and the government. The people fought for their inherent natural rights and the government went on suppressing the blacks. The country was on the verge of a civil war. The African National Congress leader Joe Modise was determined "to avoid the struggle from becoming black-versus-white."[69] The non-aligned movement appealed to the government as well as the people to sort out their differences and to find out a solution to the problem. The leaders of the NAM raised the issue in the International forums and urged all countries to pay serious thought to the issue.

Non-alignment as a movement built up by Nehru and followed by Indira Gandhi and Rajiv Gandhi stood for anti-colonialism, anti-racism and peaceful cooperation. The role India played in Harare summit consolidated the movement and gave it a positive direction. In the eighties India's policy of non-alignment sought to update the long chosen policy of Nehru. Rajiv Gandhi always worked on the settled principles, judging every question on its merit and did not show any tilt towards any Super Power. No doubt, India and the Soviet Union shared similar views but it would be utter foolishness to categorise India pro-Soviet. They shared similar views when both of them felt that they were striving for peace, disarmament and international cooperation. They worked jointly when they realised that their cooperation would be to mankind's needs. On major international issues India preferred joint actions and appealed to the statesmen to work on the principles of the NAM. This democratic diplomacy brought India popularity and the NAM as a more credible world movement. However, the BJP was not satisfied with the performance of the NAM. The BJP alleged that "the non-aligned approach and

69. *The Hindustan Times* (New Delhi), 4 September 1986.

judging of issues independently on merit is the right policy for India. In its view, in the effective application of this policy the government had failed, because the government could not ensure a coordinated execution of policy as it lacked clarity of perceptions. As a result, the party added, India had lost its credibility."[70] "India's policy of non-alignment could not be able to make a headway in the improvement of our relations with the superpowers because the government did not have a clear-cut policy."[71] The Bharatiya Janata Party condemned the way Congress government was functioning in formulating India's foreign policy. The party asserted that, "the foreign policy of Rajiv Gandhi's government had critically affected the totality of our foreign policy formulation, its conduct and all our external relations. The country's foreign policy was totally adrift: Issues of vital national importance were being so amateurishly handled as to critically affect the nation's immediate and long term interests."[72] It was surpising that the US had persistently refused to appreciate Indian standpoint on different issues, as for example, non-alignment. "Whether we like it or not, Pakistan was America's ally in the South-Asian part of the world, while most Americans considered India as a Soviet ally."[73] So the policy of non-alignment was criticised because the Western countries had never shown their support. The BJP, therefore, urged the government to revamp the policy so that India could play an influential role in the world. Being attacked from several quarters that India's policy of non-alignment was under trial and India was considered as a Soviet ally, Prime Minister Rajiv Gandhi remarked:

> "Non-aligned does not mean aligned in any way. It is an euphemism for convenience. It is really seeing the world in a more democratic way in a sense where you have the right to speak your mind without being constrained by bloc-boundaries or bloc positions on issues. Non-alignment is becoming more and more accepted in the world."[74]

Even if there were criticisms, it is beyond doubt that the non-aligned movement provided direction to Third World countries. The

70. *Two Years of Congress Misrule, A Charge Sheet,* as adopted by the BJP National Executive at Jammu on October 19, 1986, p.9.
71. *Organiser,* vol. XXXIX (12), Independence Day Number,1986, p. 26.
72. *National Executive Meeting of the BJP,* Jodhpur,October 9 to 11, 1987, p.6.
73. *Organiser,* December 20, 1987, p.2.
74. *Statement of Foreign Policy, Prime Minister Rajiv Gandhi* (New Delhi: Publication Division, Ministry of External Affairs, Government of India, May 1988), p.30.

movement ensured India to find a place in the international forums. It gave India option to retain her independent judgements in foreign affairs. India's plea for peace was not because it was militarily weak or incapable of countering threats from the imperialist forces, but because it was only one choice before the mankind to prevent calamity of extinction. As Rajiv Gandhi stated, "Non-alignment stands above all for human dignity and human rights. The exertions of the NAM have brought freedom to many of those countries who are today members of the movement. That is why we have been in the forefront of the struggle against colonialism and racism. But the struggle is by no means over. Areas of primary concern to the non-aligned movement are apartheid in South Africa, colonialism in Namibia and the destabilisation of the frontline states by the depredations of Pretoria. Our strength and our future lie in the unity, solidarity and cohesion of the non-aligned movement."[75] The Soviet Union in its fight for peace and disarmament extended full support to the non-aligned movement. The nuclear race which created conflicts and tensions was the major concern for both India and the Soviet Union. "Co-ordinating its efforts with the national liberation forces, the USSR had always been determined and uncompromising in supporting the non-aligned movement at all stages of its struggle against imperialism and colonialism and it had been consistent in rendering effective help to the people who were courageously defending and consolidating their newly won freedom. In effect, this was the joint position of socialism and non-alignment."[76]

Combodia was under the influence of China. The Heng Samarin government captured the capital and adjoining territories and the Poi regime was overthrown. The Chinese government opposed Vietnamese action and instisted on withdrawal of Vietnamese troops from Cambodia. The USSR and the US were also involved in this issue and supported Vietnam and China respectively. India's position was quite different in this regard. It was of the view that the two claimants, Sihanouk and Poi should not be allowed to have a seat in Kampuchea till the tangled issue is solved. Malaysia, on the other hand, favoured

75. *Statement of Foreign Policy, Prime Minister Rajiv Gandhi* (New Delhi: Publication Division, Ministry of External Affairs, Government of India, November 1986), pp.73-75.

76. Kovalenko, Ivan and Tuzmukhamedov, Rails, *The Non-aligned movement : The Soviet View* (Delhi : Sterling, 1987), pp.98-99.

Heng Samarin government. Other members like Laos and Vietman strongly opposed the Malaysian stand. "The AICC(I) commended India's active participation in her efforts for a peaceful solution of the Kampuchean problem and urged the government to preserve in promoting the peace process."[77] In 1989 bilateral relations between China and the USSR improved and the Soviet Union pressurised Vietnam to withdraw its troops. Subsequently the UN intervened and the Cambodian problem was solved.

The non-aligned movement strongly condemned the US policies and actions towards Third World countries. But there was no unanimity of opinions among the members and there was always an atmosphere of suspicion and allegations towards each other. In the Harare Summit Burma walked out of the movement alleging that India was Pro-Soviet. The notability, and unassociated character of of the movement was disturbed by such mutual bickerings and suspicions and so the movement was losing its credibility. The movement appeared to be lacking integrity. India, on the other hand, working for peace and amity on the lines of Mahatma Gandhi and Jawaharlal Nehru had chosen peaceful way to settle problems and kept faith on mutual co-existance and never discriminated between weak and strong nations. India never lost her faith on the policy of non-alignment and continued her efforts for relaxation of tensions that had erupted out of nuclear threats and military alliances. Even in the odd days India discouraged the developments of freezing the world into two ideological camps, communists and non-communists. With this division, there was danger for Europe and America and the poor nations fighting among themselves fell prey to the imperialist countries and joined in the game of nuclear race. The non-aligned countries had their own stake regarding non-use of nuclear weapons and so they worked for peace and cooperation. The major thrust of the non-aligned countries was to create world public opinion in favour of the disarmament issues, collective security and strategic stability. Speaking on the collective security and disarmament efforts of the non-aligned movement, Rajiv Gandhi said, "Nonalignment is the assertion of the possibility of all the diverse systems of the world living together in peace and harmony. We believe the mutual interaction of systems promotes the evolution of societies by each emulating what it finds of value in the other. The cross fertilisation of ideas and experience is an essential attribute of

77. *Resolution Passed in the AICC Meeting* in New Delhi on 4th and 5th November 1988, p.29.

peaceful coexistence."[78] There are also UN resolutions regarding non-use of nuclear weapons. But the nuclear race still continued. The non-aligned countries sought increased involvement of the United Nations to declare the use of nuclear weapons illegal and immoral. In case of any violation, proper action should be taken. But the approach of the non-aligned countries was not equally responded to by nuclear powers. Instead of disarmament they preferred arms control. The main reason why the non-aligned countries could not succeed to their satisfaction was that there were a range of issues on which there was no unanimity. They differed in their attitude and perceptions and were often unable to take firm action to solve a problem. While they relied on the United Nations and kept faith in its resolutions, at the UN meetings they differed. It was realised that in a scenario of the possibility of a nuclear war there should be no difference and to save the lives of millions of innocents the disarmament efforts must be given top priority. So the need of the hour was to demonstrate the superiority of the NAM, contrary to common criticism by the detractors of the movement. Moreover, the non-aligned movement should have to readapt and readjust itself to various power configurations in the world. The most challenging problem it faced was the policy of Western capitalist countries towards militarisation. So the strength of the movement had been dependent on the United Nations. The United Nations proved a useful forum for debating global concerns, provided ample opportunities to negotiate with one another, to mobilise world public opinion and to catalyze the world powers so that the disarmament efforts could progress. "Hence the need and the current call for transforming the UN system on their part"[79] was the most urgent task before the NAM.

In 1988, in the conference of the foreign ministers of non-aligned countries held in Nicosia they emphasised the need of nuclear disarmament. In their opinion, the Super Powers should adopt and carry out a programme for the elimination of nuclear weapons. In this period the role of the NAM was also challenging. It was accepted that the non-

78. *Statement of Foreign Policy*, Prime Minister Rajiv Gandhi, (New Delhi: Publication Division, Ministry of External Affairs, Government of India, December 1988), p.51.

79. Shingham, A.W. and Shirley Hune, *Non-alignment in an age of Alignments* (West port: Lawrence and Hill Co., 1986), pp.372-74.

aligned movement "should not only help consolidate new thinking, nor merely assist in reducing tensions between the two great nuclear powers, but also promote a climate of confidence and detente throughout the world and ensure the irreversible nature of the favourable process that had begun. Naturally, it is also impossible to avoid the question of building a new equitable and just economic order and expanding cooperation between the developing countries themselves to further their economic and social progress."[80] The other major task of the NAM was freedom of the newly liberated countries. For the newly liberated countries of Asia and Africa "independence meant the freedom for each country to choose its own individual path of development and steer its own course in international affairs unimpeded by the distorting prisons of bloc rivalries".[81] "The basic tenet of non-alignment is peaceful co-existence between different social and economic systems,"[82] and happily the Super Powers had shown their readiness to hold talks to bridge their gap as well as the differences between the East and the West.

The cold war between the USSR and the US started subsiding towards the end of the eighties. Both the Super Powers showed a greater spirit of accommodation and strived remove their bilateral differences on various issues. Despite occasional failures they continued to make renewed and persistent efforts to halt the armament race. The cold war which characterised the relations between the two Super Powers and their allies for over four decades came to an end when heads of the two governments showed their willingness to end tension on nuclear armaments. With this a new situation arose before the non-aligned countries. Since the cold war was almost over, A.B. Vajpayee spoke in Parliament, "the first and foremost task of the Indian government should be to give new relevance to the policy of non-alignment. There are certain principles of the policy on which the government should work to solve the contemporary problems."[83]

80. Vladimirov, Leonid P. (ed.), *The Soviet-Indian Phenomenon* (New Delhi: Allied, 1989), p.65.

81. *Statement of Foreign Policy, Prime Minister Rajiv Gandhi*, (New Delhi: Publication Division, Ministry of External Affairs, Government of India, September 1988), pp.9-11.

82. *Ibid.*, p.47.

83. Vajpayee, A.B., *Rajya Sabha Debates*, vol. CL (4), 27 April 1989, cols. 205-208.

Turning to the relations with the Super Powers after the end of the Cold War, a sea change appeared to have occurred in the last years of Rajiv Gandhi's reign. Personal friendship occupied more importance than the international cooperation. "There was a tendency to identify oneself with certain policies which were the products of the internal and external compulsions of one or the other side."[84] Thus, we had failed in keeping away from the Super Powers game. At the pace at which Gorbachev was moving towards disarmament proposals, non-alignment was expected to give serious thought to world economic and industrial problems rather than regional and military alliances between nations. For a healthy economic and industrial developments North-South cooperation on thes fields was the most urgent task. "If these goals are to be achieved, the NAM will have to regenerate itself and discontinue its routine exercises of updating a draft document within a rigid framework."[85]

The Ninth Summit of the non-aligned countries was held in Belgrade from 4th to 7th September 1989, here the representatives of 102 countries took part. In political sphere the summit called for solution of problems of Afghanistan, speedy democratisation of Latin America and restoration of natural rights of the Palestinians. It called for the concerned parties to convene an international peace conference to settle Arab-Israel conflict under the auspices of the United Nations. The summit also called on complete disarmament to safeguard outer space and to ban sea bed explosions. The summit called on the international community to widen the sanctions against South Africa. The economic problems also touched in the Ninth Summit of the NAM. The increasing debt burden was a major stumbling bloc for the progress of developing countries. Self reliance and economic independence which were primary tasks before the NAM can be achieved "if the non-aligned countries structurally delink themselves from the capitalist world order. It, however, does not imply any total break of the economic relationship between them. A total break is neither possible nor warranted in the present stage of world development."[86] So, first and foremost task of the non-aligned countries should be to

84. Venkateswaran, A.P., "The International Arena", *Seminar,* No. 353, 1989, pp.44-47.

85. Subramaniam, K., "NAM: New Challenges, New Goals", *World Focus,* vol.10, No.9, September 1989, p.25.

86. Bhambhri, C.P., *Foreign Policy of India* (New Delhi: Sterling, 1987), p.6.

urge the developed countries to come for result-oriented North-South dialogue to overcome crippling economic burden of poor countries.

The Tenth Summit of the NAM held at Jakarta was attended by 108 nations and it adopted the Final Document and the 'Jakarta Message'. The call was given in Jakarta for an equitable economic order, nuclear-weapons free world and for peaceful settlements of international disputes. Emphasis was given for South-South as well as North-South cooperation. Reviewing the international scenario, it was assumed that the powerful and affluent non-alinged countries like India and Singapore should come forward to utilise their resources, technical knowledge and skills for their mutual benefit. It all appeared that the Super Powers were convinced about the economic restructure of the world. The voice of the non-aligned movement was distinctly heard in the world and the Super Powers showed their support to the movement. The Soviet leader, Eduared Shevardnadze in an interview to the English daily said that, "Soviet Union had extended its support to the aspirations of the non-aligned movement not only to preserve but also to enhance its role in the world arena. He assured that the non-aligned countries would always have the Soviet Union as a partner who respects the status of non-alignment, its philosophy, its basic goals and principles."[87] The Bharatiya Janata Party recommended that India should take the initiative in solving international problems under the principles of the NAM so that NAM continues "to play a role of achieving peace and amity in the world. The party mentioned that it would urge upon people of India not to indulge in any demonstration in favour or against any side in the war."[88] "A notable feature of many non-aligned pronouncements is the disparity in the critical standards applied to the US and Soviet Union, respectively. it was the West that conferred independence on vast territories in Africa and Europe. The West has extended vast quantities of foreign assistance and afforded developing countries preferred access to its markets. Yet, on both political and economic issues, it is the West that absorbs the brunt of criticism and complaint. Although an increasing number of NAM members are concerned by this imbalance and are actively seeking more genuinely nonaligned positions, they are disadvantaged

87. Singh, Darshan, *Soviet Foreign Policy Documents*, 1989 (New Delhi:Sterling, 1990), p.126.

88. Sharma, Narendra, "Whither BJP ?", *Mainstream*, vol. XXIX, No. 7, 16 February 1991, pp.4-5.

by the practice of taking decisions by consensus".[89] "Foreign policy should be so recorded as to maximise the number of our friends abroad. Mere attendance at meetings of the Non-aligned Movement, and rhetorical statements therein, are not enough to win us friends. Our diplomacy must be more vigorous and active bilaterally, inorder to explain our point of view to seek understanding and support on matters of vital interest to us".[90] "India is continuing its positive contribution to the ongoing exercises of reorienting the role of the NAM. The Foreign Minister in September 1991 reaffirmed that the role and relevance of the movement in the changed international situation as a political forum of the developing world. While retaining its political thrust as a movement of countries that seek to preserve this independence of judgment and freedom of action, the movement decided to accord greater priority to the economic issues and to active greater coordination between NAM and G-77".[91] "However, neither has been achieved. The global economy remains firmly in the grip of a few industrialised countries. The movement has been a concrete political force. Despite all the talks of peace and cooperation, military conflicts among the non-aligned nations are not uncommon. The inefficiency of the movement was most visible during the Gulf crisis, when Iraq rebuffed diplomatic overtures from non-aligned leaders to withdraw from Kuwait, a fellow non-aligned country. Yugoslavia was on the brink of a civil war. Egypt was seen to be too closely identified with the United States. Despite its record the Non-aligned Movement is still the only grouping that by virtue of its numerical superiority in UN Organisations, can put the South interest on to the global agenda. At a time when the artificial division of the world politics into East and West is over, the distinction between the rich North and poor South is becoming increasingly clear."[92]

Inspite of all hazards, "The non-aligned movement is readjusting in a dynamic manner to the breathtaking place of global developments. The Indian goverment has reaffirmed its faith in its continued relevance."[93] "What NAM needs today is the activism. NAM should

89. *Deptt. of State Bulletin*, Vol. 87, No. 2118, January 1987, p.58.

90. *National Executive Meeting*, Thiruvananthapuram, Sept. 30, 1991, p.18.

91. *FAR*, Oct. 1991, XXXVII(10), MEA, Govt. of India.

92. *New Strait Times*, 31, August 1991.

93. Lok Sabha Debates,viii (i),Tenth Series, Third Session, February 24,1992, Cols.20-21.

proceed to lesser the burden of the United Nations and should try to do away with the bossism of the big powers. This can only be accomplished by devising effective mechanism to solve the problems of the NAM members in particular and of the third world war in general and thus becoming one ensemble. NAM should also attempt to find new answers to old problems. NAM has to show skill in turning the largely theoretical concept of the Collective Self Reliance of South into a reality by identifying and harnessing the potential of growth and developments."[94] "On intra NAM issues of a code of conduct and confidence-building and conflict-resolving mechanisms were necessary to reduce the chances of violent conflict among member countries".[95]

It is true that the changes in the world have questioned some of India's basic ideas like N.A. "Long before the non-aligned movement came into existence, India pursued a policy of essential autonomy in decision making in its external relations. Today when there are no power blocs, and no competing options being urged, it is even more important to preserve out sovereignty, to examine each item on merit against the background of India's unwavering commitment to world peace and global development, with our national interest as the determining factor. Support to the Palestinian cause continues to be cornerstone of India's policy. The AICC affirm that an enduring basis to such a settlement would be the ending of all discrimination against Israelis of Arab origin with Israel, the withdrawal of Israel from the Occupied Territories, a national thousand for the Palestinians and the establishment of amicable relations of peace and cooperation between all the states in the region".[96] Though there is breakdown of the USSR, India and Russia are keen to establish strong bond among themselves as partners in political, economic and military fields.

The Burbulis visit has opened a new chapter in relations with India by revealing that from their own experience the Russians are realising the need for rebuilding their time-tested relationship with India. "It was evident that the Russian president himself has an open mind. It was on his intervention that an eminent Indian visiting Moscow last month was assured that relations with India were of

94. *National Herald,* New Delhi, 6 May 1992.
95. *New Straight Times* (Kuala Lampur) 2 September 1992.
96. *Text of Resolution adopted at 29th plenary session of INC,* Rajiv Nagar, Tirupati from 14th to 16th of April 1992.

fundamental importance to Russia. The Russian had assured the Indian side that, as the successor state, they would honour all agreements to which the previous state was a party.[97] "The decision of the Soviet Union to modify the two year old Indo-Russian agreement on the sale to India of cryogenic engines has its political and economic significance to non-aligned India. In the circumstances, non-aligned India has no option but to go back to its time-tested policy of self-reliance in the development of technology for these engines as in other respects. It is feared that India might have to confront the United States, the sole Super power. In this situation, we need to reiterate our traditional stand, as a non-aligned state, we plan to move ahead in our economic ,technological development for peaceful purposes, that we are opposed to the norms of the discriminatory MTCR, as we have been to the signing of the NPT, and that India is determined to pursue, as before, economic and technological development for peaceful and developmental purposes.[98] "The Jakarta Summit of the NAM countries has once again established the relevance of Non-Alignment. The end of the Cold War increases, rather than reduces, the imperative of fashioning a world order that will secure the freedom of all states, the sovereign equality of all, non-interference in the internal affairs of others, democracy in international relations, peaceful co-existence and opportunities for the full flowering, through mutual cooperation and of the potential of all member states."[99] "Blindly aping an affluent economy and way of life, much beyond their means and capabilities, will mean unmitigated disaster to developing countries and erode the essence of their freedom. What needs to be realised is that poverty by itself is nothing contemptible; what is really deplorable is to ignore realities and to barter freedom for what may appear temporary gains. It would be a clear negation of non-alignment which, essentially, is the preservation of freedom and self-reliance".[100] The North-South division and differences in economic relations is the major stumbling

97. Girish Mathur, "Indo-Russian ties: Defining the Parameters," *Link,* 10 May 1992, 34(39), pp. 20-22.

98. M.S. Rajan, "Updating India's Non-Alignment," *Mainstream,* 11 Sept 1993, 31 (44), pp. 15-16.

99. *Congress marches ahead,* AICC, May 1993, Minutes of the CWC meeting, March 26-27, 1993.

100 INC, 79th Plenary session, Rajiv Gandhi Nagar, Tirupati, 14-16 April, 1992, Presidential Address by P.V. Narshima Rao.

block before the NAM. The NAM for that reason has called for an end to the economic disarray existing between North and South. "It is thus simply a matter of common sense that both sides (north-south) should recognise their interdependence and come together to fashion a joint strategy in dealing with the formidable challenges of this critical decade. It is also urged to end protectionism and an early resolution of the Uruguay Round of talks under the GATT".[101] "There is a clear nexus between disarmament and development. Global economic development will have to become one of the major international issues. A new world order will need to focus on the economic facet with sincerity and political will. If peace and stability is to be secured, the gulf between the rich and the poor will have to stop widening."[102]

The recent visit of President Boris Yeltsin of the Russian Federation "has restored the traditionally close, time-tested ties between Moscow and New Delhi. The AICC welcome the Russian Federation's reaffirmation of identity of views with India on many international issues, including issues relating to cross-border terrorist activity impinging on our territory." [103] "The challenge to Indian policy making, in the realm of international affairs is three fold:

(a) to speedily recognise the altered realities of today and to realign India's foreign policy at this critical turn of the century;

(b) to harmonise internal and external policy articulations, and the conduct of our diplomacy, so as to secure for India its rightful place and role in the commity of nations; and

(c) to address itself to the vital need for such South Asian initiatives as would establish beneficial bilateral relations will all our neighbours, thus enabling this vast reservoir of humanity to free itself from the crippling thraldom of poverty and want."[104]

The Jakarta Summit of the Non-aligned countries has once again established the relevance of Non-alignment. "The end of the Cold War increases, rather than reduces, the imperative of fashioning a world

101. *New Strait Times*, 12 May 1993, NAM Ministerial Meeting in Nusa Dua, Bali, May 11-13.

102. *Indian Express* (New Delhi), 31 Aug 1992.

103. *AICC Meeting*, Surajkund, Faridabad, 27-28 May 1993.

104. *Presidential address* by L.K. Advani, National Council Session, 18-20 June 1993, Bangalore, p.18.

order that will secure the freedom of all States, the sovereign equality of all, non-interference in the internal affairs of others, democracy in international relations, peaceful coexistence and opportunities for the full flowering through mutual cooperation, of the potential of all member states and of the human family. In pursuance of these ideals, India has also been seeking a greater role for the United Nations and its strengthening through democratisation in the character and the composition of its evital institutions."[105] "Now that the two blocs do not exist, we must unite efforts to seek peace and prosperity, Indonesian Foreign Minister Ali Alatas told a press conference. The 113 NAM members put aside political differences to form a bloc in the United Nations to pass resolutions benefiting their countries".[106] "The Prime Minister, P.V. Narasimha Rao, speaking at the non-aligned summit in Cartagene, Colombia, wanted the current negotiations for a CTBT and the convention for the cut-off of fissile material to be used to obtain a commitment to universal and comprehensive nuclear disarmament".[107] The critics allege that the foreign policy of India still lacks to be an integrated one. There are still departmental sub-divisions, disorder and inter-departmental disorientations. It has suffered from some errors and committed many mistakes. It is not functioning satisfactorily and thereby blurred the image of the NAM. Whether or not the foreign policy succeeds, it is an undeniable fact that the policy of non-alignment remains to be a `jehad' that provides a strategy to carry foreign policy forward. It is also true that the non-aligned movement has not achieved anything commendable. Even if arduous struggle it was not successful in solving international disputes.

Inspite of this, the movement is getting popular and its strength is increasing day by day. The simple reason is that the new states have no desire in the struggle for power or to influence the rest of the states. They condemmed the imperialist ambitions and hegemonic policy of the Super Powers. There are also many geopolitical reasons which prompted newly born states of the world to pursue the policy of non-alignment. Furthermore, the world has ceased to be bipolar and many Asian and African countries look for their development after a long haul of imperial exploitation. It is also true that the great powers still exercise their influences in economic and political fields. So, they are not included in the membership of the NAM aiming that they would

105. *All India Congress Committee Meeting*, Surajkund, Faridabad, 27-28 March 1993, p. 25.

106. *Times of India*, New Delhi, October 17, 1995.

not be able to overpower the weak and poor countries. The NAM has looked for disciplined members who will work to remove the potential causes of recurring wars and conflicts and to create a new world order, where the international system will be managed by democratic norms and values free from great powers' hegemonistic ambitions. The NAM is strong-willed enough to knit the world into a close associated group of nations when all the states would exercise freedom of policy and action in international affairs.

The critics allege that the aspirations and capabilities of the great powers in exercising hegemony over the rest of the world demonstrates the irrelevance of the United Nations and the NAM. Though the Super Powers are at present no longer hostile to the policy of non-alignment, though they have been sending good will to the states of the NAM, it is asserted that the movement has no relevance in the present day world, especially after the end of the cold war. However, in the view of new detente, the non-alignment is not outdated. The new detente has not changed the traditional game of power politics. The vast majority of the nations still witness great powers' financial colonialism. Recently, the United States had threatened WHO to withdraw her contribution and it was done only to prevent Palestine from being admitted to WHO and ultimately the United States succeeded. So whenever the policies of great powers get obstructed or nations go contrary to their wishes, they try to win them. So it would be improper to relate non-alignment to the cold war. We have seen the cold war blown off in the seventies but non-alignment persisted. Therefore, in the wake of periodical changes in the international scenario non-alignment showed its potential. Thus the Non-aligned movement has a bright future ahead promoting the causes of Third World countries. The only need of the hour is the non-aligned states should strike now to enforce their decisions rather than going for fresh decisions always and appealing great powers to abjure their dangerous course of actions. To protect the globe encircled by military bases, the non-aligned countries should be non-aligned both in letter and spirit. Unless they are able to focus it to a particular angle of treatment to a particular power, unless the movement becomes energetic, forceful, resonant and real, we cannot tackle the impecreating countries roaming and creating disturbances around us and there lies the future of the non-aligned movement.

107. *Times of India* , New Delhi, December 1, 1995.

Finally, the non-aligned countries "would undoubtedly benefit from careful matching of means to ends, instruments to purpose, and by concentrating more on correcting its own manifest disabilities and less on drafting rhetorical flourishes".[108] "The presents of the non-aligned movement has indeed been sturdy and concrete. Perhaps the most abiding of its achievements has been the successful propagation of an alternative vision of international relations based on independence, national sovereignty and peaceful co-existence in the peace of the concept of power blocs and confrontation".[109]

108. Mansingh, Surjeet, *India and the Nonaligned Movement, occasional Papers on History and Society* (Second Series) (New Delhi: Nehru Memorial and Museum Library, Teen Murti House, 1991), p.17.

109. *Statement of Foreign Policy*, Prime Minister Rajiv Gandhi (New Delhi: Publication Division, Ministry of External Affairs, Government of India, April 1988), pp.61-63.

CHAPTER II

India's Nuclear Policy

After the end of the Second World War the world witnessed mad race of arms among the countries to outmanoeuvre each other. The acquisition, development and proliferation of nuclear weapons were escalated. Interestingly, Third World countries instead of restructuring their economy were seeking arms. Although the developing countries claimed that they were procuring arms for self-defence, on the other hand it gave birth to fear and suspicion among the nations. With the emphasis on arms acquisition the states started producing more qualitative weapons. The Cold War between the Soviet Union and the United States was intensifying towards the end of the seventies with the Soviet intervention in Afghanistan. Several efforts to ease the tension proved useless. Both the US and the USSR started condemning each other for the new Cold War.

The eighties also witnessed antagonism between the two Super Powers. The development and possession of nuclear weapons continued at the same rate as in early decades. New weapons like I.C.B.Ms, Titan, Polaris, Minutemen and many others caused enormous destruction to the civilians. With the advent of the nuclear weapons the superpowers made them competitors spreading their influence all over the world. The large scale destruction and the huge amount involved in producing weapons and its utilisation concerned the peace loving nations. Surprisingly, the arms race escalated and sharpened further bringing the world on the verge of another world war. The mostly affected developing countries were burdened with debt and their economy was deteriorating. The United Nations which was established to ensure peace and harmony all over the world had little to do in this proxy war. Now the arms race posed threat in the form of waste of resources and hindrance to the economic development and democratic process. It diminished the existence of 'Panchasheel' and undermined a world without fear and suspicion. At this stage, the statesmen started giving serious thought to disarmament and to evolve some mechanism so that peace in the world could be restored. Middle powers, like India, also gave serious thought to end the cold war. They had their national interest in the effort of easing tension, as they needed enormous fund for their industrialisation and above all rapid economic development. Thus, India adhered to the policy of peace and disarmament.

India's peaceful nuclear programme began soon after her independence. At that time the focus was to use available nuclear energy for the development of mankind. But the Sino-Indian War and the Chinese nuclear explosion compelled Indian policy makers to reconsider their way of utilising nuclear energy. The Indian government started considering on nuclear weapons and the Indian government initiated proposals for acquiring conventional nuclear weapons. "Despite speculation about work on the design of an explosive system Lal Bahadur Shastri did not talk of a nuclear explosion. It was after the implosion of 1974 that India developed a coherent nuclear doctrine to suit the fast changing circumstances. This doctrine came to be based on the same earlier construct of the geostrategic utility and overall commitment to a peaceful approach. The eighties saw no major shift in India's position on the nuclear policy."[1] "Historically, the motivations for policy in the nuclear field have been two fold. First, there were the general attraction of a high yield field, in which the investment, although demanding, could be managed incrementally, especially if the programme could count on significant foreign assistance and technical cooperation in its less developed phases. Secondly, there was the attractions of nuclear power as a viable and prestigious proposition in a country that has been chronically deficient in terms of the total energy requirement at all points in its independent career. Sometime during the course of the late 1960s or the early 1970s, a third motivation surfaced. Marked by ambiguity andm somewhat conflicting interpretations, this is usually code worded India's nuclear options', denoting a connection with nuclear weaponry that is supposed to be both illicit and irresponsible regionally and in a global proliferation sense".[2]

The critics argue that India's advocacy of peace should be matronized with strength. It implies that the defence industry needs to

1. Azam, Kousar, J.(ed.), *India's Defence Policy for the 1990s* (New Delhi: Sterling, 1992), pp.58-59.
2. Ram, N., "The Nuclear Dispute: An Indian Perspective", in Sulochana R. Glazer and N. Glazer (eds.), *Conflicting Images: India and the United States* (Gleen Dale: Riverdale Co. Publishers), 1990, p.84.

be fortified with the weapons that the situation demands. Through proper utilisation of skills and resources available in the country self-sufficiency in defence production can be achieved. Thus, attempts of the imperialists to destabilise our nation by encouraging anti-national elements and arming Pakistan can be best tackled by utilising all resources—human and material . Moreover, the opposition should be consulted on major international issues. At the same time it must be remembered that security cannot be jeopardised on ideological differences between the opposition and the ruling party. Internal strength occupies much attention than mere acquisition or production of nuclear arms. Thus the citadel of strength is to set aside all differences and to formulate a policy to act in one mind and spirit.

The global situation in the eighties was truly alarming. The world was closely moving towards a nuclear disaster. Amidst the darkness of nuclear catastrophe Indian voice of disarmament raised the prospects of peace all over the world. India's argument of protecting the regions unaffected by the nuclear abyss was also supported by many Third World countries. Despite these seriouse efforts the arms race continued. Scarce resources which are supposed to be the ingredients of economic development diverted for producing nuclear arsenals. The peace-loving nations were forced to take the side of one or other Super Powers. The reason is that they were dependent on the Super Powers for their economic development. As the Super Powers' confrontation reached to a point of no return, the question that assumed importance whether the humanity would survive in the face of a nuclear confrontation. "To talk of a better, safer and more secure tomorrow had almost become a sacrilege. As the nuclear weapon states resorted to increased stockpiling, they spread a wave of unrest, uncertainty and anxiety among the non-nuclear countries. As the tensions grew, more and more countries were being brought into the orbit of confrontation. With the potential of nuclear weapons gaining horrendous proportions, a stage had been reached where peace and security were attributes gaining less and less priority in the calculations of major powers."[3]

On November 4,1980, Reagan was elected the President of United States of America. During Reagan's tenure, Indo-American relations deteriorated and even affected India's development. On December 29, Washington announced its decision to resume military assistance to

3. *India and the International Scene*, AICC Publication, pp.1-2.

Pakistan which concerned New Delhi. It created tension between India and Pakistan, too. Pakistan sought military help on the ground that India was planning to develop nuclear weapons. But Pakistan's suspicion about India's strategic weapons' development was baseless. No doubt Indian Government opted for demonstrating certain abilities it had, but there was no plan developing nuclear weapons or medium-range. On June 19, 1980 the Carter Administration had approved the shipments of enriched uranium for Tarapore. The Reagan Administration, on the other hand, seemed reluctant to resume the supply of uranium to India. It was a reversal of the approach taken by the Carter Administration when it approved export licenses for two fuel shipments for Tarapore. "Transmittal of Executive order authorizing export of low-enriched uranium to India for use in fuelling of Tarapore Atomic Power Station determined that it was not prejudicial to achievement of U.S non-proliferation objectives."[4] But it was not sure whether the US Government would resume nuclear fuel supply. This policy of the US shocked the Bharatiya Janata Party. "They lost their belief and confidence in the American Government".[5] "The Reagan policy added up to a sharp change in emphasis from President Carter's Non-Proliferation policy. Carter had emphasized U.S. restrictions on exports of nuclear material and equipment that would be used to build weapons. The Reagan policy emphasized the opposite".[6] In the view of the BJP, the US was reluctant to resume fuel supply to Tarapore reactor because it wanted to strengthen Pakistan to maintain balance of power. The BJP leader questioned in the Rajya Sabha "whether the government had taken any step for our security threat".[7] "The Indian government was aware that Pakistan had been trying to acquire uranium enrichment and nuclear fuel reprocessing facilities. The shipment of US made electronic equipment to Pakistan via Canada concerned the Indian government. The Government of Pakistan, on the other hand, assured that their nuclear programme was solely directed

4. CIS, Annual, 1980, vol. II, Nos 1-2, Abstracts of Congressional Publications and Legislative Histories (Congressional Information Service, INC. Washington D.C.,1981), p.228.

5. *Rajya Sabha Debates,* vol. CXV, No.11, 6 August 1980, cols. 339-49.

6. *Congress and the Nation,* vol. VI(1981-84), A Review of Government and Politics (Washington D.C., Congressional Quarterly Inc., 1985), p.138.

7. *Rajya Sabha Debates.* vol. CXVI, No. 19, 12 December 1980.

towards peaceful purposes. However, the Indian government continued to be vigilant and was prepared to take all necessary steps to safeguard the security interests of India."[8]

India was not convinced by Pakistan's plea that in case an atom bomb is made it would not be used against India. However, after getting this assurance, India had two options, either to nuclear or restrans Pakistan from going nuclear. The second choice was more valid as it would not involve risk. On the other hand, if at all India goes nuclear then it diverts from her economic development. So "India had always favoured the total elimination of nuclear weapons. In safeguarding India's sovereign rights to develop and use nuclear technology for peaceful purposes, India had continued to oppose discriminatory arrangements such as the NPT while urging the conclusion of a general convention of the total prohibition of the use or threat of use of nuclear weapons."[9] The Indian side highly appreciated the constructive steps of the Soviet Union aiming at achieving disarmament and a just and durable political settlement of the conflict situations. The Soviet view was that "India was making a significant contribution to the struggle against the nuclear war and for consolidating peace and security in the region".[10]

Detente, which India always welcomed and worked for, had been subjected to stresses and strains. There had been some developments in the early eighties, for example US supply of nuclear weapons to Pakistan, which caused concern among the peace loving nations. "The AICC noted with deep concern the developments in various parts of the world indicating the revival of a climate of cold war and confrontation. The AICC was deeply disturbed about the consequences on India's security environment. It hoped that fruitful talk between the US and the USSR would come out."[11] The BJP leader Jaswant Singh argued "if Pakistan possess nuclear weapons, it is no good saying that we are for peaceful uses of atomic energy because it would lead to strategic imbalance of the sub-continent. He wanted to know the procurement and equipping policy of nuclear weapons looking at the grave danger the country was about to face."[12] Pakistan's nuclear

8. *Ibid.*

9. Zaidi, A.M.(ed.), *The Annual Register of Indian Political Parties (Proceedings and Fundamental Texts, 1980)* (New Delhi: S.Chand and Co., 1981), p.121.

10. *Pravda* (Moscow), 8 October 1980.

11. *Resolutions adopted by the AICC*, New Delhi, 27-28 February 1981, pp.618-20.

12. *Rajya Sabha Debates*, vol.CXVII, No. 18, 11 March 1981, cols. 304-06.

aspirations carried within them dangerous potents for a serious destabilisation of the strategic balance in the sub-continent. In the view of the BJP, "the path of nuclear armament can only harm the peoples of both our lands, not benefit them in any fashion. The BJP committed itself to the concept of peaceful use of nuclear energy. At the same time the BJP refused to alyure the availability of options to the country. It retained the right to assess the requirements of the safety of the Indian nation and its people in the light of its own perceptions. In the face of these formidable challenges, the BJP remarked, the primary task was that of forging unity of purpose in the nation. The Bharatiya Janata Party demanded a debate on the subject, to take people into confidence, to consult with the opposition, to forsake its unidimensional tilt and to revert to a credible non-alignment."[13] The Indian National Congress was equally opposed to the arms race which was leading the world towards a nuclear abyss. "The AICC was concerned about the policies of the US Government. The United States in a bid to ostensibly curb the spread of Soviet influence around the world was unjustifiably creating and enlarging tension spots by massive doles of ultra sophisticated arms to Israel, Pakistan and some other countries, by embarking on the manufacture and deployment of the so-called clean 'neutron bomb' which would only bring the nuclear war closer to reality".[14] Reacting to the nuclear policy of India in the Lok Sabha, A.B. Vajpayee said that "Pakistan and other countries while trying to enter into nuclear club and particularly Pakistan if goes for nuclear explosion then we should reconsider the whole situation and our nuclear policy. As far as nuclear technology is concerned we should explore all possible ways for its exploration. We should use it for constructive ways."[15]

The prospect of friendly relations between India and the United States could not improve as the Reagan Administration struck to its policy of stopping nuclear cooperation with India. While "the Soviet Union did not mind the effort of Third World countries to acquire

13. *Resolutions adopted by the BJP's National Council Session*, at Cochin (Kerala) on 25th-27th April 1981,p.24.

14. Zaidi, A.M., *Annual Register of Indian Political Parties*, 1981 (New Delhi: S. Chand and Co., 1982), pp.606-08.

15. *Lok Sabha Debates*, vol.XXVI, No.29, Seventh Series, Eighth Session, 30 March 1982, cols. 401-04.

16. Chaudhury, S., "Can India maintain equidistance from the Superpowers", *India Quarterly*, vol.37,No.4, October-December 1981, pp.586-87.

nuclear capability".[16] Rather the USSR extended its help to Third World countries to meet their requirements in the defence field. It is noteworthy that the US position on supplying enriched uranium to India was definitely against the principles of Indo-American nuclear cooperation agreement of 1963. "The lack of consistency in its approach to Israel, South Africa, China and even Pakistan on the one hand and to India on the other had only led to the dilution of the credibility of the US policy on control of nuclear technology. America's nuclear policy towards Pakistan revealed that the NNPA and other non-proliferation rules had been repeatedly given a go by in the interest of cultivating a close relationship with that country which was reported to have progressed towards making the nuclear bomb. On the other hand the same act was invoked to bar continuance of the existing commitments and programs to non-nuclear and friendly countries like India, who expressed their commitment to use nuclear energy only for peaceful purpose."[17]

It has been noted that the fundamental disagreement between India and the United States was the Nuclear Non-proliferation Treaty. The treaty contemplated against proliferation of nuclear weapons to non–nuclear states to preserve global peace and security. Thus the motive behind the treaty was to prevent the emergence of more nuclear weapons states. It objected the transfer of nuclear explosive devices also. The signatory states were agreed not to involve any non-nuclear states to manufacture or otherwise acquire nuclear weapons. However, the treaty granted the right to develop, to produce and use nuclear energy for peaceful purposes. Another source of discongruity between India and the United States was the Nuclear Non-proliferation Act. The Reagan Administration stopped the resupply of fuel to Tarapore reactor on the ground that it would be contrary to the terms and conditions of the NNPA. Moreover, the USA viewed that the world-wide nuclear proliferation can be checked by observing the NNPA safeguards. But India was displeased with the American stand as India had always used it for peaceful purposes. However, the discord was settled when France agreed to resume supply of fuel to India. With this USA and India emerged as unreliable friends. From an Indian perspective, the NPT was discriminatory for nuclear disarmament. The treaty did not solve the problem and it did not put restraint to possess

17. Vinod, M.J., *United States Foreign Policy towards India* (New Delhi: Lancer Books, 1991), pp. 119-22.

nuclear weapons by the nuclear powers but only prohibited its acquisition by the non-possessing states. So India, ab initio, objected the NPT.

The Indo-American relations on nuclear fuel supply to Tarapore was settled after France agreed to supply enriched uranium to India. "But France as a supplier of enriched fuel could be expected to act under US instruction and ensured that Indian Atomic Energy Programmes are monitored and controlled to American expectations".[18] Though Indo-American relations were said to be cordial after the visit of Indira Gandhi to Washington, "It did not guarantee that India and the US would grow closer to each other for the US concession was under pressure from several quarters".[19] The BJP considered that the agreement on Tarapore was not in nation's interest. In its view if India agreed to receive third party help why it did not do it independently but did it at the American instruction. In its resolution the BJP said, "it was incomprehensible why we had chosen to keep the agreement of 1963, alongwith all the attendant conditionalities, alive, whilst simultaneously opting to accept the additional ones of the IAEA and those to be imposed by France when we eventually finalised the supply of uranium from it. It was misleading to suggest that our options of reprocessing of the spent fuel were encumbered. The whole matter had been rushed through against the expert advice of our Atomic Energy Commission. This also affected the Mixed Oxide (MOX) method of reprocessing adopted by our scientists. So any further nuclear fuel supply arrangements should have a penalty clause for default in supply of raw materials and we should not accept inspection of our nuclear facilities consequent upon the application of the 'pursuit' clause".[20] Moreover, France was not agreeing to supply the stuff without full safeguards. The point was that "France was demanding the fulfilment of terms and conditions on the basis that it was a member of the London club which imposed on India such conditions".[21] At this crucial moment, in the Indo-Soviet Summit the Soviet Union extended her desire to supply nuclear fuel to India.[22] "The Indo-Soviet Summit of 1982 was characterised as a summit for

18. *Organiser,* 8-14 August 1982, p.1.
19. *Ibid.* Independence Day *Number,* 1982, p.13.
20. *Resolutions Passed by the BJP* in its National Executive Meeting, Bangalore, 28-30 August, 1982, p.18.
21 *Organiser,* 19 September 1982, p.13.
22. *Ibid.*, 3-9 September 1982, p.1.

world peace and against madness of nuclear war. Both the leaders showed great determination to extend the areas of world peace and the Soviet leadership made concrete offers to the NATO powers for the reduction of world tensions. The Indo-Soviet friendship was a warning to the imperialists that the forces of peace would exercise their full weight in the international meetings and regional forums against militarism."[23] On 30th November 1982, both USA and India exchanged notes confirming the understanding about the substitution of the US by France as a supplier of nuclear fuel for Tarapore power station. The exchange of notes paved the way for the future resumption of fuel supply for Tarapore Atomic Power Station through the signing of an agreement with the Government of France. "The exchange of notes thus helped to resolve the impasse created by the US failure to supply nuclear fuel for Tarapore as provided in the 1963 agreement".[24]

Suspicion and antagonism among the countries affected the world more in the eighties than ever before. The Super Powers' strategy of global domination and subjugation took precedence over other consideration. The arms race outmoded the assured desire of endurance. The mad race for acquiring armaments was leading the world towards a nuclear holocaust. While the world was running without food, shelter and many other essential commodities the nuclear power, were spending million of dollars on acquing nuclear armaments. In this situation "the BJP believed that it was incumbment on the superpowers to move purposefully towards nuclear disarmament. What was at stake were not just their respective domains, but it was entire humanity. So until the non-aligned countries agree on a mutual reduction of their spendings on arms, their pleadings for peace and disarmament would be lacking in the needed credibility".[25] "The Government of India attached great importance to the idea and the potentialities of the world disarmament campaign, in the ceaseless quest of mankind for a lasting, genuine world peace based on the achievment of disarmament. It was clear recognition of the fact that unless the common people everywhere, particularly in the nuclear-weapons states and other militarily signifi-

23. Bhambhri, C.P. "Relevance of the Summit", *Link,* vol.XXV, No.8, 3 October 1982, pp.10-11.

24. *Lok Sabha Debates,* Seventh Series, Eleventh Session, vol. XXXVII, No.40, 28th April 1983, cols. 80-83.

25. *Resolution in the National Executive Meeting* on 13th-14th April 1983 in Vigyan Bhavan, New Delhi, pp.1-5.

cant states, are actively concerned about the imperative and urgent need to halt and reverse the mad arms race and to make meaningful progress towards disarmament, the human race would continue to face the grave danger of self-annihilation."[26]

Mrs. Gandhi went to the USSR on a week's visit on September 20,1982. She discussed with the Soviet leaders her three suggestions made at the disarmament conference, "first, a convention on the non-use of nuclear weapons; second, a freeze on nuclear weapons and total stoppage of further production, and third, immediate suspension of nuclear weapons test. She drew the Soviet attention to the militarisation of India's neighbourhood.... The US had begun to use Pakistan for an opening into China; Pakistan and China had reached military understanding directed against India, and the US was jumping into the ring. Both Moscow and New Delhi were inexorably drawn closer together by compulsion of circumstances created by their common foes."[27] It was also reported that the USSR had agreed to assist India in importing a large quantity of heavy water and then gave their technology for making heavy water in India. According to the BJP "the USSR and other European powers being the members of the London Club would be under tight surveillance terms if they want to have supplies of nuclear material. So India should grab the Russian offer. On the contrary, the suggestion of the Atomic Energy Establishment of Tarapore to scrap the Tarapore plant as the dependence on the Soviet assistance would be contrary to India's policy of self-reliance. The decommissioning of the plant would release India from the tension of finding enriched uranium and it would save India to depend on West for spare parts in the reactor."[28] The suggestion however, did not appeal much to the Indian government. The reason was simple. A nation, being threatened by its neighbours by acquiring nuclear weapons, cannot decommission its nuclear plants. Again Russia had never put any string by giving aid. So accepting the Russian offer was not at all harmful to India's security. Rather it could be said that the fuel supply first and then technical knowledge was the demand of the time to become self-reliant. Moreover, "Soviet-Indian relations are

26. *Foreign Affairs Record*, August 1983, pp.147-49.

27. Gupta, M.G., *Indian Foreign Policy: Theory and Practice* (Agra: Y.K. Publishers, 1985),pp.188-96.

28. *Organiser*, 13-19 November 1983, p.1.

based on the fruitful basis of the treaty of peace, friendship and cooperation. Those relations had stood a good test and both sides valued that treaty and friendship. The Soviet Union stood for the strengthening of friendship with India."[29]

In 1984, the US offered nuclear weapons to Pakistan which obviously meant to arm Pakistan, it shows America's intention of helping Pakistan in case of any Indo-Pakistani nuclear war. Now it was clear that Pakistan had turned into a US bastion to pursue that any help to Pakistan would not be used against India was not to be reckoned with. This act ostensibly justified Pak-American unfriendly attitude towards India. So only one option was left for India — to go nuclear, either receiving nuclear weapons from the USSR or to develop her own nuclear weapons.

The threats of chemical and biological weapons and their proliferation assumed a global dimension as in any case proliferation of a particular kind of weapon would have a disastrous effect on the whole world in case of a war. Thus the security question was not regional but global, may it be in South Asia or West Asia or elsewhere. It was realised that unless there is a remedy to the large scale proliferation, security will be endangered. Notwithstanding the fact that the proliferation of chemical and nuclear weapons was manifested everywhere, there was no concerted international consensus to look into the adverse effects of acquiring nuclear weapons. It is because nations are free to act and think for their security, national security acquired more attention than the global security. In case of India and Pakistan, if Pakistan is on the verge of producing an atom bomb India cannot ignore the importance, it cannot pursue a non-violent policy of not acquiring nuclear weapons.

Nobody could ignore the fact that the South Asian security environment had become worse in the mid-eighties. Detente and disarmament had been displaced with cold war. The dialogue between India and Pakistan for arms limitations had been deadlocked. The arms race and arms transfer to the Indian peninsula had acquired dangerous dimensions. Installations of cruise and pershing missiles affected disarmament drive. In this situation the Indian government had to take initiatives to save the region from being turned into a 'Conflict Zone'. But the BJP was dissatisfied with the policies of the Indian govern-

29. Singh, Darshan, *Soviet Foreign Policy Documents, 1983* (New Delhi: Sterling, 1984), p.148.

ment. It believed that "instead of pursuing a uniform policy with regard to those issues India adopted double standards which would neither enhance its prestige nor would it able to serve the cause of peace and disarmament.... The foreign pressure would increase if India fails to keep its house in order. The Congress government, in the opinion of the BJP, miserably failed in discouraging the primary obligation."[30] "Pakistan's continued efforts to achieve uranium enrichment and spent-fuel reprocessing capability raised doubts about her declared policy of use of nuclear energy for peaceful purposes only. Inspite of all these, Indian government had been exercising utmost restraint and preserved its policy of peace with Pakistan."[31] The Indian government adhered to its peaceful use of nuclear energy and appealed other countries to observe the canons of the international agreement on disarmament. The Indian government was watchful on the point that the nuclear programmes of both India and Pakistan remain peaceful. As the BJP leader Jaswant Singh observed, "the transformation of a peaceful nuclear programme into a military utilisation was not that difficult and it was not that it involved any great change of technology. The real debate on the nuclear energy was for peaceful purposes and in that context the government should consider it, initiative should be taken to realise it."[32] In its neighbourhood, India faced unfavourable developments. The growing build up of arms by Pakistan was a matter of concern to India and contrary to the Indian proposal of peaceful nuclear policy. It posed serious threat to Indian security when the US started pouring lethal and sophisticated weapons to Pakistan. The Congress party hoped that "the Government of Pakistan would realise that peace, friendship and cooperation with India was in Pakistan's own interest and in the interest of stability of the region".[33] Besides Pakistan, China's role in acquiring nuclear weapons was also shocking. China had asked for nuclear power technology from the outside powers and the US agreed to supply equipments and spare parts to China. Moreover, the USA also agreed to supply F-16 aircrafts to Pakistan. The Indian reactionaries condemned the double game USA played. In case of India the US Government

30. *Presidential Address by A.B. Vajpayee in the Fifth National Council of the BJP in Indore* on 6th-8th January 1984, pp.9-10.

31. *Rajya Sabha Debate*, vol.CXXX, No.12, 8 May 1984, cols. 271-72 (Speech of R. Venkataraman, Minister of Defence).

32. *Ibid.*, cols.276-77.

33. *The Foreign Policy of the Indian National Congress*, The AICC Publication, p.24.

violated the contractual obligations of supplying fuel and vital spare parts to Tarapore, but in case of Pakistan or China it accentuated the flow of nuclear power technology. The American's argument was that Pakistan would not go for producing nuclear weapons if they are supplied with necessary spare parts and informations. It was clear that American intention was to isolate India in South Asia as the later was close to the Soviet Union, even if the US Government denied the allegations. "India was in fact isolated in the international arena. The superpowers and their satellites were in a position to deny nuclear fuel and spares because the Indian nation was not united. So to the BJP, India should go nuclear for an enlightened notional interest lest it would be a grave danger to its security."[34]

So the eighties witnessed prolonged turbulence, mutual suspicion and rivalries among the nations. National security acquired importance in front of nuclear threat by other countries. In this situation, India's "main security problem was how to shield ourselves and our developmental process, from the turbulence around spilling into our own territory. Our neighbours said they had the same problem vis-a-vis India and they had to shield themselves. The critics argued that if centuries of war, Germany and France could bury their hatchet and today people can travel from one place to another without visa; why should not such a development take place between India and Pakistan."[35] It is not appropriate to take the examples of France and Germany in case of India and Pakistan as the situation is altogether different. Under the prevailing situation in South Asia this can be said that "We should try as much as possible to promote better relations. We have to go a long way to start the process. It would be unrealistic if we overlook these basic differences and thought that there were no problems at all. Good security management lies in anticipating the problems in advance and taking the necessary counter measures to limit the damage these problems might cause us."[36]

In the General Election in 1984 the Congress party won a spectacular victory and Rajiv Gandhi assumed the office of the Premiership. The critics now raised many questions about India's role in interna-

34. *Organiser,* 27 May 1984, p.1.

35. Subramaniam, K., Zuberi, M., and Ramanna, *R., Problems of living in Nuclear Age* (Chandigarh: Centre for Re-search in Rural and Industrial Development, 1985), p.7.

36. *Ibid.*, pp.7-8.

tional affairs. However, India's policies carved out during Jawaharlal Nehru and followed by Indira Gandhi, continued during Rajiv Gandhi's era in India's functioning in world. Among other issues nuclear disarmament was indeed an alarming one. So Rajiv Gandhi's objective to mobilise world public opinion against nuclear weapons was primary in India's overall nuclear policy. India had consistently urged to ban the vertical proliferation and substantial reduction in stockpiling chemical weapons. Rajiv Gandhi carried this campaign to various international as well as regional fora.

Rajiv Gandhi presided over the Second Summit of the six nations in 1985 comprising Sweden, Mexico, Greece, Tanzania, India and Argentina. The main objective of the summit was to dispose of further production and proliferation of the chemical, biological and all other nuclear weapons. The Delhi Declaration was signed at the end of the summit where it was unanimously accepted that all nuclear tests using outer space must be scrapped and the outer space should be used for benefit of the mankind. The summit demanded elimination of nuclear weapons of the two Super Powers to ensure peace and security in the world. Above all, they suggested for verification under the auspices of the United Nations to further the process of disarmament. Unless there is a complete halt of production of nuclear weapons and reduction in conventional weapons there cannot be a nuclear-free world. The participating nations in the summit stressed on the halt of all types of testing, production and deployment of nuclear weapons. They believed that only such a step would facilitate to come out of danger of nuclear war. "Two specific steps required special attention that time: the prevention of an arms race in outer space and a comprehensive test ban treaty. In their view, outer space must be used for the benefit of mankind as a whole, not as a battle-ground of the future. They further urged the nuclear weapon states to immediately halt the testing of all kinds of nuclear weapons and a treaty on nuclear weapon test ban. Such a treaty would be a major step towards ending the continuous modernisation of nuclear arsenals."[37] However, the summit declaration was not supported by other Third World countries. The critics also argued that India, in its effort of disarmament, was left alone without much support of the non-aligned countries. The BJP believed that "India was being driven more and more into a loan blind ally as far as international support was concerned."[38]

37. *Foreign Affairs Record*, January 1985, p.9.

38. *Organiser*, 10 February 1985, p.16.

The international situation was tense in the second half of the eighties. So the AICC(I) urged the nuclear powers "to find a common ground for reversing the disastrous lurch towards mutual destruction. The tremendous potential of scientific and technological development could be harnessed for human welfare only if the astronomical spending on armaments is halted."[39] The Soviet Union also stressed on complete disarmament and put the task before nuclear powers. It also supported Indian call for an early convention of an international meeting with the participation of nuclear as well as non-nuclear states. "The Indian government highly valued Soviet declaration not to be the first to use nuclear weapons. Both sides considered that the adoption of such an obligation by all nuclear weapon states would be an important step towards the complete ban on the use or threat of use of nuclear weapons. The two sides stressed the importance of a freeze on nuclear weapons on a global basis beginning from a specific date and under appropriate verification."[40] The common approach of both India and the USSR on major international issues testified that "after Rajiv came to power new orientation had been given to India's policies. There was no doubt that India became the centre-piece of the Soviet Union's policy in Asia and also in its global strategy and there was no question of leaving India in lurch."[41]

The Indian scientists and researchers were hopeful of discovering new routes in searching techniques to accelerate nuclear research programme. As the Indian problem was to get enriched uranium from foreign countries, they were set up to produce required uranium for the uranium-powered reactors. "The peaceful efforts had been chosen by BARC covered magneto-hydro-dynmics, lesser fusion, uranium enrichment and the PNE. The MHD process for the production of power involves the conversion of energy released by burning coal directly into electric current, thus dispensing with costly boilers, turbines and generators which are needed in a conventional thermal station. In 1985, Asia's first MHD generator, a 30 MW experimental prototype, was commissioned at the Tiruchirapalli complex Bharat Heavy Electrics Limited (BHEL) in collaboration with BARC and the High

39. *Resolutions Passed in the AICC Meeting* held on 4th and 5th May, 1985 in Delhi, AICC Publication, pp.19-20.

40. *Foreign Affairs Record,* May 1985, p.134.

41. *Organiser,* 26 May 1985, p.1.

Temperature Institute Moscow."[42] India's nuclear policy was aimed at peaceful uses of nuclear energy. At the same time the Indian government alleged Pakistan's nuclear activities and the US role in supporting Pakistan's role by supplying sophisticated arms. India urged both Pakistan and the United States to refrain from bringing nuclear war into South Asia. The Rajiv Gandhi government was equally concerned about media report that Pakistan possessed necessary capability to make the bomb. However, President Zia refused the allegation. He extended his hands in disarmament programmes being carried out by India. On 18 December 1985, both the heads of India and Pakistan agreed not to attack each other's nuclear stations. The declaration was definitely a welcome step. Of late, during Benazir Bhutto's reign, the US started to assert itself infavour of India. The Reagan Administration advised Pakistan to search out amicable solution in the spirit of Shimla Agreement. The US even stopped military and economic aid to Pakistan due to its desire of acquiring nuclear weapons. Despite these initiatives taken by the US administration the Pakistani government did not give up its clandestine nuclear activities.

The strategic tie between Pakistan and China was another source of conflict between India and Pakistan. China was an unfriendly neighbour since the 1962 war and it was trying to boost military strength of Pakistan. With the support of China on the one hand and the US on the other, Pakistan was becoming much stronger posing threat to India's security. In July 1985, Pakistan had tested krytons, had been purchasing beryllium and this way its nuclear capability went increasing as the US administration did not pay any heed to world criticism against military aid to Pakistan. Thus, the pace at which Pakistan was attaining a nuclear weapon capability affected the peaceful atmosphere of the Indian sub-continent. Developing strong ties with the nuclear weapon states and more particularly with the US, with the help of modern missiles, F-16 aircrafts and enriched uranium it was planning to strike Indian cities. Pakistan's navy was strengthened, had Hawkeye Airborne Early warning aircraft to strike at Indian fleet, coastal and offshore installations.On the other hand, China was moving ahead with its nuclear programme. China's attempt to produce neutron weapons and battle field tactical nuclear weapons instead of neutralising nuclear threat in Asia was alarming. The critics argued

42. Vas, E.A., *Op. Cit,* p.186.

that Sino-Pakistan nuclear collusion would create an asymmetric situation in South-Asia. It was revealed that in 1984 China had supplied sensitive nuclear weapon design information to Pakistan.

The BJP was concerned on Pakistani programme of manufacturing nuclear bomb. "It was no doubt that despite Pakistan's protestations, the acquisition of such nuclear weapon could only be intended to intimidate India and could pose a serious threat to its security and integrity. The BJP was convinced that the country could no longer afford to adopt a policy of drift and escapism in that serious matter involving the country's unity, integrity and security. The BJP would like to declare that it could not even conceive the idea of countering Pakistan's threat by willy-nilly pushing India into the umbrella of any superpower, one or the other. The BJP, therefore, urged the government of India to take people into confidence on the vital question. An immediate response to Pakistani Nuclear Bomb was necessary. The BJP called upon the government to take immediate steps to develop our own nuclear bomb."[43] "So the requirement was to maintain parity, it not superiority of arms with her enemies. If Pakistan achieved nuclear weapons capability and China earlier, India could see imminent danger in her frontier. We, therefore, should build up our own nuclear weapons and bomb delivery system to achieve something like parity of effectiveness, so far as China and Pakistan were concerned."[44]

The Bhopal gas tragedy of 1984 created fear among nations on the question of nuclear rector safety. India agreed with the United States about the importance of reactor safety standards and practices. The critics alleged that if India pursued parallel policy with the United States it would hamper her nuclear research and her self-reliance drive in that field. If at all India seeks foreign advice, Canada or Japan or Soviet Union might be reliable friends rather than the US. It is also argued that because Chinese nuclear weapons do not pose any threat to India and Pakistan, the disarmament efforts should be confined to India and Pakistan. Any Indian move to acquire nuclear weapons or any research in that matter would be evaluated seriously in Pakistan. So the nuclear controversy can be solved if India abjures its nuclear

43. *National Executive Meeting of the BJP,* 19th-21st July 1985, Bhopal, BJP Publication, pp.9-10.

44. Bankeshwar, S.S., "Why India Should go Nuclear", *Orga niser,* vol. 37, No. 13, 11 August 1985, p.9.

policy unilaterally. However, this choice was not supported. If at all India announces such a policy it is not sure that Pakistan will follow it. So it can be said that so long there is no end in world nuclear race, so long the Super Powers pursue their ambiguous policies, India must adopt a strategy of ambivalence. It must watch the situation in West Asia and Diego Garcia where US interests lay and take appropriate steps to meet threat.

It is beyond doubt that suspicion and fear encouraged Pakistan to go for nuclear arms. India realised that Pakistan's drive to acquire nuclear bomb was due to the American military ambition. America's foreign policy had become to affect India on the one hand and to conspire Pakistan's nuclear programme on the other. Washington's occasional warnings to Pakistan to defer it from acquiring a nuclear bomb was a mere eye-wash. India's requests of not spending money after nuclear weapons and arms manufacturing were not receiving importance to the Pakistani government. Thus, the preparations for making bombs were going and scarce economic potential of the developing countries was being spent after unproductive causes. In this situation, "politicians can play help the detached intellectuals in this matter by creating a congenial atmosphere through the adoption of travel restriction between the two countries and also the promotion of regular trade and exchange of ideas. At the same time the two countries must have a provision for the mutual inspection of their nuclear facilities, and a mini-Nuclear Non-Proliferation Treaty of their own."[45] It was also argued that "our real enemy being poverty and backwardness it would be an act of sheer madness and jingoism to embark on the road to nuclear weapons and this would have disastrous effect on our economy, destroying ourselves from within".[46] "Nuclear arms race would also increase our dependence on the advanced countries and thus would compromise our political independence. National resources would be diverted to non-productive and non-usable weapons programmes and the process would become irreversible".[47] However, on the other hand, if Pakistan acquires the bomb, it would leave India insecure, but, at the same time, Pakistan's strategists

45. Dhar, N., "Indian Defence and Social Sciences", *Radical Humanist,* vol. 49, No.5, August 1985, pp.13-15.

46. Sinha, S.K., "Our Nuclear Compulsions", *Ibid.*, p.23.

47. Sharma, D., "India's N-Bomb Decision Cann't be secret", *Ibid.*, p.29.

must realise that any atomic attack against India should be away from the border of Pakistan lest radioactive waves from the explosion would affect its own people as well.[48] Thus the nuclear option was dangerous for both India and Pakistan. That's why the Bharatiya Janata Party "pledged to build up India as a strong and prosperous nation drawing inspirations from India's age-old culture and values. It would help India to emerge as a great world power playing an effective role in the comity of nations for the establishment of world peace and a just international order".[49] The options, therefore, available to India were of either a resolute, purposeful, controlled nuclear weapons programme or an equally purposeful but a joint programme for non-nuclear South Asia.[50]

South Asian countries having low per capita income should not unnecessarily divert their scarce resources for acquiring nuclear weapons. Instead of it they should endeavour to raise their economic standard first of all. "From this perspective the level of poverty is so great that the horrors of war: thus such expenditures in the West are not.

Therefore, either a programme of education or pressure, or both, is justified on the part of the liberal West in dealing with Indians, Pakistanis and others who wish to purchase advanced jet fighters, tanks or nuclear fuel from the West."[51] It is an undeniable fact that war is dangerous to both the developing and the developed countries and particularly Third World countries cannot afford their scarce economic resource to go waste. So it was expected that the Super Powers should take immediate steps not to deteriorate world environment further. As all wars, small or big, carry the danger of escalation of nuclear weapons, the non-aligned countries appealed great powers not to get involved into regional as well as global conflicts. "Nevertheless,no arms build up can be sustained unless the population is sufficiently docile and accommodating to accept the costs involved. The key to disarmament lies in people shedding the very docility which has permitted rearmament of such monstrous proportions in the first place. In other words, it lies in what Einstein once called the chain reaction

48. Bose, D.K., " India's options in the Nuclear World", *EPW,* vol.20, No. 38, 21 September 1985, pp.1594-96

49. *Resolutions as adopted in the National Executive Meeting of the BJP* on 9 October 1985 in Gandhi Nagar (Gujrat),p.2.

50. Speech by BJP M.P. Shri Jaswant Singh, See *Rajya Sabha Debates*, vol. CXXXVI, No. 16, 10 December 1985, col. 233.

51. Jain, B.N.(ed.), *Reflections on India's Foreign Policy* (Jaipur: RBSA,1990), p.50.

of awareness; and therefore in mass agitation. In the words of Olof Palme it is very unlikely that disarmament will ever take place if it must wait for the initiatives of governments and experts. It will only come about as the expression of the political will of the people in many parts of the world. It seems reasonable to argue that in view of the mounting costs of rearmament, manifested, for example, in an exorable inflation, the political will of the people cannot remain dormant for long."[52]

Inspite of all odds India had always endeavoured for the cause of peace and international cooperation. The Plenary Session of the Indian National Congress thus acknowledged the role played by Indira Gandhi and also Rajiv Gandhi and demanded total nuclear disarmament. The session noted that while the Geneva Summit was a positive step, purposeful and determined action, yet there could be no rest for India until peace is won completely and permanently".[53] To the contrary, the United States refused to any measure of limiting and restricting production and proliferation of nuclear weapons in any case. So all resolutions that had been agreed in Geneva proved fruitless. "Thereby the United States created an artificial impasse in the nuclear weapons question and showed once again Washington's real attitude to the talks on nuclear and space in Geneva, the absence of readiness and desire on USA's part to reach agreements on real steps to prevent an arms race in outer space and to stop it on earth."[54] It should be realised that practical measures in the field of disarmament would release enormous funds for mankind's peaceful development. For this reason India has struggled for restoring peace in South Asia as well as in the world. The Soviet Union also highly praised India's toil for peace and disarmament in the subcontinent and also throughout the world. "The Soviet side was convinced that the friendship between India and the Soviet Union and their common endeavour to preserve peace was an important factor in ruling out the threat of thermo-nuclear war and protecting life on earth".[55]

It is correct to say that India's nuclear programme was designed to use available nuclear energy for peaceful purposes. The environmental concern was another factor which prompted Indian government

52. Attar Chand, *International Relations* (Delhi:Anmol, 1992),p.136.

53. *Inaugural speech by Congress President Rajiv Gandhi and Centenary Resolve at Congress Centenary Session* at Indira Nagar in Bombay on 28 December 1985, p.33.

to go for peaceful nuclear energy programme. Side by side, India's nuclear energy programme aimed at achieving status of a nuclear power. So "India's nuclear energy and space programmes are essentially of dual purpose. India's development of missiles in particular is believed to entitle it to a voice in the corridors of world power, necessitating Indian participation in, for example, future arms control negotiations."[56] The American and Chinese reaction to India's nuclear programme was less shriek due to India's policy of peaceful nuclear explosion. It had also no impact on the world nuclear programme. It's adherence to utilise nuclear power for peaceful purpose was, however, taken seriously by the Pakistani government. Other nuclear powers like Britain and France did not react sharply to India's nuclear policy as they were much concerned about Super Powers nuclear race.

On 17 December 1985, the Indian Government concluded with the Government of Pakistan an agreement not to attack each other's nuclear installations. The BJP held the view that "the agreement conferred on Pakistan not just immunity in its military and nuclear programmes but also it conceded to Pakistan a nuclear status equal to ours".[57] The prime motive which actuated India throughout the turbulent years was that the Indian leaders had been deeply conscious about peace, progress and development and India's policy within the Third World had always been based on the principles of sovereign equality, peaceful coexistence, mutual respect for a more just, peaceful society where each human being can develop the totality of high potential.[58] "India's adherence to a peaceful approach prevented her from translating the PNE capability into a weapon capability. India had a dual advantage: it retained the right to prescribe disarmament, and at the same time Indian non-nuclear status remained safe. It gave India the deterrent capability in Asia. By not going in for a weapon programme, India legitimised this nuclear capacity and also retained the diplomatic advantage of a non-nuclear weapon power".[59] "The Indo-Soviet

54. *TASS,* 5 September 1985.

55. *Pravda* (Moscow), 7 September 1985.

56. Thayer, Carlyle and Ramesh Thakur, *Soviet Relations with India and Vietnam* (London : MacMillan, 1992), pp.162-63.

57. *Presidential Address* by L.K.Advani, Plenary Session of the BJP, Ekatmata Nagar, New Delhi, 9 May 1986, p. 18.

58. Faleiro, Eduardo, "India and the Third World," *Secular Democracy,* vol.XIX, No.8, August 1986, p.41.

59. Paranjpee, S. ''India's Nuclear Status : A Policy Note", *Asian Affairs,* vol.13(2), Summer 1986, p. 58.

bilateral cooperation during Rajiv-Gorbachev era was marked by cordiality and "constituted an important sphere of the diversified friendly relations between the two countries and also had great international importance as a powerful factor in the struggle of all peace-loving force of the planet against the war threat, for durable peace and security. It was with profound satisfaction that the genuine friend of India had welcomed the statement made by the Prime Minister Rajiv Gandhi that India would continue to be guided by the ideals bequeathed by Pandit Nehru and Indira Gandhi. This was a guarantee of future victories in the consolidation of national independence and in the advancement of the active role of the republic in world affairs."[60] Mikhail Gorbachev arrived in New Delhi on 25th November, 1986. Both the heads met without aides where they discussed about Pakistan's nuclear programme and acquisition of sophisticated weapons from the United states.[61]

Perhaps one of the highest watermarks in Indo-Soviet relations since Rajiv Gandhi came to power was the official visit of Mikhail Gorbachev to India in November 1986. In their meetings the two leaders issued 'Delhi Declaration on principle for a Nuclear Weapons Free and Non violent world.' "For India, to seek the evolution and establishment of a non-violent world order was not surprising because of its traditiition and philosophy. But for the Soviet Union to subscribe to the idea of a non violent world was something novel.... It indicated India's influence on Soviet thinking. It was a happy coincidence that there was considerable harmony in their thinking on world affairs which was based on their respective national interests. Their policies with respect to peace and disarmament had many common points. That is why in India, Governments changed, different political parties came to power, but our relations with the Soviet Union continued to grow."[62]

The overriding question mankind confronting was whether the humanity would survive before the threat of nuclear race. Under these circumstances regional as well as global efforts of nations were considered to be best weapons to counter the threat of nuclear war. "In

60. Banerjee, B.N. *India's Political Unity and Soviet Foreign Policy* (New Delhi: Paribus, 1985), p.217.

61. Satish Kumar (ed.), *Year book on India's Foreign Policy, 1985-86* (New Delhi : Sage, 1988), p.61.

62. Misra, K.P.,"Indo-Soviet Relations: An Overview", in Vinod Bhatia (ed.), *The October Revolution and 70 years of Indo-Soviet Relations* (New Delhi: Panchasheel, 1987), pp.85-87.

the contemporary integral, inter connected and interdependent world, a policy should draw from the cultural treasures of each nation and the entirety of human civilisation. A policy should be fertile with thoughts of human destinies and be founded on humanistic principles. And it was by this type of policy that both India and Soviet Union were guided in international affairs."[63]

The Indian government was anxious to implement the Delhi Declaration as it would help in ushering in a nuclear weapon-free and non-violent world. "Rajiv Gandhi's plan which coincided with Mikhail Gorbachev's statement of January 15, 1986 in many respects, is based on four provision: one, there should be a binding commitment by all nuclear-weapon and non-nuclear weapons in stages; second,all nuclear weapons and non-nuclear weapon states must participate in the process of nuclear disarmament ; third, to demonstrate good faith and build the required confidence, there must be tangible progress at each stage towards the common goal; fourth, changes are required in doctrines, policies and institutions to sustain a world free of nuclear weapons. Negotiations should be undertaken to establish a comprehensive global security system under the aegis of the United Nations."[64]

The reason why there was no relief in Indo-Pakistan nuclear race was a matter of concern. The critics argue that it is because of Pokharan Explosion that has led to tension between the two nations. It is first India that went for nuclear weapons and as a countermeasure Pakistan was bound to acquire atom bomb. Inspite of their irregular attempts to establish cordial relation the overall estimation proves that India and Pakistan both have passed through a tense phase throughout the eighties. It is a moot question why both of them are so eagerly inviting a nuclear war into a peaceful region even if they are aware of the consequences that would cast on their inhabitants. Reasons are multidimensional. It is because there is no international procedure for inspection of nuclear research programme. Again, unless China is brought in, any serious measure for disarmament would not yield good result. Pakistan suggested that the nuclear dispute with India was a bilateral affair and opposed any sort of foreign intervention. Reacting to the Pakistani opinion Rajiv Gandhi said that "the nuclear problem

63. Vladimirov, L.P., *op. cit.*, pp.116-17.

64. Glebivashentsov, Nikolaikolstov, "For a World Without Nuclear Weapons and Violence", in Leonid P.Vladimirov, *The Soviet-Indian Phenomenon* (New Delhi : Allied,1889), pp. 62-63.

was a global problem and Pakistan had a role to play in it. It should not act a proxy of the United States. It was not a bilateral issue. On the other hand, when the imperialists said that Pakistan and India should sit together to solve the nuclear was irrelevant."[65] So Pakistan's nuclear programme was the most important issue before the Government of India. It was an indirect threat to India's security. "It was not like that USA would help to create a congenial atmosphere or Pakistan would defer from its action, if India sticks to her peaceful approach to the use of nuclear energy. So India had only one option, that is to go nuclear and to make nuclear bomb not because China or Pakistan did it but to be recognised as a world power in the international scene."[66] Even if the US warned Pakistan to stop military aid in case Pakistan goes for nuclear bomb, yet surprisingly when Soviet Union did the same USA in opposition to Soviet warning extended aid to Pakistan with an aim to check Soviet influence. It testified American intention of not forcing Pakistan to abide by its promise not to produce nuclear weapons".[67]

The Soviet Union highly valued India's position and its approach on the issue of the complete halt of all types of nuclear tests everywhere. International security was the most important task before the Soviet Union. India also supported Soviet desire of establishing a comprehensive system of international security. "A high degree of humanism was also evident in the policies of the two countries. Both the Soviet and the Indian people thought not only in terms of their own security or interests, but also related them to universal security and the aspirations of the whole mankind. Only the elimination of nuclear arms would provide the necessary resources for improving the life of nations, would provide for abolishing hunger, poverty, illiteracy and other social and economic ills".[68] "It is clear that India continued to play a key role in Soviet strategy and ideology. The Indo-Soviet relations in Gorbachev-Rajiv era demonstrated special ties with each other. On its arms control position vis-a-vis the United States, the

65. *Lok Sabha Debates*, Eighth Series, Seventh Session, vol.XXI. No.3, 6 November 1986, col.395.

66. Speech of Pramod Mahajan, BJP M.P. in Rajya Sabha, see *Rajya Sabha Debates*, vol.CXL, No.4, 7 November 1986, cols. pp. 311-14.

67. *Organiser*, 30 November 1986, p.13.

68. Gorbachev's Address to Joint Session of the Indian Parliament, see Darshan Singh (ed.), *Soviet Foreign Policy Documents*, 1986 (New Delhi : Sterling, 1988), pp.480-85.

Soviets had New Delhi's support to the hilt".[69] "It is observed that Indo-Soviet and US-Pakistan relations stood on very different footing. While the US used Pakistan card to pressurise India, the Soviet Union had never asked India to play its proxy. The different positions of the two states of our subcontinent clearly explained the US hostility to India."[70] India had played its independent role considering both national and international situations. Neither it sought Soviet support to dominate or influence other countries. On the other hand, Pakistan never showed its independent judgement and actions and everytime Washington directed Islamabad to toe US line.

The security environment around the country had considerably degenerated. The Government of India in this circumstances favoured disarmament, a nuclear free world and pursued a peaceful non-aligned policy. But the BJP was not satisfied with the policies of the Indian government. In his presidential address, L.K.Advani remarked, "When dangers face the country our response should not be half-hearted and unconvincing. Considering fully the pros and cons of the issue the BJP was of the view that India must go in for a nuclear deterrent of its own."[71] Besides, it is not that we shall neglect our economic development or ignore peace and disarmament. Our efforts should be to strengthen the movement of peace and disarmament to avoid nuclear war. So the main tenets of the BJP's foreign policy approach were that "the money and energy should be spent to remove poverty and illiteracy instead of spending after nuclear arms, its manufacture and proliferation".[72]

No doubt, India should increasing activity in taking initiatives and advancing proposals intended to help normalise the situation on the globe, to achieve disarmament and to reduce the nuclear danger; when the Soviet people supported India's struggle for a world without nuclear arms".[73] There had been all sided cooperation between the two

69. Banerjee, J.,"Moscow's Indian Alliance", *Problems of Communism*, vol.XXXVI, No.1, January-February 1987, p.11.

70. Bhambhri, C.P., "US view of Indian Security : Glaring contradictions "in Rakesh Gupta (ed.), *India's Security Problem in the Nineties* (New Delhi: *Patriot,* 1989), p.111.

71. *Ninth National Council of the Bharatiya Janata Party* In Vijaywada (Andhra Pradesh), 2-4 January 1987,p.20.

72. Statements of Sri Kalpanath Roy in Rajya Sabha, *Rajya Sabha Debates,* vol. CXLII, No. 9, 27 April 1987, cols.255-57.

73. Alekseyev, Aleksandr, "USSR-India: Cooperation for the benefit of the peoples", *International Affairs* (Moscow), (5), May 1987, pp.48-49.

countries. But the United States, in its strategy to restore balance of power in South East Asia and to counter India's link towards Russia, started strengthening India's two border states, China and Pakistan. If Pakistan by any means becomes a nuclear power, our security would be threatened. As the BJP observed, "Soviet Union, no doubt, had been a good friend in need but when gratitude and our national interests come into conflict, the later would be more important and on that account a change in our policy was urgently needed".[74] India had all capabilities to manufacture bomb. But the only question was whether India would reverse its policy of Peaceful Nuclear Explosion? "Because India owed the United States a pledge of peaceful use and safeguards in perpetuity for Tarapore plutonium and to safeguard and restrict to peaceful use of the plutonium from Madras and Dhruva".[75]

Looking at the security scenario in the eighties, there were two sections of people giving two different opinions. While some argued that if India goes for a bomb it would increase the danger of proliferation as in the case of Europe or America. The other section differ with this sort of stand by India viewing Pakistani attempt to possess a bomb. It must be noted that the Government of India being attacked from several quarters reiterated its faith in peaceful nuclear policy and strived for disarmament. Thus the policy India picked up during Jawaharlal Nehru continued in the eighties. This stand of India was commendable world wide. It was not that India was not bothered about her security as Pakistan had opted for nuclear bomb, but her effort was to deliver humanity from the nuclear holocaust, and to bring about a durable trend towards a healthier international environment. The Indian government was also critical of the America's policies in Pakistan and South Asia. But the United States did not even listen to India's appeal. In South Asia and West Asia, USA had vital interests and it did not want to lose its hold in these regions. "Pakistan's Islamic status enabled it to influence happenings in the Persian Gulf and served as an alternative cold war defence site. So close link between the US and Pakistan became a necessity and therein came the problems between India and the US. The US attempts at balancing the Indian and Pakistan claims though did not always meet

74. Ratnam, P., "Aiming US equidistance between India and Pakistan", *Organiser*, 2 August 1987, p.4.

75. Milhollin, Gary,"Stopping the Indian Bomb", *American Journal of International Law*, vol.81, No.3, July 1987, pp.608-09.

with success, yet the US government could able to wield its influence in South Asia."[76]

The disarmament treaties between the US and the USSR was regarded as a historical importance on the ground that since the dawn of the nuclear race there was no formal treaty between the two Super Powers. The INF treaty between them was an uphill task which would inspire Third World countries to think on disarmament. "The BJP highly appreciated the efforts of the two superpowers which could lead the mankind in this field".[77] On this occasion the Government of India extended its warm support. India had always stood for peace and disarmament efforts. The Indian government always supported all steps taken in this regard. Shri K.Natwar Singh, Minister of State for External Affairs, in the plenary session of Conference on Disarmament declared, "We, in India firmly believe that the time has come for the international community to engage in some collective introspection on our present predicament.... We urge that serious consideration be given to the changes of doctrines, policies, attitudes and institutions required to realise the prospects of a nuclear weapon free world that has opened up now. We have to develop means to channelise these applications into a stabilising mode. In order to do so, we need continually to assess the implications of these developments for security. We also need to develop appropriate institutional mechanisms which are capable of understanding this task."[78]

Even if the Super Powers agreed to reduce their nuclear weapons, other nuclear powers went on producing nuclear arms. They were not bound by any treaty like the INF. So danger did not come from the Super Powers but from other nuclear powers. In case of India, the Indian Government refused to endorse the proposal for a nuclear weapon free zone in South Asia because of Pakistani and Chinese nuclear programmes. "What was necessary that time was that USA should deter Pakistan from going in for fissionable material or producing uranium of weapons grade".[79] On many occasions, the AICC(I) had taken serious note of Pakistan's persistent efforts to acquire nuclear capability and urged the Government of India to take all appropriate

76. Paranjpee,Shrikant, *US Non-proliferation Policy in Action : South Asia* (New Delhi: Sterling, 1987), pp.90-93.

77. *National Executive Meeting of the BJP*, 1-3 January, 1988, Ernakulam(Kerala), p.11.

78. *Foreign Affairs Record*, vol. XXXIV, No.3, March 1988, pp.72-75.

79. Kaul, T.N.,"INF Agreement, Nuclear Disarmament and India", *Man and Development*, vol.X, No.1, March 1988, p.16.

steps to meet the threat.[80] So the call of the hour was to cover up regional conflicts and to develop regional dialogues and mutual understandings between states. "Then it would be possible not only to wince the "nuclear syndrome" but to achieve a breakthrough in combating poverty, protecting the environment, hunger and other large scale disasters".[81]

There was no significant development in Indo-Soviet relations in 1989, perhaps because "some of India's leading nuclear scientists had demonstrated little enthusiasm for Soviet nuclear facilities, particularly in comparison to alternative sources in the West and Japan or in India's own advanced nuclear-energy programme".[82] Another fact was that, even if the USSR offered assistance in India's peaceful nuclear energy programme, the Soviet leased submarine to India in 1989 created unhappiness in USA. The US was also opposed to sell a nuclear powered submarine to a country like India as it would create fresh tension between India and Pakistan. But the US administration did not stop the transfer of high-tech to India, for it did not want to displease India as it did not in the case of Tarapore. Later, towards mid-1989, on the visit of Frank Carlucci, American Secretary of Defences. "India conveyed him its apprehensions about Pakistan's nuclear weapon programme",[83] and the US assured India to look into the matter. It shows that inspite of divergencies, ups and downs in US-India bilateral relations. Cordial relations grew up towards the end of the eighties.

We have also seen that the world military expenditure was stepping up neglecting the developmental process. Though the liabilities were increasing day by day, yet there was no cut on defence expenditure. The nuclear weapons were accumulating in a greater scale. Those steps definitely affected the research works, economic and scientific developments of not only the develcping countries but also the developed nations. Despite the sincere desire of India and other concerned nations the Super Powers went on increasing their defence build-up, as for example, Table 1 shows that the United States spent

80. *Resolution passed in the AICC Meeting* held on 23rd and 24th April 1988, at Maraimalai Nagar (Tamil Nadu), p.33.

81. *TASS*, 18 November 1988.

82. Bouton, Marshall M., and Phillip Oldenburg(ed.), *India Briefings, 1990* (San Fansisco : West View Press, 1990),pp.55-57.

83. Satish Kumar (ed.), *Yearbook on India's Foreign Policy*, 1989 (New Delhi: Sage, 1990), pp.60-61.

as much as \$300 billion in 1989 whereas \$134 billion in 1980. We can assess the increase of defence expenditure in just ten years, a three-fold increase of expenditure. Table II shows the rapid increase of defence expenditure by the US Government. In 1990 it was at the peak, though later due to sufficient initiatives taken by the world leaders, the US defence expenditure toward down in 1991 and 1992. We can argue that the money spent after the production and proliferation of weapons could have been directed to the poor countries struggling for raising their standard of living. A liberalised trade and official aid could have ameliorated the conditions of poor Third World countries. Thanks to the agreement of both the Super Powers the nuclear weapons were decided to be reduced in phases.

The Geneva Conference succeeded in mobilising public opinion against the production and proliferation of nuclear warheads. New ideas and proposals were also tabled in the special session. India proposed an Action Plan in this regard which envisioned that nuclear disarmament cannot be attained till the nuclear weapons are committed to observe the doctrines of deterrence. If the proposed regulations of the conference are not strictly observed and till the reduction of nuclear arms are not taken under immediate effect the world cannot be regarded safe. So, "India's Action Plan was based on the premise that the process of disarmament cannot be confined to USA and USSR, but there should be a binding commitment by all nations to eliminate nuclear weapons".[84] India's approach was to eliminate the nuclear weapons by 2010 A.D. and to establish a non-violent, nuclear-weapon free world, so that the mankind would survive.[85] To sum up, "Rajiv Gandhi's foreign policy was based on the principle of `pacification' rather than `pacifism'. Pacifism generally means elimination of force; pacification on the other hand, refers to the belief that violence is unjustified. He was not a pacifist in a sense that he did not believe that in interstate or international affairs, resort to force has already been eschewed. The threats are there.... There have to be defence ministries, defence budgets and defence forces. But they are only for `defence' and never for committing aggression. We have to have nuclear programmes,

84. Text of speech delivered by Mr.K.Natwar Singh, Minister of State for External affairs, see Satish Kumar (ed.), *Yearbook on India's Foreign Policy, 1990-91* (New Delhi: Tata Mc Graw Hill, 1991), pp.224-25.

85. *Election Manifesto* , Congress (I), 1989, p.57.

but only for peaceful purposes."[86] "China has categorically stated that it would take part in nuclear disarmament process only when the arsenals of the big nuclear powers are reduced to its own level. India could conceivably take the same position that it would consider joining the non-proliferation regime only when China becomes a political part of the nuclear disarmament process and when Pakistan's existing capability is dismantled".[87] "Whether Pakistan goes or does not go for the last bit of her bomb, Sino-Pak axis remains a formidable threat... India's nuclear policy can be evolved largely in the context of China and not of super-powers or Pakistan and that was what, ironically, paralyzed the real exercise of option in the past. This is more true today with Pakistan having the bomb with Chinese assistance. China has never given up her dream of domination in Asia".[88] ".... a South Asian nuclear approach with explicit and implicit backing from the existing nuclear powers may be effective to stabilize the arms race in this region. Once there is nuclear deterrents in the military arsenals of both India and Pakistan, the arms race between them would cool down because nuclear deterrents would remove their mutual phobia and make war a permanent no-option for them. The existing nuclear states should recognize India's and Pakistan's rights to acquire nuclear weapons and help stabilize the security system of the region".[89] "Peaceful uses of nuclear energy in India are woefully underdeveloped. India, which is way ahead of most third world countries due to advanced scientific capability on different areas in nuclear research and experience of advanced technology has yet to achieve the target it set for itself for utilization of nuclear energy for peaceful purposes in the economy and medicine. India's plan to become a powerful force in the international nuclear market has been seriously affected due to weak political leadership. If India wishes to use nuclear energy for peaceful purposes, it must seriously re-examine the limitations which have forced this country to abandon the modest target energy output".[90] "Pakistan is now a nuclear-weapon state and this fact changes the military equation in the Indian peninsula. The Government of

86. Gupta, M.G. Rajiv Gandhi's Foreign Policy : A study in Continuity and change (Agra : MG Publishers, 1987), p.216-17.

87. Dutt V.P. "India's answer to NPT", *Monthly Public Opinion Survey,* xxxvii (6×7), March-April 1992, pp. 3-4.

88. Sethi, J.D., "The Bomb and NIT", *Ibid,* xxxvii (10), July 1992, pp. 17-19

89. Md. Nuru Zaman "The arms Race in South Asia : Some Approach to stability}, *Bass Journal,* 13(4), October 1992, pp.425-50

90. *Patriot* (New Delhi), 30 August 1991.

India must take all measures, including the exercise of the nuclear option, to meet Pakistan's challenge to India's unity and territorial integrity. We should re-double efforts to pursue a vigorous defense R&D programme including the development and deployment of modern missiles to reinforce our defense preparedness".[91] "The US Senate decided to delete the Legomarsino Amendment which has sought to make US assistance to India on the same basis of Pakistan. India has always maintained that its nuclear programme is an entirely clandestine programme which has nuclear proliferation. The official spokesman of the MEA expressed India's satisfaction that the efforts to equate between India and Pakistan have been removed and the Pressler Amendment on India's nuclear programme will not be applicable to India".[92] "The Americans would be happy if India opens all its nuclear facilities to IAEA inspection and agrees to a nuclear weapons free zone in South Asia. If we allow that say for the West, there is no doubt India would be asked to tone down its nuclear programme and would be asked to take western and rather than develop on its own and at great cost nuclear technologies. The essential discrimination in the NPT is that the US, Britain, France, Soviet Union and China can have nuclear materials, but India cannot".[93] "In seeking to prevent nuclear and ballistic missile proliferation in South Asia, the United States' objective is first to cap, then over time reduce and finally and try to eliminate weapons of mass destruction and there means of delivery. Her aim is also to help reduce tensions and avoid conflict which could escalate the use of nuclear weapons. The United States, therefore, seeks to help create a climate in which the sense of security of both India and Pakistan is enhanced through tension reduction and confidence-building measures and where both the countries perceive distinct advantages in rejecting nuclear weapons and ballistic missile delivery systems, and recognize the disadvantages inherent in their possession... As a matter of fact, the US strongly emphasizes non-proliferation in her relations with both India and Pakistan and considers its to be the major issue in her relationship with both the countries".[94] "In relation to non-proliferation control mechanisms, India and the US must seek to find ways of cooperating. India could strengthen these international mechanisms

91. *National Executive Meeting* held in Thiruvardha Puram, September 30, 1991, p.18.

92 *Foreign Affairs Record,* xxxvii (a), p. 157

93. *Organiser,* december 1, 1991, p. 15.

94. Bose, T.C., "The United States and South Asia : The Nuclear Proliferation Dimension", *Strategic Analysis,* xvi(12), March 1994, pp. 1597 -1616.

by lending active support to them, while the United States must review the procedures on technology transfer to facilitate easier Indian access to strategic technologies".[95]

But the US administration continues its old policy of using Pakistan to contain and constraint India. "By massive arming of Pak continuously over the last 40 years, the US has been responsible for unleashing a burdensome arms race between the two countries. And when it still found Pak suffering from security complex, it allowed it to go ahead with its N-bomb project".[96] "Besides, China has a sizable stock of nuclear warheads stationed in Tibet. These have to be destroyed to remove India's apprehensions, which are legitimate".[97] "The real dimension of international security today is that of the possible loss of control over nuclear arsenals. The proliferation issue has assumed a qualitatively and frighteningly new dimension. In the view of the AICC, "the only logical route available to us is to pursue a global approach based on a new international consensus on non-proliferation. To be effective, this global non-proliferation regime must be universal, comprehensive and non-discriminatory. Its goal should be full and complete nuclear disarmament. There should be no reservation on this goal".[98] "In a world which is reducing nuclear arsenals and where it is increasingly recognized that nuclear weapons are not usable except as a deterrent, it is necessary to engage in a dialogue with our potential nuclear adversaries, irrespective of our nuclear status. While India should continue to wage a relentless struggle for nuclear disarmament, elimination of all nuclear weapons, and for outburning of these weapons, it is also necessary for India to join in the arms control negotiations with other powers. While strategically aiming at outlawing and eliminating nuclear weapons, we should have tactical plans for arms control. We should not enter into such discussions out of fear of big power economic pressures".[99] "The BJP firmly believes in the principle of sovereign equality of nations. As long as nuclear weapons are not outlawed for every country in the world, India must not only retain its nuclear option, but must immediately manufacture and deploy such weapons. At the same time, India

95. *Hindi* (Madras), March 5, 1992.

96. *Organiser*, March 22, 1992, p.3.

97. Kamath, M.V. "Nuclear Blackmail", *Organiser*, April 15, 1992, p.4

98. *Presidetial Address* by P.V. Narasimha rao, AICC, 79th Plenary Session, Rajiv Gandhi Nagar, Tirupati, April 14-16 1992, p. 29.

99. Subramaniam, K., "India's Nuclear Policy", *World focus*, vol. 13(8), August 1992, pp.8-10.

must accelerate its programme of development of missiles and rockets for military and civilian purposes. India must make it clear to the international community that in matters relating to India's security, there can be no compromise".[100] "The end of the cold war has not resulted either in the end of nuclear weapons as such, or of nuclear threats to nations. Globally, there has been welcome movement forward; regionally, however, the problem of proliferation has got aggravated. With Pakistan self-declaredly a nuclear weapon state, given the reality of China and the aspirations of some nations in the Gulf, India has to address itself to this question principally as one of national security concern.

The BJP presents a four-point formulation as the basis of the party's nuclear policy. The BJP

(i) shall not compromise on national sovereignty and security;

(ii) subscribes to the principle of a comprehensive, universal and non-discriminatory treaty of non-proliferation;

(iii) would be willing to explore the articulation of a 'no first use' statement. Simultaneously, it would examine all aspects of cooperative security, extension of other confidence building measures and the goal of nuclear restraint in the entire region -- Central, South, West and East Asia;

(iv) holds that India cannot abjure its peaceful missile development programme".[101] "Precisely, the movement towards nuclear free world would be facilitated if all nuclear weapons states agree to universal force on future development and deployment of nuclear weapons. India shall continue to work together with other like-minded parties towards establishing a co-operative world order based on truly non-discriminatory non-proliferation and disarmament with the objective of establishing a nuclear weapons free world".[102]

100. *Political Resolution* adopted at the Nation Executive Meeting, New Delhi, December 23-24, 1992, p. 10

101. *Presidential Address* by L.K. Advani, National Council Session, June 18-20, 1993, Bangalore, pp.19-20.

102. *Foreign Affairs Record,* xxxix(7), pp. 221-222.

But the Clinton administration stands on the way. It "wants India and Pakistan to agree to a verifiable halt to all aspects of their nuclear weapons programme as an important contribution to global non-proliferation efforts. The US objective, it is said, was first to cap, then reduce and finally eliminate the possession of weapons of mass destruction and their means of delivery. It also sought to help reduce tensions and avoid conflicts which could possibly escalate to the use of WMDS or ballistic missiles. It also actively discouraged third countries from exporting WMD related equipment and technology to India and Pakistan".[103] "Looking at the grave scenario, India made it clear that the question of closing nuclear options did not arise. Pakistan has acquired nuclear weapons and in such a situation, it is unrealistic and unacceptable to foreclose India's nuclear option. Moreover, New Delhi has insisted that non-proliferation measures must be universal, comprehensive and non-discriminatory".[104]

However, India has put efforts to establish a nuclear free world and in all international seminars, meetings, the Indian delegates express the Indian anxiety over escalated nuclear supply to South-Asia. With the support of other like-minded countries progress has been made "in establishing an international consensus for banning nuclear weapons testing and halting production of fissile materials for nuclear weapons purposes. India and the US have worked closely together in helping to forge this international consensus. To consolidate these gains, further meaningful stress should be taken towards de-nuclearization which the international situation now allows".[105] On his visit to India, the US President, praising India's efforts, showed his willingness on disarmament issue. "Both the leaders called for a new partnership between India and the US. They offered their strong support for efforts towards the non-proliferation of weapons of mass-destruction and their means of delivery and towards their progressive reduction, with the goal of elimination of such weapons, which are among the most pressing challenges to the security of states in the post cold war era".[106] "The Prime Minister, Shri Narasimha Rao has repeatedly voiced his total endorsement of India's position in this regard at every opportunity. We hope for a fully nuclear-free world and are prepared

103. *Times of India* (New Delhi), February 16, 1994.

104. *Patriot* (New Delhi), April 18, 1994.

105. Text of the Address of Prime Minister P.V. Narasimha rao to the Joint Meeting of US Congress at Washington, *Indo-US Relations on the Threshold of a Bold Era*, AICC, May 1994, pp.6-7.

106. *Times of India* (New Delhi), May 21, 1994.

to join in any initiative which sincerely tries to achieve this globally. The AICC notes with satisfaction the support of Prime Minister Rao and President Clinton for efforts towards the non-proliferation of weapons of mass destruction with the eventual elimination of such weapons".[107]

In these years, the US government "appears hopefully of India singing the proposed Comprehensive Test Ban Treaty [CTBT] despite a change in New Delhi's stand on the sensitive issue. Under Secretary of State for Arms Control and International Security, Ms Lynn E. Davis said, India would be well served by signing the CTBT which the five nuclear powers were determined to deliver by the end of 1996".[108] India achieved another milestone and it "becomes a force to reckon with in the global satellite launch vehicle market with the successful launch of PSLV-D3, the country's third and last developmental polar satellite launch vehicle from Sriharikota Range".[109] "Strenuous last minute efforts by India and some other developing countries stalled concerted moves by nuclear powers to bulldoze the text for a new CTBT which seeks a freeze on the nuclear programme of threshold states without any matching gesture on their own huge stockpiles. It, however, depends how for these developing countries succeed in their efforts to bring about a CTBT to help the progress towards total elimnination of nuclear weapons". Strangely,[110] "it was the fond hope of the people of India that the end of the cold war would usher in an era of peace, cooperation and all round development of friendly relations among the nations of the world. That hope has been belied and there is still conflict and tension in many parts of the world. The attempt to impose a new world order based on the military and economic strength has vitiated the international atmosphere. The US is preparing to reward Pakistan for its development of nuclear weapons by supply dozens of F-16 aircrafts".[111] "The BJP is of the firm view that India should continue to develop and deploy an indegenous missiles system... in order to provide absolute security against aggression, urgently commence the process to manufacture and arm defense forces with nuclear weapons".[112] "The BJP demands that the Government of

107. AICC Meeting, Talkatora Indoor Stadium, New Delhi, 10-11 June 1994, p.32.

108. *Time of India* (New Delhi), December 1, 1995.

109. *Hindu* (Madras), March 22, 1996.

110. *Hindustan Times* (New Delhi), March 25, 1996.

111. *National Executive Meeting* held on 8-9 June, 1994, Vadodara, p.7.

112. *National Executive Meeting* of the BJP, Patna, 15-17 September 1994, pp. 12-13.

India clearly state that it will not accede to a Comprehensive Test Ban Treaty nor agree to fissile materials cut-off for weapon purposes nor accept the provisions of discriminatory Missile Technology Control Regime and unless a treaty is established for the total elimination of nuclear weapons universally within a stipulated time frame".[113]

The supreme objective of a nation is to promote its national interest. So foreign policy is formulated and implemented considering a nation's desire. Sometimes global interest is also taken into consideration. Then only a foreign policy is good and effective when it contains the contents of other nations's interests. It must think for friendly countries, but may have to be unfriendly for the adversaries. Adoption of suitable means and tactics at the right moment can only testify the validity of a country's foreign policy. No doubt, Pakistan and China both moved against India and their drive for nuclear bomb concerned Indian diplomats. On the contrary, India had to receive nuclear weapons from the Soviet Union. In this situation, South Asia was moving towards grave danger which would escalate arms race to an unprecedented scale.

In such a situation, the critics argue whether India should go nuclear and seek nuclear weapons or should it go without nuclear weapons? Acquisition of nuclear weapons as it understood cannot leave off their hostilities, rather it would affect their good relations. It would besprinkle fear and suspicion. To solve these unresolved problems the focus should be fixed on the elimination of nuclear and chemical weapons, to let the people live peacefully. It should be realised that the risk of employing nuclear weapons implies destruction. Without an Indian willingness to move on this issue, other states like Pakistan cannot do a lot as they are aware of India's nuclear capability. However, it does not mean that it is unnecessary to keep our defence equipment prepared but surely it does not say that we should keep on arming ourselves with the weapons the developloped countries eager to proliferate.

There is another section who argue that if Pakistan and China go nuclear and bring nuclear warheads to our border, why not India? If they have not made nuclear weapons sufficiently to their advantage, they can get it elsewhere or else they can make it tomorrow, because they have that capability and technology and if not, they can get it to make it. So the critics stress that India should think of her future now itself. It should not hesitate to acquire sophisticated weapons

113. *National Executive Meeting* of the BJP, New Delhi, 23-24 December 1995, p. 17.

being supplied by the developed countries. May they earn by exporting nuclear weapons to the Third World, but security is much important than considering one's income. We shall have to aware of the danger of nuclear confrontation. So, it is a moot question whether India should go nuclear or not ? If India, at all, wants not to go nuclear and seeks to normalise relations peacefully with China and Pakistan, it would endanger its security because Pakistan might not do it. so the weapon system has to be acquired, the nuclear weapons should be stockpiled only to deter Pakistan.

TABLE I

US NATIONAL DEFENCE EXPENDURE OUTLAYS, FOR 1980-89

(Figures are in US $ billion)

	1980	1981	1982	1983	1984	1985	1986	1987	1988	1989	1990	1991	1992	1993	1994	1995
Personnel	40.9	47.9	55.2	60.9	64.2	67.8	71.5	72.0	76.3	78.2	78.9	84.2	79.2	84.3	85.8	86.7
O & M[a]	44.8	51.9	59.7	64.9	67.4	72.4	75.3	76.2	84.5	85.4	88.3	90.9	92.4	95.2	97.6	98.4
Procurement	29.0	35.2	47.3	53.6	61.9	70.4	76.5	80.7	77.2	80.7	81.4	71.7	60.5	60.1	59.2	60.1
RDT & E[b]	13.1	15.3	17.7	20.6	23.1	27.1	32.3	33.6	34.8	37.0	36.5	36.2	36.9	36.7	37.1	37.8
Energy, defence	2.9	3.4	4.3	5.2	6.1	7.1	7.4	7.5	7.9	7.9	9.7	11.6	12.0	12.8	13.3	14.1
Other	3.3	3.8	5.1	4.7	4.7	7.9	10.4	12.0	9.6	9.7	8.5	9.0	8.2	7.3	6.8	7.2
TOTAL	134	157.5	185.3	209.9	227.4	252.7	273.4	282.0	290.4	298.3						

a. Operations and maintenance.

b. Research, development testing and evaluation.

Source: SIPRI DATA BASE

TABLE-II
US Dept. of Defence and National Defence Expenditure. Budget authority and outlay. FYs 1990-93

Figures are in US & Billion, Current and Constant (1993) Prices

	1990	1991	1992	1993
Deptt. of Defence				
Current Price				
Budget Authority	293.0	290.9	276.3	267.6
Out Lay	279.8	262.4	294.7	278.3
Constant Price				
Budget Autority	226.4	308.8	286.6	267.6
Outlay	333.5	278.2	305.6	278.6
National Defence				
Current Price				
Budget Authority	303.3	303.6	289.2	281.0
Outlay	299.3	273.3	307.3	291.4
Constant Price				
Budget Authority	337.9	322.3	299.6	281.0
Outlay	334.2	298.8	318.1	291.4

SOURCE: SIPRI YEAR BOOK 1992-93

TABLE III
(Percentages)

Demographic variables	No. of Res-pondents	TABLE IIA Agree stron-gly	TABLE IIA Agree some-what	TABLE IIA Dis-agree some-what	TABLE IIA Dis-agree stron-gly	TABLE IIA No. opin-ion	TABLE IIB Agree stron-gly	TABLE IIB Agree some-what	TABLE IIB Dis-agree some-	TABLE IIB Dis-agree stron-what	TABLE IIB No. opin-on gly	TABLE IIC Agree stron-gly	TABLE IIC Agree some-what	TABLE IIC Dis-agree some-what	TABLE IIC Dis-agree stron-gly	TABLE IIC No opin-ion
SEX																
Male	827	33.1	14.6	7.0	37.1	8.1	59.3	22.0	8.1	7.3	3.4	58.5	22.9	7.1	5.0	6.5
Female	673	36.4	17.5	7.3	27.8	11.0	53.0	27.5	6.5	5.6	7.3	54.7	30.5	4.5	2.5	7.9
AGE (in years)																
21 to 35	855	37.8	15.2	7.7	31.3	8.0	60.0	22.3	7.0	6.5	4.1	58.7	27.6	5.1	3.4	5.1
36 to 50	424	31.1	18.6	6.8	32.1	11.3	50.9	29.5	6.6	6.6	6.4	50.9	25.9	8.0	5.0	10.1
Over 50	221	29.0	13.6	5.4	40.7	11.3	53.4	23.1	10.4	6.3	6.8	60.6	21.7	5.0	3.6	9.0
EDUCATION																
Primary or less	76	19.7	3.9	2.6	36.3	47.4	44.3	13.2	6.6	5.3	30.3	40.8	19.7	6.6	1.3	31.6
Some secondary	151	34.4	15.2	4.0	31.5	13.9	52.3	23.2	6.6	4.6	13.6	55.0	21.9	3.3	4.0	15.9
Secondary completed or some university	523	37.3	15.7	5.4	34.8	6.9	57.0	26.2	7.5	6.7	2.7	52.6	28.9	8.6	4.6	5.4
University degree or more	750	34.3	17.5	9.5	32.4	6.4	58.1	24.7	7.7	6.9	2.5	61.7	26.0	4.5	3.6	4.1
OCCUPATIONS																
Professionals	77	33.8	19.5	7.8	31.2	7.8	49.4	35.1	6.5	6.5	2.6	54.5	27.3		10.4	7.8
Businessmen and retail traders	240	36.3	15.8	3.8	33.8	10.4	62.9	24.2	6.3	3.3	3.3	47.5	25.4	7.1	6.3	13.8
Government officials & business executives	69	27.5	15.9	20.3	34.8	1.4	56.5	18.8	11.6	8.7	4.3	60.9	30.4	7.2	1.4	-
While collar workers	349	30.4	20.9	9.5	33.0	6.3	54.7	28.1	8.0	7.7	1.4	59.3	27.7	7.7	2.6	2.6
Skilled workers	74	28.4	12.2	6.8	40.5	12.2	68.9	16.2	4.1	6.8	4.1	62.2	18.9	5.4	6.8	6.8
Unskilled workers	31	29.0	16.1	9.7	19.4	25.8	51.6	29.0	3.2	6.5	9.7	29.0	35.5	12.9	6.5	16.1
Housewives	351	38.2	11.7	6.0	29.1	15.1	48.4	27.1	7.1	6.0	11.7	52.4	30.8	3.1	3.1	10.5
Students	144	42.4	11.8	6.9	34.0	4.9	65.3	13.9	8.3	9.7	2.8	72.9	17.4	5.6	2.1	2.1
Others	15	33.3	33.3	-	26.7	6.7	46.7	46.0	6.7	-	6.7	33.3	33.3	20.0	6.7	6.7
Not working retired/unemployed	150	34.0	16.7	4.0	49.3	6.0	60.0	19.3	8.7	6.7	5.3	65.3	20.7	6.7	2.0	5.3
CITY																
Bombay	375	32.0	17.9	8.0	34.1	8.0	66.9	17.9	6.7	3.7	4.8	59.7	25.6	5.3	1.9	7.5
Calcutta	375	34.7	11.2	9.6	36.5	8.0	54.4	28.5	6.4	8.0	2.7	70.1	19.5	2.7	5.1	2.7
Delhi	375	33.6	9.3	5.6	38.7	12.8	53.6	30.6	4.0	12.8	8.0	54.9	25.9	7.2	2.9	9.1
Madras	375	38.1	25.3	5.3	22.4	8.8	50.9	29.9	12.5	1.6	5.1	42.4	34.1	8.5	5.6	9.3
TOTAL	1500	34.6	15.9	7.1	32.0	0.4	54.5	24.8	7.4	8.8	5.1	50.4	26.8	5.9	3.9	7.1

Source: *Monthly Public Opinion Survey, XXXVII(1), October 1991.*

CHAPTER III

Arms Trade and Security

Security stands for the means of being secured and a step taken to protect the homeland from the enemy's attack. For its accomplishment several means have been undertaken throughout the ages, arms acquisition being one of the most important means. In the medieval ages the security was not threatened so much as at present. There was non-existent of sophisticated weapons as the present day world witnesses. However, it cannot be denied that there was no arms transfer that time, but it was not a consistent feature as at present. So, since the dawn of the concept of security protection arms production is a well-known feature, but after the end of the Second World War the confrontation between the two Super Powers aggravated the fear of destruction by developing more and more sophisticated arms. Now the quality of the arms occupies a prominent place.

It is important that throughout the eighties there was no direct clash among the great powers. But the proxy wars brought tension and fear among the peace loving states. Instead of accelerating the pace of detente there was transfer of large scale arms to the developing countries and this way the great powers tried to show their strength and potential. This in turn threatened the congenial atmosphere of many Third World countries, retarded their economic growth and diverted attention from developing economy to destroying the opponent. In fact, in the initial years arms transfer to the third world was mainly from the US side. Later other European powers jumped into the fray. France and Great Britain were confined mainly to the European powers and their colonies. The Soviet Union was already the most developed country among the WARSAW countries and concentrated its arms transfer to the communist countries and later to South Asia. So this strategy of the big powers was overshadowed by two broad factors. First, the ideological differences and Second, the economic and strategic considerations. They saw transfer of arms a convenient way of reducing their cost of production on arms and to correct their adverse balance of payment situation. It is noteworthy that in the eighties global military expenditure was almost doubled from the sixties. The United States spent billions dollar every year in the mid eighties and the Soviet Union almost equal to the United States, both of them accounting sixty percent of total global military expenditure. On the other hand, Third World countries has shown a four-fold increase in their defence expenditure.

After the loss of Iran and the Soviet invasion of Afghanistan, America started prevailing upon some of the South-West Asian countries. So the strategic consensus of America focussed on South and South-West Asia for which Pakistan acquired significant position. The sheet anchor of American policy was to threat Soviet presence, but it served dual purpose. The other one was to weaken India which had already started acquiring weapons from the Soviet Union. It is often considered that India was a Soviet ally and Pakistan as an American supporter. Being universally condemned as a strap to America, Pakistan had no option but to support American strategy in the region. But by acting upon America's South-Asian plans Pakistan posed threat to India's security. Apart from, Pakistan was not only supporting American strategy or acquiring weapons only to pose threat to India's security but also it had indirect consequences in India. "From its very inception Pakistan had constituted a strong element in India's security calculus not only because of the aggressions committed so often by Pakistan against us but because of the fundamental ideological contradiction of the two nation states. It was a clash of ideologies of a theocratic authoritarian state versus a liberal democratic secular state. US policies of supplying high technology weapon systems to it had been one of the major causes of friction between India and the US. US policies in pursuit of its strategic objectives unfortunately led Pakistan to acquire exceptional military capabilities. The power structure in Pakistan was dominated by a military-bureaucratic feudal elite, who had acquired a vested interests in propagating and sustaining an adversal relationship with India in order to provide legitimacy to its own hold on the power structure. So it would be India's interests to establish stability and integrity, cooperation with Pakistan as this is conducive to Indian security interests also."[1]

The acquisition of sophisticated military hardware by Pakistan introduced destablisation in the Indian sub-continent. India differs

1. Singh, Jasjit (ed.), *Indo-US Relations in a changing world* (New Delhi: Lancer International, 1992), pp.96-97.

with Pakistan's claim of gathering weapons is a right for her security interests. In fact, the large quantum of weapons Pakistan acquired far exceeded the requirements forced on it by the Soviet invasion of Afghanistan. It was a threat to the regional security environment. "It also makes Pakistan more and more recalcitrant and indifferent to the process of normalisation with India and Afghanistan".[2] For this purpose, the military budget of Pakistan also increased to unusualness. In this case the responsibility of the NATO cannot be ignored alongwith some of Third World countries who aggravated the worsened situation. "That was the result of the attempts to break the equilibrium of forces that was established in the world and to impose its will upon people from the position of military superiority".[3]

The Afghanistan problem remained in the main agenda of Indira Gandhi's foreign policy which also determined India's relations with the Super Powers. Of course the relations with the Super Powers did not start from a new slate but the developments before her entry to the Indian Parliament had impact in it. The Western powers were vehemently opposing the presence of Soviet army in Afghanistan. Whatever might be the terms and conditions of the Soviet-Afghan agreement, it was opposed because the Soviet troops threatened American interests in the region. On the other hand, it was implicit from the Soviet move that it was interested in checking American policy of creating more satellites in South-West Asia, even if undeclared. So the Afghan rebels were migrating to Pakistan because of Soviet invasion, some of them for replenishment of supplies of weapons. In this situation, America tried to prevail against Pakistan to encounter Soviet move. The US-Pakistan strategy started giving military help to the rebels. The complex situation was a matter of concern for India. The immediate response of India was that it had no particular objection to Soviet invasion caused considerable embarrassment for the US. But later the Indian government clearly stated that all foreign troops should be vacated from Afghanistan and the country must be allowed to remain non-aligned. The foreign policy experts were surprised at the shifting stand of India on Afghanistan issue. The reason why India took such a stand was "perhaps the Indians did not believe that the Soviets would pull out of Afghanistan and their dependence on Moscow for advanced military hardware contributed to their reluc-

2. See *India and International Scene*, op. cit., pp.3-4.

3. Speech by L.I. Brezhnev in the Indian Parliament, See Darshan Singh (ed.), *Soviet Foreign Policy Documents, 1980* (New Delhi:Sterling, 1981), p.112.

tance to pressure the Soviets. Initially, some Pakistanis warned against Indo-Soviet attack, but Washington never accepted the argument. The American judgement was not that India would not help much on Afghanistan but that it would not be serious hindrance to either the effort to counter the Soviet forces or to Pakistani and American diplomatic activities."[4] The Soviet Union, to the contrary, opposed such a step of India which was expecting a pro-Soviet stand by the Government of India. But their differences on Afghanistan did not affect their bilateral relations at all. It was because of the fact that India was ready to expand Indo-Soviet bilateral relations and the Soviet Union was equally willing to be a close ally with India. Once the mutuality of interests bad been established and subsistent, the two countries made no secret to pursue their policies for optimum realisation. When the Afghan issue came to the floor of the United Nations the Indian envoy declared that, "India cannot look with equanimity on the attempts by some outside powers by training, arming and encouraging subversive elements in Afghanistan....We are against the presence of foreign troops and bases in the country.... The Soviet government has assured India that its troops went to Afghanistan at the request of the Afghan government and it will leave at Afghan government's request".[5] Mrs. Gandhi also declared that the Soviet presence in Afghanistan would constitute a threat to India's security. She said that "there were no reason why Soviet Russia should do anything against India. But it was Pakistan who has acquired arms and power from America used against India"[6] "The Government of India on the other hand condemned the US role in South Asia which had gripped it in danger. The Soviet move in Afghanistan was, therefore, a countermove to US action in the sub-continent. So it was powers like USA, China and Pakistan those must be blamed, not the Soviet Union".[7] However, India, as Indira Gandhi declared, was not happy with the Soviet Union in Afghanistan and urged the USSR to take its troops away from Afghanistan.[8]

4. Gould, H.A. and S. Ganguly, *The Hope and the Reality (US-Indian Relations from Roosevelt to Reagan)* (San Francisco: West View Press, 1992), pp.141-45.
5. *Times of India* (New Delhi), 13 January 1980.
6. *Daily Mail,* 14 January 1980.
7. *Los Angels Times* (Los Angels), 14 February, 1980.
8. *Amrit Bazar Patrika* (Calcutta), 22 February, 1980.

War, in any form, was not beneficial for the economic development and for that reason it should be avoided. "The best way to win war was to prevent it. That is why India had been trying so hard for peace. That was also the rationale behind India's policy in Afghanistan".[9] The BJP was opposed to presence of a foreign military presence in the soil of another non-aligned country. The party urged the Government of India to take positive initiative in this matter. "It hoped that the non-aligned nations could make a move in finding a solution which would bring moral pressure on the Russians to vacate the aggression, the military occupation of Afghanistan. Of course, America was pumping more arms to Pakistan. The Americans seemed to be bungling in their foreign policy, so far as they assessed India's in their foreign policy, so far as they assessed India's need and Pakistan's need to be equal". [10] The Bharatiya Janata Party stressed that "Pakistan ought to understand that the threat to its security posed by the presence of Soviet troops just beyond the Khyber pass could not be met simply by trying to grab arms and armaments. India too must realise that it is in India's own interests that there should be strong and stable Pakistan between India and the USSR as a buffer state. The Governmennt of India should take an initiative to overcome the setback in our relations with Pakistan. In the fast deteriorating situation, India alone could play a meaningful role if it expressed itself clearly and unhesitatingly agaist any encroachment upon the freedom of nations, any violation of frontiers and any interference in the internal affairs of other peoples".[11]

In 1981, the United States announced the reduction of developmental assistance to India by 8.5 billion dollar. On the other hand it started exporting lethal weapons to Pakistan in pursuance with its West Asian and Indian Ocean policy. Table 5 shows that Pakistan received highest military aid from the US than other South Asian countries. The sale of F-16 aircrafts, Vulcan Phalanx air defence systems, guns to be mounted on destroyers and harpoon anti-missiles ships were items that indeed caused consternation. The Indian ambassador in the US conveyed India's concerns over American supply of war items to Pakistan.

9. *Selected speeches and writings of Indira Gandhi*, vol .IV, op. cit., p.198.

10. The speeches of Mahavir Bhai, the BJP M.P. in Rajya Sabha, see *Rajya Sabha Debates*, vol.CXV, No.11, 6 August 1980, cols. 339-49.

11. See the *Text of the Presidential Address* by Shri A.B.Vajpayee delivered at the 1st National Convention of the Party held at Samata Nagar in Bombay on 28-30 December 1980, p.20.

The subsequent meetings between the two heads of government was also preoccupied with this problem.

The AICC reiterated its commitment of friendship with all our neighbours and urged that the process of normalisation of relations with Pakistan should be accelerated. "The AICC strongly opposed any effort in creating instability in the sub-continent through massive US arms aid to Pakistan".[12] In the view of the BJP "the US arms assistance to Pakistan was based on faulty prognosis. From Turkey, through Saudi Arabia to Pakistan, the US was creating a corndorn sanitaire in its attempts at containment of USSR. It viewed any massive supply of arms as contributory to a heightening of tension in this region. The BJP believed firmly that the peace, security and progress of the region lay in friendship between India and Pakistan".[13] In such a totality when threat to our peace and security was obvious, the Indian government was urged to lodge strong protest against such developments which posed serious threat to our unity and integrity. "So defence build-up was considered as a priority to our security".[14] "The country's defence preparedness would not achieve the required degree of self-reliance until the defence production base is widened. The BJP expressed its concern at the low level of expenditure in defence build-up. Even the low level of investment was not bearing fruit because of inefficiency and corruption in some of our defence laboratories".[15]

Being attacked from several quarters on the performance of the Congress Party and mainly on our defence area, Prime Minister Indira Gandhi reacted sharply. She was aware of the fact that building of defence industries at the behest of developmental efforts would not give tangible results. She realised that through the gift of armaments, the centre of decision and policy-making would have moved out of our hands. In her words, "In the early years, we had neither resources, nor the desire to get entangled in the rivalries and conflicts of the blocs and their war preparations. The gigantic proportions of our problems needed our total attention. Only in conditions of peace could we

12. Resolutions adopted by the All-India Congress Commit tee, New Delhi, 27-28 February 1981, p.620.

13. *Resolutions of the BJP,* National Council Session, Cochin (Kerala), 25th-27th April 1981, pp.21-22.

14. Kriplani, J.B., "Our Diplomatic Response to US arms in Pakistan", *Organiser,* vol.XXXIII, No.3, 7 June 1981, p.4.

15. See *Resolutions of the BJP,* n.13, p.23.

concentrate on development. A small country could and some did achieve growth through large scale aid. For us, self-reliant development was not only desirable but it was the only possible way".[16] The number and size of the armed forces does not determine the strength of a nation, not even the possession of sophisticated weapons. But the real strength lays how far a nation brings all her resources to utilise in case of a war. Further, the state of defence preparedness of a nation has great bearing on her ability to prosecute an independent policy in foreign affairs during peace time. The Indian government was worried of its ability in development and production capability of a combat aircraft. It was a matter of satisfaction that the defence research and development laboratories had made spectacular progress in tank technology and took up steps to develop Guided Missiles Systems. Other scientific institutions also extended their help to the DRDO in attaining self-reliance in our defence field. "The armour developed by the Defence Metallurgical Research Laboratory, Hyderabad, was designed to with-stand anti-tank weapons providing a very high degree of immunity to the tank. A totally indigenous and an extremely accurate gun which can fire FSAPDS and HESH Ammunition was also developed by ARDE, Pune. The Instruments Research and Development Establishment, Dehra Dun, had developed fire control system incorporating stabilised sight for the gunner, panoramic sight for the commander and low light level television for navigation to provide high first round hit probability. The aim of the government, therefore, was to organise a well founded indigenous defence science and technology base which could respond adequately to rapidly evolving needs".[17]

Defence preparedness was a constant friction between the government and the opposition. No doubt, there was no laxity to safeguard the sovereignty of India against external threats. In this direction the Indian government showed alertness in preparing our army, navy and air force to meet the threats of advanced countries across our border. "All aspects of defence preparedness had been reviewed including the strengthening of our defence against enemy air-raids, importing strategic installations and such other measures as were warranted by sudden escalation in the threat environment. As a long term measure, government was involved in perspective planning in regard to defence

16. Inaugural speech at Silver Jubilee Celebration of the School of International Studies of the Jawaharlal Nehru University, New Delhi, 30 October 1981. See *Selected Speeches and Writings of Indira Gandhi,* vol.V, op.cit., p.499.

17. See *Self Reliance in Defence,* AICC Publication, pp.1-7.

needs with proper balance between manpower, equipment and facilities for the most cost effective defence management and to maintain full defence preparedness at all times. The department of defence supplies placed orders on indigenous items. Supplies were received in 3989 cases of the total value of Rs. 58.93 crores during the year 1980-81 and 1656 items of the value of Rs.31.53 crores during the year 1981-82. The value of purchases from small sector by Mazagaon Decks Limited and GSL during 1980-81 amounted to Rs.350 lakhs and Rs.20 lakhs respectively".[18] Though the total value of military sales from the USSR to India was not published, yet it was estimated to be more than sixty percent of the total military imports by India. This degree of dependence on Soviet Union made both the countries to be linked strategically more than any other field. There were several reasons why India chose Soviet Union in this field. The main cause was perhaps the low price of the items. Besides, the credit terms available, subsidy granted and the payment in soft currency encouraged India to explore relationship with the Soviet Union. Again the Soviet Union allowed India to produce Soviet designed weapons under licence. This helped India to produce arms and equipment in her domestic factories.

Clearly the United States' relationship with Pakistan offered best opportunity to the latter for her security programme. But Indira Gandhi did not allow Indo-American ties to go out of hand. It was realised that without American aid India could not be able to achieve a self-sufficient economy and, therefore, India was reported to have established rapport with America. In pursuance of this approach, Indira Gandhi visited Washington in 1982. She explained India's stand on Afghanistan and also conveyed India's apprehension over the US supply of arms to Pakistan. The United States agreed to the Indian need for increased external assistance to maintain the pace of development. Thus, while the convergence between India and the United States remained over many political and strategic issues, the economic relationship continued to improve. In 1982 India was the second largest trading partner of the US. So, India's primary concern being economic development and to realise it, the Indian government thought it proper to maintain cordiality with both the Super Powers. In a hostile regional environment with many delicate problems to be handled India did not want the relationship to be uneven. Her long

18. Verma, Srikant, *Seven Hundred Days (An Appraisal)*, AICC Publication, January 1982, pp.57-59.

cherished policies of maintaining independence and autonomous capacity in making decisions was also maintained and cordial relations with the Super Powers were continued and good will of the Super Powers retained.

The Government of India was really concerned with the Super Power rivalry leading to confrontation among the South-Asian countries. "It was believed that if conscious efforts were not taken to make an end to superpower rivalry and arrangements were not made then the South Asian countries would go under foreign hegemony".[19] A.B. Vajpayee argued in the Lok Sabha that, " We should be prepared for any type of danger. We should be vigilant about our security and integrity. But this does not mean that we should create an atmosphere of suspicion and fear. Each nation, after all, should endeavour to settle the dispute amicably".[20] He regretted that the government was not enough vigilant towards these points. The BJP had all along stood for and reiterated its commitment to improve bilateral relations with the neighbouring countries. "Regional cooperation was a logical corollary to a policy of peace with neighbours. India could convincingly espouse the cause of detente abroad only by actively working for it nearer home. Personal rapport between leaders could cement relationships, but what was urgently needed was an institutionalised understanding of what each country stood for. The BJP urged Pakistan that it should give up for ever the path of conflict with India. It must realise that mere acquisition of weapons would not give security and the raising the bilateral issues in international forums would not normalise relations".[21]

The Reagan Administration considered India and Pakistanin equal in the spheres of arms strength. Though it never made any cataclysmic statement against India, on the contrary inspired Pakistan to pursue a aggressive posture. Thus, a series of offers were made in favour of India to seal off past divergencies. Offer of super computers, weapon systems, fighter air crafts and defence technology were made in this connection. While Pakistan got massive aid all it wanted to get, India got supply to counter Pakistani military build up by the traditional ones. President Reagan clarified his position that the weapons of Pakistan would not be used against India, which could not satisfy the

19. *Organiser,* 21 March 1982, pp.8-9.

20. *Lok Sabha Debates,* Seventh Series, Eighth session, vol.XXVI, No.29, 30 March 1982, cols. 389-90.

21. Resolutions in the BJP National Executive Meeting, 28th-30th August 1982, Bangalore, *op. cit.,* p.17.

Indian government. In contrast, the Soviet Union desired to see a friendly and strong India, with capability to meet the challenges of the West. In reality both the Soviet Union and India wanted to develop an atmosphere free from security threat. A mutual cooperation, peaceful co-existence and healthy competition could creat a peaceful world. So they were against all types of sophisticated weapons to protect the humanity from mass annihilation. The Soviet Union highly valued India's contribution to peaceful international community and the constructive initiative taken by India. It is noteworthy to state that the USSR had also desire to see a peaceful and violence free Asia. Security in Asia was of vital importance to the Soviet foreign policy. In this context, the Soviet leaders stated that Asian-Pacific regional security must be attained so that all nations could act freely. Instead of joining in hostile camps and inviting mutual bickerings, free association of all nations based on the fundamental principle of peaceful co-existence seemed to be the guiding factor of Soviet foreign policy. It was the Soviet Union who shared India's views on Pakistan's attempt to gain military supremacy over India. It was because of Western apathy towards India, that its defence preparedness suffered heavily for a long time. Both the US and Britain were reluctant to provide military weapons even at higher prices. So India quickly turned towards Soviet Union and later Soviet assistance helped India to develop modern arms and equipment. For instance, Vijayanta tank was designed and built due to Soviet supply of necessary technology. So whenever India wanted any type of help economic, political and military, the Soviet Union extended her hands without superimposing herself in any manner. The Soviet assistance in ship building industry can not be ignored likewise.

It was not that India and Pakistan had difference and they did not strive for solving those divergencies. In 1983 Pakistan's relations with India took a somewhat different path. Both of them accused each other of creating tension in other's territory. However, Indian and Pakistani foreign secretaries expressed the desire of their respective governments to live in peace and cooperation. Pakistan agreed that Kashmir could now be covered in a no-war pact between the two countries. The Pakistani statement should a sign of improvement in their bilateral relations.

The Soviet observers carefully noted the exchange of political and military visits between Pakistan, USA and China. It maintained that China and America were secretly acquiring base facilities in Gwadar and other points on Pakistan's Baluch coast in the Arabian Sea. Pakistan had a key role to play in the operation of the US Rapid Deployment Force. On the other hand China sought access to the Indian Ocean via the backdoor of Karakoram Highway. In such an environment Moscow seemed to be the only reliable friend of India. Indeed, "the top Soviet leaders repeated Moscow's anxiety to see India's defence capabilities further improved".[22] But the Soviet Union did not take measures to fulfill Indian needs. It was felt that Soviet strategic assistance was not conducive to Indian interests. "It was observed that complete reliance upon Russia for military imports has done us damage. With more and more ties with the Soviet Union our foreign policy lost its flexibility. The worst that has happened is that supplies from the Soviets have not been accompanied by full indigenisation techniques. The West on the other hand came forward with handsome terms".[23] The US had always been more willing to sell arms. George Schultz told the Indian press that "misunderstandings about Indian purchase of US arms had been removed and that the US was prepared to sell military hardware to India".[24]

Negotiations and preliminary agreements on arms deal between India and the United States were under discussion in 1983. Though India was in need of artillery guns, the Indian policy makers realised that the United States had feared that any technology transfer to India would lead to a leakage to Moscow. "Indian defence analysts believed that neither of the superpowers would give a country defence technology unless there was a convergence of strategic interests and there was no such convergence between New Delhi and Washington".[25] The US military expenditure in the eighties amounted to thousand dollars which exceeded the income of many Third World countries. The overall global military expenditure surpassed the income of South Asian countries. Therefore, India had always stood for demilitarisation and disarmament. India had made enormous strides in this direction. India's objective was to utilise the military budget in the head of economic development. " Most important of all, Indira Gandhi pledged to preserve India's peace and disarmament legacy and worked for a united, strong and prosperous India. The Soviet Union gave all

22. Banerjee, Jyotirmoy, "Moscow's Strategic Link with New Delhi: An interim assessment", *China Report*, Vol.9, No.1, January-February 1983, pp.7-20.
23. *Organiser*, 8 May 1983, p.7.
24. *Organiser*, 10 July 1983, p.3.

possible help in this direction. Both countries, with confidence and conviction, strived to give new directions and new dimensions to their policies. India and the Soviet Union also showed the world how a warm kinship could be established between neighbours whatever the differences in their domestic, economic and social systems".[26] In February 1983, India and the Soviet Union signed a protocol for cooperation in space technology and space research. In March, Indo-Soviet planning group discussed about cooperation in fuel, energy and water resources. In June, the Soviet Union agreed to help India in extracting oil from Gujarat belt. The foreign minister of the Soviet Union, Gromyko declared that "the Indo-Soviet relations have stood the test of time and could establish peace in Asia and in the whole world. He expressed that Soviet Union would continue to strengthen the Indo-Soviet relations further".[27] When Dr. Ramanna visited Moscow , the Soviet Union agreed to assist in setting up two atomic power plants in India.[28]

From the perspective of US attempts to establish its hegemony over the world, a nation even if non-communist and non-aligned had to consider the interests of the United States. Moreover the American activities of apotheosisation of America was understandably a policy of Soviet containment. Any power refused to come under the influence of any Super Power had to face serious economic and strategic constraints. The occasional rally of Third World countries to stay away form the Western world weakened their position. So the regional powers had to follow the lines of the big powers for the sake of their higher interests. As for example, Pakistan looked for military aid not only because Pakistan wanted to contain India but also she needed economic development. Russia was not a comfortable partner for Pakistan as India was a close ally of the USSR. On the other hand USA wanted Pakistan to play a proxy role in the Indian sub-continent. So Pakistan followed the directions of the Reagan Administration. As a result it received military and economic aid. India on the other hand depended on the USSR as the Soviet Union's interests coincided with that of India. The Soviet Union fully respected India's progressive

25. Singh, S. Nihal, *The Yogi and the Bear (Story of Indo-Soviet Relations)* (New Delhi: Allied, 1986), pp.212-13.

26. Banerjee, B.N., Peace, *Friendship and Cooperation* (Delhi : BR Publications, 1987), pp.6-16.

27. *Pravda* (Moscow), June 17, 1983.

28. *The Statesman* (New Delhi), 16 December 1983.

democratic principles and independent foreign policy. It had never compelled us to toe the Soviet line in the international affairs. Rather it wanted to see a prosperous, self-reliant and strong India and helped it in this direction. In fact, the United States did not recognise India's importance and status in South Asia nor it allowed her to emerge as a power in the sub-continent. The balance of power that existed in South Asia was well suited to American policy. So the US did not want to disturb it. As a result the Reagan Administration remained absolutely adamant on arming Pakistan at an accelerating rate. What disturbed the American administration was that whenever the US expected, India refused to fall in its scheme despite all pressures. It was also believed that the US aid was aimed to be used as a political lever against India. On that account India also refused to lay aside her independent foreign policy. It was Pakistan which got massive aid because it acted as an US satellite and Washington by all means used Islamabad to its advantage. And on Pakistani side, it had become able to acquire lead in some sector of sophisticated weapons due to the US aid.

It can be stated that in many ways Pakistani became the central point of contrary between India and USA. " Washington found the Pakistani connection more valuable than the friendship of non-aligned India. It had been the United States efforts all along to retain Pakistan as an ally, against whom was a subsidiary question. The alliance with Pakistan was useful first against the Soviet Union and then against both Soviet Unoin and China. But the fact cannot be washed away that this connection provided to Washington a useful lever of pressure against India".[29] "There was also regional factor that influenced the pace of change in American policy. The Indian and Pakistani bureaucracies treated Americans in very different ways and Americans, especially those not very familiar with the region, responded accordingly. Representatives, bureaucrats, journalists and politicians routinely received red-carpet treatment in Islamabad and met with officials several grades above their own level. This contrasted sharply with the cool, indifferent and sometimes outright hostile treatment in New Delhi of Americans who were not certified friends of India. Pakistan even had good ties with important Gulf states that were friendly to Washington and may have served as a conduit to American approaches to Iran. Moreover, India's performance at the United Nations

29. Dutt, V.P., *India and the World* (New Delhi: Sanchar Publication, 1991), p.68.

and its shrill attacks on modest American additions to Islamabad's arsenals made it seem highly unlikely to American policy."[30]

The BJP opposed any exclusivity to Super Powers' interests in South Asia. It was committed to the concept of peace with the neighbours. In its view "an enduring peace on the sub-continent can only be achieved through the process of improving bilateral relations. In that context, the institution of a joint Indo-Pakistani commission was to be welcomed. The BJP was of the view that Pakistan must not rooted in the prejudices of the past. It must abjure the established pattern of overarming and of commenting on India's internal affairs. A mutual agreement between our two countries about non-use of force can no longer be put aside. Therefore, the BJP urged the government for an early conclusion of a comprehensive treaty of peace and friendship with Pakistan."[31] The Minister of External Affairs stated that the contention of American government for the supply of Harpoon Missiles to Pakistan was appeasable. The American administration assured that those weapons would not be used against India. Even after the assurance it was realised that if those arms are utilised against India, America would find itself either helpless or unwilling to check Pakistan from doing so. So "it was not a major question of one Harpoon Missile that was given to Pakistan. Pakistan would get supplies from somewhere. Problem was we have to replenish our own stock, to start with our own competence, development of our own competence, to equip ourselves militarilrily for our defence".[32]

While endeavouring to cope with these development effectively, India continued her efforts for peace and friendship with Pakistan. The AICC (I) hoped that "the Government of Pakistan would realise that peace, friendship and cooperation with India was in the interest of stability in the region".[33] "The Congress Party urged all the patriotic forces in the country to realise the threat being posed to the security of India by large-scale induction of arms to Pakistan. India had no aggressive designs towards any country. The Congress government was committed to policy of peace and friendship with all Countries and believed that the Pakistan government would reciprocate India's

30. Gould, H.A. and S.A. Ganguly, *op.cit.*, pp.141-45.

31. Fourth National Council Session of the BJP held in New Delhi, 15th-17th April 1983, see A.M. Zaidi, *Annual Register of Indian Political Parties*, 1983, p.59.

32. *Rajya Sabha Debates*, vol.CXXVII, No.15, 12 August 1983, cols.220-22.

sincere desire which would contribute to stability in the entire region".[34]

In 1984 the Indo-American relations were at their lowest ebb. Starting from 1st October till the brutal assassination of Indira Gandhi both India and USA attacked each other on major international issues. For the US, India was creating imbalance in the sub-continent by opting for production and acquisition of arms. India, too, criticised American policy of containment. Importantly, the US patronage to the Sikh extremists and her continued supply of arms to Pakistan slide down their bilateral relations. Yakub Khan visited Washington towards the second week of October 1984. In his visit he asked United States for AWACS and Hawkeye, a high-flying plane and F-16 fighter bombers. India urged the United States to consider Pakistani demand for more sophisticated weapons as it carried danger of arms conflict in the sub-continent. Pakistan also showed her eagerness to acquire nuclear weapons on the ground that India was planning to attack Pakistani nuclear installations. However, India outrightly rejected such an allegation. Moreover, what displeased India was the American ambassador Deane Hinton's statement projecting India as an aggressor. Mrs. Gandhi accused USA for arms supply to Pakistan. It was an American attempt to bring more states under its control. The Anglo-American attempt to bring more base facilities along the coasts so that it could meet Soviet threat. So the Anglo-imperialistic attempt in the Indian sub-continent to create a hostile atmosphere attracted the attention of the non-aligned countries. The non-aligned countries unanimously condemned US action which directly aimed against India and Soviet Union. They also alleged Reagan administration for its overlook to the UN decisions that the Mariana islands be declared independent where the US was building new military base. Thus the entire world saw the danger of escalated cold war. The Indian Peninsula was totally unsafe and threatened. In the context of Anglo-imperialist menace the Soviet Union expressed her anxiety. It was significant that Moscow showed her willingness to transfer Soviet technology and Soviet arms. In his visit to India, the Soviet defence Minister Marshal Ustinov said that "the Soviet Union regards with understanding the striving of the Indian government to strengthen country's defence capability. We want to see friendly India strong,

33. *Resolutions passed in the AICC meetings* held in Bombay on 20th-21st October, 1983, p.22.

34. *Resolutions adopted at the 77th plenary session* of the Indian National Congress in Calcutta, December 1983, pp.29-30.

non-aligned state struggling for peace—The time is not far-off when a space flight of a joint Soviet-Indian crew will be made. It will open another facet of close and friendly relations between our two countries and our two peoples".[35] Marshal Ustinov in an agreement with India agreed to supply the improved version of MIG-31 to India which was considered to be superior to F-16 aircrafts. The Soviet Union also agreed to supply advanced technology aircraft to Indian Air Force and latest sensing systems to increase the capabilities of sight, surveillance and detection of naval ships. Both sides also agreed to increase the capability of Indian navy to meet threat in the Indian Ocean. To counter the US militarisation of the Indian Ocean, Moscow had agreed to upgrade operational capability of Indian navy. Simultaneously, the Indian Air Force acquired MI-25 helicopter gunships which had capability to carry a crew of eight fully equipped troops and 1275 kilograms of bomb weight. The Soviet Union also agreed to supply AN-32 aircraft and giant tactical transport aircraft submarines IL-76 by the end of 1984, new surface-to-air missiles, supply of T-80 tanks and importantly MIG -29 aircraft which had fighting capability like F-16 aircrafts.

It is clearly evident from Table 2 that huge money was being spent for military preparedness. The Third World countries were acquiring more and more weapons due to their mutual suspicion and hatredness. Besides the Middle-East countries, the two South Asian countries India and Pakistan were also diverting their economy towards military budgets. The Super Powers were investing their capital to produce more and more sophisticated weapons. The argument is valid on the ground that the money could have been utilised for the developmental activities of the Third World. To examine the argument on the other angle "the key elements in the Indian decision to accept MIG-29 was the realization that an Indian produced supersonic aircraft for the 1990s would simply be not available. France, though highly desirable as a weapons supplier, is a medium sized power and hence was unable to match the credit terms of a superpower and India had resource constraints together with the goal of self-reliance".[36] And acceptance of military aid was unavoidable for her security interests. Likewise, Pakistan also did not find any logic to halt arms acquisition as India was interested to increase its defence capability. That is why India opted for Soviet arms and Pakistan for US weapons.

35. *Die Welt,* 16 March 1984.

36. Singh, S. Nihal, " Why India goes to Moscow for arms", *Asian Survey,* vol.24, No.7, July 1984, pp.710-20.

But the Indo-Soviet cooperation testified time-tested friendship. It came more successful than the US-Pakistan alliance. The Soviet Union showed her willingness to help India in checking terrorist activities in Punjab. The Western press, however, narrated this cooperation in a different way. Moreover, they remarked that the Indo-Soviet military cooperation would be detrimental to peace and nuclear free South-Asia. The Western imperialists characterised it as an attempt of the communists to contend India so that it could use India to its advantage. India rejected the plea for the Soviet Union had never put any hurdle to its aid programme. To the contrary, the Indo-Soviet military cooperation was a defensive arrangement to counter the US strategy. Preservation of security was of utmost importance to India and in the face of US-Pakistan military threat India had no option but to go for Soviet arms. Inspite of acquiring sophisticated arms India had not shown any desire of threatening Pakistan's security. In the midst of constant danger India always appealed to Pakistan to settle their bilateral differences through mutual negotiations instead of inviting the Super Powers to intervene. At the same time it would be wrong not to consider Pakistan's concern on India's strength on nuclear weapons. So it was Pakistan which showed hostile attitude than the US and so it adopted Israeli type of activities by indulging itself in state terrorism by arming and training to the Afghan rebels and the Sikh extremists. However, the strong hands of the CIA were already there. It was only India's security alertness that avoided any serious attack on India. The Anglo-imperialists' abortive attempts were frustrated. Thereby, United States always wanted to keep back India in every possible way. That was the reason why India's sincere and serious requests against American military aid to Pakistan was not considered seriously.

It was a fact that the Pakistani army had been deployed on our border. Pakistan had also taken up a programme of development of roads and other infrastructure close to our border. Pakistani troops had also been resorting to firing across the line of control. Violations of our air space by Pakistani aircraft were also not uncommon. Inspite of all these developments India had been exercising utmost restraints and preserving our policy of peace with Pakistan. In such a situation, the BJP leader Shri Jaswant Singh spoke about his party's position. He said that the BJP expressed concern about Pakistan's massive arms acquisitions and threatening our security. He added, " The real danger we are facing is not an Indo-Pakistan situation developing on account of want of incentives. But the real danger we are facing is the introduction, is the importation in our region of the concept of proxy wars. If we, India and Pakistan, become an instrument of superpower conflict or the superpowers policies being played therein as agencies of the super powers interests, then we will be committing grave ill and a grave crime to the peoples of both these nations".[37] "For that purpose, the BJP urged for a South Asian Regional Summit, which would ensure its independent, non-aligned status without any outside intervention or interference".[38] The Indian government also realised that our security preparedness "must be from all sides of this vast subcontinent, not only from land borders but also from our long shore line. That is why India must be self-reliant in defence production, because to give our people not just the security but the knowledge that they could live secure. For this the Indian government was prepared to use its own inventives and also to learn the knowledge and the researches garnered from all other parts of the world".[39] The Super Powers wanted harmony between India and Pakistan as long as it served their interests. For example, the United States wanted concord so that it could face Soviet Union and China; on the other hand Soviet Union supported friendly relations among the South Asian countries to challenge the U.S. hegemony in this region. "So the dire necessity is that if we cannot ignore superpowers interests we should consider our amity with reference to our own interests, not with reference to the interests of any external power including the course of the superpowers".[40] Therefore, the BJP urged "to pursue a policy of peace, friendship and cooperation with neighbouring countries, to reestablish India's Asian identity emphasising on a policy of constructive cooperation in South and South-East Asia. Moreover, the BJP declared to resolve the social and political turmoil in strategically sensitive border states. To the BJP, internal cohesiveness and a united and determined national will was the foundation of a nation's defence preparedness".[41] " So the real challenge to our foreign policy lay in the success of our diplomacy in Islamabad, Kathmandu, Colombo and Dhaka and not

37. *Rajya Sabha Debates,* vol.CXX, No.12, 8 May 1984, cols. 271-75.

38. Speech of Suraj Bhan Singh. See *Lok Sabha Debates*, Seventh Series, Fourteenth Session, vol.XLVIII, No.52, 9 May 1984, cols.414-17.

39. *Selected speeches and writings of Indira Gandhi:* vol.V, op. cit., pp.64-65.

40. *Organiser,* 14 October 1984, pp.5-6.

41. *Election Manifesto* of the BJP, Lok Sabha Election 1984, pp.20-22.

the capitals of big powers. Through sensitive and patient diplomacy, we could slow down the extravagant militarism in the sub-continent, we could carry greater credibility in urging detente, disarmament and international social justice".[42]

After the assassination of Mrs. Gandhi, the Congress government again emerged under the leadership of Rajiv Gandhi. Rajiv Gandhi's accession to power, however, did not premonish any radical changes in the foreign policy of India. His vision of leading India into the 21st century without much reliance on foreign capital was an astounding task. His pragmatic approach for rapid industrialisation and technological development was considered to be a commendable task. At the beginning the Soviet Union seemed to be slightly suspicious about this Indian effort. The Soviet suspicion was that India might go to West for transfer of technical knowledge and massive aid package. Though the Indo-Soviet strong bond of relations continued to be dominated in the foreign policy approach of Rajiv Gandhi, his economic policies inevitably led India closer to the Western countries. While retaining the traditional Indo-Soviet relations, India found no contradiction of entering into the West, particularly to the United States. Despite the differences on America's supply of military weapons to Pakistan and divergence on Afghanistan issue, the newly elected Indian Prime Minister opened the door for a better relationship with the United States.

Pakistan also showed its interest in aligning itself with the United States. The Indian Ocean littoral countries like Philippines, Indonesia and other countries of the SEATO group, too, showed their spontaneous feeling of a fear of India's domination and they were also supporting the United States. In all cases, they had their economic stakes behind supporting the US policies. They wanted rapid economic growth and thereby ingress of dollar was valuable for them. Since its inception Pakistan served as a link between Central Treaty Organisation and the South East Asian Treaty Organisation, even if it did not join the groups. Despite the rapidly changing political and strategic environment in the eighties, Pakistan continued to minister to US strategy. The Shimla spirit has survived but its virility has been lost over the years. To the contrary, India is still guided by her policy of non-alignment and the famous 'Panchasheel' still proves its potency for India. Thus, it appeared that Pakistan's fear of India's policies

42. Mehta, Jagat S., "Revitalising India's Foreign Policy", *Monthly commentary on Indian Economic conditions,* vol.XXVI, No.5, 305, December 1984, p.50.

would not come to a halt unless there was radical transformation of United States' policies in South Asia. "Unlike the 1950s and the 1960s, US power politics in India-USA relations was no longer tempered by a tinge of idealism. In the 1950s, however, though the United States armed Pakistan, US policy-makers repeatedly said that for them India was equally important and extended to it large economic aid. In the 1980s, they had repeatedly stated in unequivocal fashion that India no longer needed concessional borrowings from the IDA and the IMF. Initially, the United States pursued its power politics while at the same time economically aiding India. But in the eighties, it was power politics simple and pure. The change in attitude was because India was fast building itself as a major power comparable to China. Hence there was the unstated purpose of limiting India's power, especially when it was perceived to be leaning towards the Soviet Union".[43] Although the United States showed her willingness to discuss Indian requirements on arms assistance, and economic aid, nothing came out of it because of Indian reservations on the standard of US contract. For instance, the US refused to release night sights for TOW. The Indian inhibition was clearly demonstrated when Rajiv Gandhi expressed his insensitiveness on US arms supply. He said that " He did not visualise any defence deals because of US undependability".[44]

So both India and the United States found barriers in their bilateral relationship. At the same time they did not show any direct confrontation also. So both of them were pursuing double-track policy. The United States did not let down Indo-American relations, rather it encouraged Indian government for its independent and non-aligned status. It did not show eagerness to supply military hardware to India but on the other hand could not ignore American interest of developing good relations with India as the later provided market for US products. It also did not stop military aid to Pakistan but continued to state that it would not create threat to India's security. India, on the other hand, did not want to sacrifice her independent course of action but sought American aid for its military build-up. It was a well known fact that the US would not change her policy towards Pakistan. So India had nothing to do but to put certain limitation to it. India could not ignore Soviet Union's aid at crucial juncture but also could not put aside America's higher technology export to India. On the other hand,

43. Kamath, P.M.(ed.), *Indo-US Relations: Dynamics of Change* (New Delhi: South Asian, 1987), pp.50-53.

44. *Washington Post* (Washington), 14 June 1985.

from the American side they "were trying to buy time from India for the Pakistani military regime at a time when their growing expectations of the Pakistani people that the Indians should help to ovethrow their warlords and restore human rights and democracy. The western countries were also quite active in keeping India worried on Sri Lankan front so that India could not retaliate against Pakistani sabotage in the north-west".[45] " In the immediate neighbourhood of South Asia, India's policy was directed towards promoting mutual trust and extending cooperation. India was determined to resolve problems with the countries on the basis of mutual respect, sovereign equality and friendship. It was on India's interests as well as the interests of the region that the South Asian countries should work together and build up relationship based on equality, mutual respect, benefit and non-interference and non-intervention. More importantly, India sought cordial and cooperative relations with Pakistan on the bases of sovereignty, equality, non-interference and mutual benefit".[46] "Pakistan was also equally hopeful of cordial relations with India and other neighbouring countries. Particularly with India, Pakistan reaffirmed that there would no weakening of efforts to develop a relationship of mutual trust and confidence. Pakistan reiterated that it was not in competition with India in an arms race and the arms it acquired was meant to achieve partial replacement of its obsolete defence equipment. Rather it showed willingness to grasp the hand of friendship that India extended for establishing good neighbourly relations".[47]

Indian efforts and societ unions writtingness hold a special place in readucing the threats of arms race. The Indo-Soviet relations were marked by the desire of peaceful co-existence and both India and the USSR worked on those lines for stronger peace and security of the mankind. "Before an irreversible situation created the Soviet Union urged all peace loving states to raise their voice against the new danger, the danger that brought the world to the threshold of a new spiral in the arms race".[48] The basic consideration of India's foreign policy was to develop very close relationship with the USSR. The USSR had shown its desire of establishing good relations with India

45. *Organiser,* 3 March 1985, p.1.

46. *Foreign Affairs Record,* April 1985, pp.95-101. (Minister of state for External Affairs, Khurshid Alam Khan's speech in the Lok Sabha on Demands for Grants of the Ministry of External Affairs in New Delhi, 9 April 1985).

47. *Public Opinion Trends, Analyses and News Service (POT),* (Pakistan series), New Delhi, vol.IX, part 187, pp.2152-53.

48. *Pravda* (Moscow), 22 May 1985.

over many decades. Looking at the satisfactory progress of Indo-Soviet relations the AICC (I) remarked that "the most significant feature of Soviet attitude towards India was their emphasis on continued good relations and hoped that their relationship would continue in the mutual interests of both countries".[49]

On the other hand, during Reagan-Rajiv era the Indo-American relations entered the phase of increased misgivings and mistrust. The U.S. administration was not worried if India's security would be endangered by US-Pakistan alliance. "Also the US was not serious of India's apprehensions that the US encouragement of Pakistan and other neighbours of India had resulted in a virtual encirclement of India".[50] The main thrust of U.S. policy in South Asia was to weaken India. "The idea of projecting India as one of the many South Asian Countries which should busy themselves with development was part of the U.S. policy to neutralise India in some manner or the other".[51] As a leading American editor observed, " the Americans were unusually itchy about India and found it more irritating than many other countries with which the United States also had substantive differences. Moreover, the United States had incorrectly defined its interests in South Asia on the basis of an increasingly outdated assessment of India's power potential. As a result, there was growing possibility that American policies would lead India to identify its geopolitical interests more strongly with those of the Soviet Union, posing serious dangers for the United States. In particular, a hostile Indian navy, possible nuclear armed, could greatly complicate American use of the United States Navy's 850 million dollar base complex at Diego Garcia as well as other aspects of American military access to Indian Ocean and Persian Gulf".[52]

The United States was not supporting India's policy of non-alignment. India proclaimed that it was a true champion of the non-aligned movement. The Soviet Union supported India's non-aligned status and tried to show that it was a natural ally of India, while the

49. *Resolutions passed in the AICC Meetings* held in Delhi on 4th and 5th May 1985, AICC(I) Publication, pp.21-22.

50. Viswam, S., "India and President Reagan", *Mainstream,* vol.XXIII, No.12, Nehru Birthday Special, 1984, p.48.

51. John Cherian, "Foreign Policy: Shifting Sands?", *Mainstream,* vol.XXIII, No.39, 25 May 1985, p.6.

52. Glazer, Sulochana R. and Glazer, N. (eds.), *Conflicting Images: India and the United States* (Gleen Dale; Marry land: Riverdale Co. publishers, 1990), pp. 57-61.

United States wanted India to be more inclined towards the West. India, to the contrary, in various non-aligned conferences condemned US actions in South Asia. Perhaps this stand of the Government of India dissatisfied America and thereby the US administration tilted towards Pakistan and tried to project the latter more militarily stronger than India in South Asia.

On the other hand, "Unlike our defence deals with the West which were largely in the nature of outright purchase, the Soviet cooperation had by and large helped in indigenous defence production. It appeared that the extent of mutual confidence between the two countries was such that there was no nagging insistence on safeguards against transfer of technology as one had to encounter in any deal for strategically sensitive items, the kind of safeguards the U.S. insisted upon".[53] " Since the Soviet Union's dominant concern was to weaken the military alliances which the US and Western Powers were building around its borders, it countered this by pursuing a policy of arms transfer involving support to the non-aligned movement, liberation movement and countries asserting independence vis-a-vis the western alliance system like SEATO and CENTO. This served two purposes—undermining Western influence and at least neutralising the neutrals, if not winning friends".[54] Gorbachev praised India's contribution to the struggle for peace and security in Asia and the whole world. He declared that the "friendship and cooperation between the USSR and India and their commitment to peace was an important factor in preserving life on earth".[55] The Soviet leader shared India's concern about Pakistan's acquisition of atomic weapons. He reaffirmed that "Soviet Union had great respect for India and it would support India in case of any need"[56], even in the event of conflict between New Delhi and its neighbours.[57]

India's relations with the neighbouring countries started deteriorating after Rajiv Gandhi assumed power. With Pakistan our relations was so unpleasant that Pakistan started differing with India in international as well as bilateral issues. To add fuel to fire Pakistan started encouraging terrorist activities in the border states of India. The

53. Chakravorty, Nikhil, "No Room For Illusions", *World Focus,* vol.6, No.7, July 1985, p.4.

54. Khan, R. ''NAM and Global powers", *World Focus,* vol.6, No.7, July 1985, p.17.

55. *Soviet News* (Moscow), 11 September 1985, p.324.

56. *Tagesspiegel,* 28 October 1985.

57. *The Muslim* (Lahore), 12 November 1985.

Bhartiya Janata Party held the view that "a logical corollary of those hostile actions was dependent on India's diplomatic steps to discipline Islamabad. But the government had neither will nor the vision to take any effective action".[58] In such a totality when there was large scale military exercises, it was meant to weaken India because India had to divert her resources from economic development to military awareness. "It was not alone Pakistan that India had to contend with, but it was the force behind Pakistan that had to be tackled, i.e., the US strategic consensus which aimed to build Pakistan a militarily strong nation".[59]

India, a truly non-aligned state, was following the principles of the non-alignment as guiding factors of its foreign policy. The Indo-Soviet relations improved observing the principles of non-alignment. "The reasons for Soviet support was based neither on formal alliance nor on ideological-political affinity. Soviet Indian relations were clearly based on realistic recognition of each other's capabilities, on enlightened mutual interests and on the hard-headed premises of international interdependence and international co-existence. Experience of national life and world affairs had confirmed for both the countries the basic validity of their policy premised toward each other. Its most outstanding attribute had been that it had never been focussed against any other country deliberately, notwithstanding however inevitable fall out of any policy projection as an unavoidable corollary due to the inter-meshing of international politics".[60] The Indo-Soviet relations reflected the role of Soviet Union and India in world affairs and their moral right to save the world. "Their relations based on freedom, equality and non-violence and was a major contribution for peaceful world order".[61] The Delhi Declaration was described as a historic document, a truly extraordinary document. The Rear-Admiral Pushkin pointed out that "a nuclear war can not be won. The Delhi Declaration representing the interest of people everywhere should be heard also everywhere. There was no other way to peace".[62]

To the contrary, the policies of the United States had been

58. *Two years of Congress Misrule : A charge sheet*, adopted by BJP National Executive at Jammu, 19 October 1986, p.9.

59. *Lok Sabha Debates*, vol.XXI, No.3, Eighth Series, Seventh Session, 6 November 1986, cols. 373-78.

60. Khan, Rasheeduddin, "Defence of Indian Sovereignty and the Role of the Soviet Union", in Vinod Bhatia(ed.), *The October Revolution and 70 years of Indo-Soviet Relations* (New Delhi : Panchasheel, 1987), pp.116-17.

61. *The Statesman* (New Delhi), 28 November 1986.

62. *Novosti* (Moscow), 2 December 1986.

motivated to limit India's role and influence in the region. The United States was aware of India's growing strength and power that it had acquired. So it was feared that India would dominate the developing states of South Asia which was inimical to American interests. It was an established fact that India was not as much close to the US as Pakistan was, so the United States opposed India's actions in a number of cases. In fact, the US contention was far from reality. India had no intention of playing as a dominant state in the region nor was it capable enough to thwart US actions in the sub-continent. The American interests were no doubt hostile to those of the Indians as it were projected by the critics. Occasional frictions overshadowed their bilateral meetings because of America's global equation. The South Asian region was of much importance to the United States. So also it was highly vulnerable to other outside powers. The Soviet Union was equally attracted to this region what the United States could not allow. Any other attempt was acceptable other than to see a Soviet dominated South Asia. This was perhaps the fundamental flaw in Indo-American relationship. On important global and transregional issues both India and the United States found themselves at odds while Indian policies converged with the USSR. The Government of India showed its enthusiasm on disarmament issues. It appealed all the powers for disarmament and for establishing a peaceful world order. So the alignment between India and the USSR demonstrated unity on a variety of issues. India shared Soviet concern that the Indian subcontinent would turn to a battle-field if the United States did not show any interest in that matter. The Indian perception was that the US could not able to manage the South Asian security and integrity. So instead of blaming India or the USSR, the US should encourage the regional countries to solve their bilateral problems. And the countries of South Asia would come for an understanding and could play satisfactory role in international fora, if they are allowed to determine their future by themselves. On the other hand, India persuaded Pakistan and other countries of the region of not entrusting them to the outsiders who were least concerned of their progress and development.

No doubt the Reagan Administration was interested to forge closer ties with India as it expected India to be a major military partner of the United States. It also showed its willingness to export military hardware to India. Sometimes, both sides made significant steps in overcoming their divergencies and Indo-American relations were likely to grow. Policies were set up to suit both sides. The most important deal concluded in 1987 was to supply 11 general Electric FE-404 engines to India which was described as the most recent combat-aircraft engine. Again USA was agreed to supply radars to equip Chandipur test-firing range in Orissa. Mr. Gandhi's visit to USA in October 1987 gave further initiative to the proposal of supplying military weapons. Perhaps India had made request for submarine launched missiles during his visit. So Indian doubt about US supply of weapons had been settled down. The US-India military linkage was strengethening. "The Indian government's propensity for alignment with the West was not the result of haphazard moves determined by the merits of various economic and political questions. India received its military equipments from the US and its officers got their training from the British commonwealth and the United States".[63]

The acquisition of early warning radar system by Pakistan would bring insecurity to India and so the Indian government had decided to produce weapons and to prepare the country for any aggressive action of outside powers. Once it gets support from a big power, it was believed, and all material strength were united, then threats of the imperialists would be faced. It was felt that in any case any local conflict would bring third world war or a major catastrophe what non-aligned India was not ready to face. On the possible sale of sophisticated early warning radar planes to Pakistan, Rajiv Gandhi reacted sharply. He said, "... the sophisticated early warning systems will be used by Pakistan against us. Their military deployments have always been focussed on our borders. Afghanistan has not changed what really bothers me is that the introduction of these systems will escalate the arms race to a qualitatively new level. It will add to tensions and mean a serious set-back to our efforts at normalising relations with Pakistan. And it will divert move our scarce resources from development".[64] Thus, the Indo-American relations were upset by Washington's strategic relationship with Islamabad. "While all sorts of conditionalities were being put by the US for the sale to India of a super computer for peaceful purposes, it was significant that the US authorities were not going to stop their increased arms supplies to Pakistan, despite the widely publicised Symington Amendment in the U.S. Congress".[65]

63. Hagelberg, Gerhard, *What Path for India* (New York: Far East Reporter, 1989), pp.13-14.
64. Interview with Mr. Pranoy Gupte of "News Week", 31 March 1987. For details see statement on *Foreign Policy of Rajiv Gandhi* (New Delhi: Publication Division, Ministry of External Affairs, 1987), p.23.
65. Chakravorty, N., "India and the world", *World Focus*, vol.8 Nos.7-8, July-August 1987, p.11.

Never before had India faced such external threats as it was in the later part of the eighties. India was being squeezed between pressure-tactics of two Super Powers. "The Soviet Union had agreed to supply matching aid of arms to Pakistan as it was received from the US".[66] "So we were likely to face situation in which all the three superpowers and their satellites would be encircling India with their mighty military force stationed within striking distance of our major cities and the BJP condemned that the government had been found wanting in meeting this challenge. So the BJP considered to pay special attention to the development of relations with our neighbours and to encourage regional cooperation in South Asia in the common interests of all states in the region so that the superpower rivalry would be checkmated."[67]

Dr. Maulana Abul Kalam Azad had rightly observed, "Mr. 11. Jinnah and his followers did not seem to realise that geography was against them.... It was one of the greatest frauds on the people to suggest that religious affinity can unite areas which are geographically, economically, linguistically and culturally different."[68] So the way Pakistan was moving and acting in collusion with the SuperPowers demonstrated its motive to further destabilise the sub-continent. The destabilisation movement in Punjab, Jammu and Kashmir were dangerous for India's security. If we accept Uncle Sam's conception that India and Pakistan were equally responsible for their desolation, we shall be on wrong boat. Starting from the partition of India, the Indian leaders had been opposed to any division of India, but the saboteurs destroyed the unity of the country. So further spoilage of the sub-continent was detrimental to the interest of the people of both India and Pakistan.The critics argued that Pakistan's acquisition of military weapons was not conducive to its economic development which Pakistan could not realise. Her anti-India stance only promoted the military regime to go for United States' military aid. The foreign policy experts also viewed that the situation in the sixties and the seventies was similar to the eighties as far as US-Pakistan alliance was concerned. As the Table 1 shows the US military aid to Pakistan in 1982 was less compared to total aid to other countries. It started increasing in 1983 and it was quite high in 1985, Though the US

66. *Organiser,* 8 November 1987, p.2.

67. See *Our Five Commitments,* BJP publication, op.cit., p.19.

68. Azad, Abul *Kalam, India Wins Freedom* (Bombay : Longmans Press, 1959), p.227.which is totally unnecessary. We need it for much more creative

administration was in favour of building a strong American base in Pakistan, due to pressure from the Third World countries of the Indian sub-continent supported by some big powers, the arms aid started reducing since 1986 and in 1990 it was almost same as it was in 1982. The acquisition of arms by Pakistan has only one reason behind it, i.e., to counter India. The anti-Hindu air prevailing there only encouraged her to go for war with India. All these developments are not favourable for the developing economies like Pakistan or India. Though the political situation was not much changed in the eighties, due to the world economic crisis a large amount of military expenditure was surely inimical to the developing countries especially. So the critics argued that instead of concentrating her resources to counter India, Pakistan should think of her economic development. Moreover, the arms aid to Pakistan which posed a serious challenge to the peace and development was not the US responsibility solely. The critics argue that it would be wrong to state that Pakistan would not have gone for arms had there been no US arms. Other big powers were there to provide arms to Pakistan. What was a matter of concern was that despite several talks between the great powers to reduce their expenditure on defence, the US continued to export and the US spent around 40 percent on its defence accounts of the total government expenditure. In 1987 the defence outlay was 274 million dollar out of 1,004.584 billion dollar which was $130.976 billion in 1980. So within a span of seven years the defence expenditure was more than double. It was the desire to acquire more sophisticated weapons that invited the United States to use Pakistan in its game of power politics. So the attitude and response of Pakistan reflected more security challenge to Indian. If we probe little deeper into the issue we could see Pakistani eagerness to maintain parity of arms with India. The sooner, Pakistan is motivated to come out of its chosen path, the better it would be for the growth and security of South Asia.

Mr. K.C.Pant, Indian defence minister visited Moscow in 1988 February. In his discussion with the Soviet leader he expressed "India's concern about Pakistan's military build up arms assistance by the US, which brought the ashes of cold war into the region".[69] India was "not worried about the arms aid per se, because that is really bilateral between the US and Pakistan. But what it means is that we have to spend a lot of our funds on defence which is totally unnecessary. We need it for much more creature activities, development activities,

69. *Tagesspiegel,* 17 February 1988.

rather than defence. The second thing is that it freezes a lot of Pakistan's own finances for their own nuclear programme which is now very clearly established as a military weapon programme."[70] It would be totally wrong if Pakistan is blamed alone. For the protection of its interests in the Indian Ocean and Persian gulf, the United Sates went on stockpiling arms and strengethened Pakistan on nuclear field. Therefore, the US had increased its arms aid from 85 million dollar in 1979 to 500 million dollar in 1985, a eight-fold increase in a period of six years. So the US had certainly succeeded in furthering its aims in the region,though it could not be able to solve the major problems confronting the world that time. At least it succeeded in preserving the military regime in Pakistan which was friendly to American policies. It must be noted that the US was equally interested to support the democratic uprising in Pakistan but it was skeptical of equal response from Prime Minister Benazir Bhutto. The United States wanted to further its image in Asia and also the Pakistani military regime wanted to remain in power as long as possible. Their two perceptions coincided and matched due to various reasons. The United States was disillusioned with Indian foreign policy and sought to block the prospect of cordiality between India and Pakistan and so it gave her unstinted support to the Zia regime. On the other hand the conflicts between India and Pakistan conflict of dominance in the sub-continent, encouraged Pakistan to accept willingly American friendship and military support to achieve parity with India. Therefore a 'marriage of necessity' was the guiding factor for both Pakistan and USA. The American announcement to give 4.2 billion dollar during 1988-1993 showed the enhanced American interest in Pakistan. Besides India too be blamed because (as the Table 2 shows) the import of weapons by India was the largest among all the countries over the world. Further, Table 4 shows that defence expenditure of India in 1986 was $ 8.35 billion which started increasing since 1987 and it stood at $ 9 billion in 1990. Per capita defence expenditure is quite high in case of a country like India. Only since 1989 it started decreasing. So it is neither desirable nor necessary to spend huge amount after defence when we are striving for uplifting our economy. Even after spending money for defence preparedness it could not fulfil our defence requirements. In this situation, the BJP remarked that "the total mishandling of our security arrangement made our foreign policy episodic and

70. Prime Minister Rajiv Gandhi's interview with USA TODAY in New Delhi on 15 March 1988, see *Statements of Rajiv Gandhi on Foreign* Policy (May 1988), Op. Cit., p.23.

adhoc. The principal and immediate anxiety of the BJP was the strategic imbalance of our armed forces. Defence capital expenditure for 1987-88 had actually been cut down by almost Rs. 100 crores, whereas the defence revenue expenses had gone up by Rs. 700 crores. In other words, we had spent more on the peripherals at the cost of modernization, upgradation and the future combat effectiveness of our armed forces. Moreover, our relations with neighbours had been strained and India's position had been reduced to a status of almost regional inconsequence."[71] No doubt Indo-American relations improved that time, but difference on US arms supply to Pakistan aggaravated. From the US side a change in political strategic approach in the international arena was observed. "There was a change in US attitude because of Rajiv Gandhi's pursuit of high-tech from the developed countries."[72] The AICC(I) expressed its satisfaction in India's relations with the United States. "There had been noticeable increase in the interest shown by US industry in seeking collaboration with Indian partners. High technology areas of cooperation were being explored and trade both ways had increased. But the AICC(I) remained concerned at the continuing massive US supply of sophisticated arms to Pakistan. It called upon the government of the United States to review its policy with a view to deescalate the arms build-up in the region."[73]

Pakistan was receiving arms from the United States on the pretext of tackling the Afghan rebels, but it started channelising those arms to the terrorists in Punjab. Therefore, "the Indo-Pakistan relations had reached to a low level and the United states was condemned for this conflagration".[74] So US military assistance to Pakistan affected the Indo-Pakistani relations more than the Indo-American relations. The danger of cold war was not far away from the South Asian region. "The continuous deposit of US arms in Pakistan had led to certain pernicious developments which impinged on India's foreign policy. Apart from US arms assistance inevitably whetting the appetite of military dictators in Pakistan which had never shed its aggressive adventurist

71. *Presidential Address by L.K.Advani*, Fourth Plenary Session, Deen Dayal Dham, Agra, 8 April 1988, pp.12-14.

72. Hari Kumar, K.N., "Trading Non-Alignment For High-tech: Rajiv's Record US visit", *Economic and Political Weekly*, vol.23, No. 17, 23 April 1988, p.853.

73. *Resolutions passed by the AICC Meeting* held on 4th and 5th November 1988, New Delhi, p.29.

74. *Organiser*, Commerce and Industry Special 1988, pp.13-14.

designs in the sub-continent."[75] As Gursharan Singh has rightly pointed out, there were three main obstacles to Indo-USA security ties: "First, India's non alignment policy and consequent refusal to join in formal military pacts or even to acknowledge the communist states as a global military threat ; Second, Pakistan's objections that US arming of India may prove detrimental to its own security, together with US willingness to sustain such objections and third, the political,financial and technological terms offered by Washington for the sale of US arms or the transfer of military technology to India".[76] Shift in US attitude towards India is clearly seen after the signing of the Memorandum of Understanding (MOU). "Though both sides were interested in carrying out the beginning they had made, the conflicts between NSDD 147 and NSDD 99—which set out the broad guidelines governing security assistance to Pakistan to help it improve its overall defences would continue to be potent threats particularly to Rajiv Gandhi's ability to carry out the Indian public opinion with him".[77]

The Bharatiya Janata party made it clear that "the principal challenge India faced in the field of external relations was regional. India's national and security interest would be served only through a larger awareness of the regional demands, regional needs, regional fears and regional sentiments of South, South-west and South-East Asia. So proper ordering of our relations with all neighbours was the need of the hour."[78] The BJP further differed with the government "in which it had been dealing with crucial issues of national security, particularly in the context of Pakistan. It was a matter of deep concern that Pakistan continued to aid and supply arms to anti-national elements in Jammu and Kashmir and to the terrorists in Punjab."[79] The BJP held the view that "national security is a primary responsibility of a state. Safety of nation is an integral whole; an amalgam of the internal, the economic and the social, political, the military and diplomacy. The BJP alleged that the conduct of diplomacy by Rajiv Gandhi had left India's foreign policy in tatters. It viewed that India

75. Chakravorty, Nikhil, "Evolution of Indian Foreign Policy", *World Focus,* vol. 9, No.8, August 1988, p.14.

76. Dhanjal, G.S., "Security factor in Indo-US Relations", *Mainstream,* vol.XXVII, No.26, 25 March 1989, p.18.

77. *Ibid.*, p.35.

78. *Resolutions adopted* by the National Executive Meetings of the BJP, Palampur (Himachal Pradesh), 9th to 11th June 1989, p.10.

79. *Presidential Address* by L.K.Advani, Eleventh National Council Session, Shanmukhananda Hall, Sion, Bombay, 25th September 1989, pp.12-13.

was facing challenges in the field of external relations, arose from a re-assertion of the altered importance of non-alignment in a rapidly transforming world. The BJP was committed to mutually beneficial aims of good bilateral relations with all our neighbours and a strengthening of SAARC. It stood for normalisation of relations with China, honourable solution to the border problem and comprehensive settlement of all outstanding matters with Pakistan and Sri Lanka. Thus, the BJP stood for a foreign policy committed to world peace, disarmament and a non-exploitative new international economic order. The party added that it would work towards re-imparting dynamism to the non-alignment movement; a policy of peace, friendship and cooperation with neighbouring countries and to thwart superpowers dominance in South Asian region."[80] "We should make vigorous efforts to remove irritants in our relations with neighbours. Without sacrificing on matters which affect our security, unity and integrity of India, we must show generosity in our relations with our neighbours."[81] "The essential pre-requisite of a military cooperation between India and the US is that it should help in bringing about the disappearance of the military threat on India's border with Pakistan in Kashmir which is worsening everyday with the Pakistan aided infiltrators and militants. So any defense tie with the US could serve India's interests, if the military threat to its security and integrity is made to recede".[82] "Pakistan continued to pursue procurement of military hardware and technology from other countries far beyond its legitimate defence requirements. In addition, it continued with its clandestine and weapon-oriented nuclear programme and its efforts to acquire ballistic missiles and technology".[83]

Pakistan's total thrust to its armed forces and public was on creating an anti-India tirade and this was evident from the syllabi being followed by Pakistan army training institutions.[84] The Indian National Congress strongly condemns the blatant interference of Pak in the internal affairs of our country. Having started three wars which brought it nothing but misery, Pak has now launched a fourth war against India: a proxy war, through a well-financed, well trained and

80. *Election Manifesto of the BJP*, Lok Sabha election 1989, pp.38-39.

81. BJP *National Executive Meeting*, Thimvanthapuram, September 30, 1991, p.19

82. *Hindu* (Madras), 11 October 1991.

83. *Lok sabha Debates*, Tenth Series, First Session, vol. 4 (39), September 5, 1991 lok. 362-63.

84. *The Statesman* (New Delhi), January 17, 1992.

well-armed fifth column. No nation can tolerate repeated provocation from across the border beyond a point. India will always strain every nerve to ensure peace. At the same time, the exercise of self-defense is an inalienable right of every nation".[85] "Pakistan has been acquiring sophisticated and modern military weapons, namely, Harpoon Missiles, Mohawk and Hawk Eye reconnaissance plane and electronic arms. India wants peace and friendship with all, particularly with its neighbours; but it cannot be at the cost of our security, territorial integrity and national honour. India believes in equality and non-interference and her foreign policy is based on the five principles of Panchasheel".[86]

On the other hand, "with the likely loss of its military bases in the Philippines and the growing concern of the US at the possible emergence of a Pan-Islamic Power, the United States seems to be keen on projecting India as a regional power capable of serving its strategic interests. India too seems to be ready to play ball as, for the first time after independence, its own security concern, coincide with that of the United States".[87] "The cryogenic engines and related technology are meant for our civilian space programme. They do not and cannot have any military application. In offering its cryogenic engine, centaur, to the ISRO, General Dynamics of the US had confirmed earlier that *Centaur is a non-upper stage and is not practicable as a weapon*. So, they themselves have certified that what we were really seeking to obtain from them was entirely peaceful. I assure of our continuing commitment to achieving self-reliance in the field of high technology particularly in areas like space which have a major bearing on our economic development. We have had very fruitful cooperation in peaceful application of space technology with several countries including the erstwhile Soviet Union, France, and the United States and now Russia. We would like to continue such cooperation to our mutual benefit".[88] "Another step towards closer cooperation between India and the US in the sphere of defense has been taken with the visit of General Jimmy V. Adams. US delegation was headed by Lieutenant-General Johnnie H. Corns and the visit of Admiral Frank B. Kekes, at which it was decided to set up a Steering Committee for naval

85. *Text of Resolution* adopted at 79th Plenary Session of INC, Tirupati, 14-16 April 1992, p. 34.

86. *Pakistan War Posture*, AICC Publication, pp. 3-4.

87. *The Indian Express* (New Delhi), January 18, 1992.

88. *Lok Sabha Debates*, vol. xi (37), tenth Series, Third Session, April 23, 1992.

cooperation. With the two navies having established communication at sea and a possibility existing of joint exercises being conducted in the not too distant future, the Air Force too could find an opening to participate in a joint Air Technical Information Distribution System".[89] "Indo-US defense cooperation is likely to grow in view of the convergence of geo-political and strategic interests in the Asia-Pacific region. In this context, the American offer of its highly sophisticated AN-TPQ-36 and TPQ-37 Scanning Radars assumes significance".[90] "The aim of Kicklighter proposals is to gradually strengthen ties between the two armies, through expanded cooperation and partnership by the end of the decade. This would be worked out by high level exchanges, visits and periodic policy reviews between US and Indian Army officials".[91] "The economic crisis and a lack of clear political direction in Russia during the past one year have created an air of uncertainty around India-Russia ties.... Moreover, India's efforts at achieving self-sufficiency in this regard has not made much headway. Even though, India has been producing domestically many equipments under license from the former Soviet Union, its dependence on the latter and now on Russia for the supply of spares on a regular basis, constant up gradation of equipment through technological innovations, technology transfer and other related after-sale services is enormous. As Russia has made moves towards a market-led economy, Russian factories are demanding payments in hard currency. After Yelstin's visit, Russia has made three proposals in response to the concerns expressed by India. First, Russia would seek to improve the functioning of its factories which supply equipment and spares to India. Second, joint ventures would be set up to co-produce spare parts either in India or in Russia or in both the countries. Third, technology transfer to India for production of spares. The Russian affirmation to continue the past commitment is a positive outcome. In the short-run even if Russia is unable to promptly deliver the promises, India has very limited choice. But in the long-run India has a choice; it can diversify its sources of arms supply without any adverse impact on its defense preparedness or, it can move firmly in the direction of self-reliance by not only developing its own R&D base but also by acquiring technology".[92] "The Russian decision to conduct all foreign

89. *Statesman* (New Delhi), March 4, 1992.

90. *Times of India* (New Delhi), 21 November 1991.

91. *Ibid,* Ib October 1991.

92. Subramanian, K., "Changing contours of New Delhi-Moscow Defence Tiles", *Link,* 14 February 1993, pp. 19-21.

trade with India in hard currency from 1989 has major implications for arms imports by India which has traded on a soft currency basis in the past. There was also another rationale for India buying arms from the USSR--obtaining political support from a super power.... India has no choice in the future except to rely on its R&D activities in the area of defense production era as the Soviet Defense Ministry is proposing co-production of select aircraft like the SU-37, YAK-141 and MG-31. There can be little doubt that by virtue of the relations between New Delhi and Washington being strengthened, there could be further collaboration in the field of defense. One such collaboration is the Light Combat Aircraft [LCA] for which the F-404 engines were imported from the General Electric Company in the USA.''[93] "Mr Drukov emphasized the continuing importance of Indo-Soviet ties inspite of uncertainties about the future of his country. Seventy percent of all our defense supplies come from the USSR. Will such levels of cooperation and supply continue? And will we continue to receive spare parts we require"?[94] There is need to develop indigenous skills to maintain and improve India's security. India may not get enough spare parts to maintain its armed forces which has got over 70 per cent of its weaponry from the Soviet Union. Even though both nations renewed the Indo-Soviet friendship treaty, from the indicators of change, it is evident that India cannot count on its Soviet military ties the way it had got accustomed to over 25 years.[95] Contrary to the apprehensions expressed in various quarters about a deep rupture in the supplies of defense equipment from the erstwhile USSR, efforts were on to reduce the present dislocation.[96] In the new situation two schools of thought have emerged one is for the wholesale switch over to the Western system, especially to the US. The second school of thought is for giving a big chance to the Indian effort. The DRDO can be geared up to meet this unprecedented challenge.[97] "Russia has offered to produce jointly with India MIG-29 aircraft and T-72 MI tanks. Joint production means sharing equally the finances, joint research, development and exports. Moscow is also willing to negotiate about the T-72 S Tanks and has offered to sell its MIG-21 production-line. But the joint production will provide a good oppor-

93. Subramaniam, R.R., "India, US and Russia in the changing world order ", *Strategic Analysis*, vol xv(12), March 1993, pp. 1239-50

94. *Indian Express* (New Delhi), 13 October 1991.

95. *National Herald* (New Delhi), 18 November 1991.

96. *Hindustan Times* (New Delhi), 28 December 1991.

97. *Ibid*

tunity for both India and Russia to achieve self-reliance. It will strengthen Indian defense-industrial base which is being under-utilized".[98]

"For decades, cooperation with India has a major factor in maintaining the geo-strategic balance in the region".[99] "The biggest advantage of the proposed Indo-Russian military cooperation offered by Moscow and largely confined to technical cooperation is that it will elevate India's status from a client state to an equal partner [Russian offer puts India on better footing]".[100] "Less than ten months after the Soviet Union's disintegration, India's domestic arms production and defense preparedness have been badly affected by a disruption in military supplies from the ex-Soviet states. The country has been forced to cut back production of some weapon systems. This crisis forced Defence Minister, Sharad Pawar to travel to Moscow".[101] "India is emerging as one of the main buyers of Russia's wide ranging defense equipments which Moscow is currently marketing as part of the major effort to obtain foreign currency. Sales by the erstwhile Soviet Union were often made at low cost to the customer or were given to the client state as part of a complete package of economic, defense assistance in return for political favours".[102] "Difficulty had arisen in implementing the commitment of the Government of Russian Federation regarding the transfer of technology of production equipment under the agreement on cryogenic stages and technology transfer signed in January 1991. The Government firmly believes in self-reliance in our launch vehicle programme and development of cryogenic technology is an essential part of it. Our space engineers have been simultaneously working to develop technologies for our own design of cryogenic engine. If the agreement cannot be implemented, we are quite confident of our space scientists and engineers who would be able to develop our own technology".[103] "The US is pressurizing us to accede to a discriminatory NPT which is no less than a direct attack on our sovereignty. The US is forcing us on a defence regime of their choice".[104] "For a conducive atmosphere, in which any meaningful

98. *Time of India* (New Delhi), 23 January 1992.

99. *Tribune* (Chandigarh), 2 February 1992.

100. *Indian Express* (New Delhi), 13 September 1992.

101. *Bankok Post* (Bangkok), 16 September 1992.

102. *Statesman* (Calcutta), 24 April 1993

103. Narasimha Rao's statement in the Rajya Sabha, *Rajya Sabha Debates*, 18 August 1993.

104. *Organiser*, 24 April 1994.

discussions are to take place, Pakistan must cease its active and sustained support to terrorism and subversion directed against India. Pakistan should eschew the path of confrontation and the adversial frames of its mind-set which is hardly conducive to peace and harmony in the region".[105] "Our defense prepardeness is now a matter of grave concern. There has been a sharp increase in military spending in the region. Pakistan continues to spend disproportionately high percentage of its GDP on defense as does China. As against this, in India there has been a total neglect of military updating. Whatever be the status of the Pakistani nuclear programme, one thing we can now be sure is that the Indian programme has been capped, as has the Agni Missile Programme... unless we update our weapons, and have a technical edge over opponents, our country will face dire consequences".[106] "Since 1989 an accelerated dissolution of the cold war situation and the disappearance of one of the power blocs has rendered the international situation considerably more complex. There was an inherent restraint and predictability in the earlier situation: this has now been replaced by uncertainties and a considerable measure of confusion. A new era of global peace has not dawned: an acute regional disparities and fierce territorial conflicts persist. The end of the cold war has not resulted either in the end of nuclear weapons nor of nuclear threats. The problem of proliferation has got aggravated. With Pakistan self-declaredly a nuclear weapon state and the turmoil and uncertainties in the CIS, India has to address itself to this question principally as one of national security concern".[107] "Pakistan is getting sophisticated arms worth more than one billion dollar from the United States as against the 368 billion dollar sanctioned following the Hank Brown Amendment. India has disagreed with the US administration that the military sales under the Hank Brown Amendment and cleared by the US Senate, would not tilt the military balance in favour of Pakistan in the subcontinent".[108] "Despite vigorous opposition from a number of senators and congressmen, the administration has been of the view that it is essential to carry on an 'ongoing dialogue' with Pakistan thus 'enhancing US influence' over Islamabad.[109] "The Clinton

105. *Foreign Affairs Record*, xxxix(2), 19 February 1993.

106. *A chargesheet against Congress Government*, released by BJP at Patna, 17 September 1994, pp. 20-21.

107. Presidentail Address by L.K Advani, *National Council Session of the BJP*, 18-20 June 1993, Bangalore, pp. 7-9.

108. *Times of India* (New Delhi), 4 December 1995.

109. *Times of India* (New Delhi), 21 March 1996.

administration intends to implement in the most responsible way the Brown Amendment. The Sino-Pakistan nuclear weapons related transaction is apparently in violation of the US anti-proliferation law, resulting in the demand in Congress for putting in abeyance the implementation of the Brown Amendment".[110]

In the second half of the eighties India received arms worth 19,300 million dollar (See Table 5). It was quite high compared to other countries. The other nations, as shown in the Table 5, also equally received arms from the developed countries. But in case of India, being a developing country, it should spend its scarce economic resources for socio-economic development of the country. It is being felt that a nation cannot be militarily strong if it has surmounted socio-economic problems. So the critics argue that development, poverty alleviation and other socio-economic tasks are equally constitute important strategy package alongwith acquisition of arms and nuclear weapons. War is no longer a viable instrument of national power, the military preparedness is treated a less significant component than the socio-economic development now-a-days. But it cannot be denied that military security constitutes a perceptible necessity for national defence. A nation cannot just ignore military preparedness in the current international scenario, specifically when frequent threats to its security is forcefully imposed as we have seen in the case of India and Pakistan. So defence preparedness should come only after a country overcomes its socio-economic problems.

In the ninties when the Super Powers realised the necessity of disarmament and demilitarisation the countries of the Indian subcontinent were looking for arms for their national security. Occasional divergencies no doubt skill-fully sorted out, but it was realised that well managed defence structure was the only adequate solution to meet the armed confrontation in the future. So the defence experts suggested that India should form a national body which would examine the situation time and again and would suggest how to handle the crises diplomatically. They did not see any impediment of receiving arms from the Super Powers but the dire necessity should be to increase indigenous defence production. Besides the defence management practices, they argue, India should go nuclear at all hazards. And if India goes for arms import then Soviet Union seems reliable partner. It seems that the economic and strategic links of India and the USSR have benefited both the countries. The USSR had political

110. *Hindustan Times* (New Delhi), 30 March 1996.

advantage of strong Indo-Soviet ties as it opened up the opportunities to get access to the Third World market. Similarly, India visualized advantages of scientific and technological transfer of knowledge and also availed latest technology from the USSR. So unless a radical change takes place that could harm both the nations of any international impulsions, the Indo-Soviet cooperation was expected to grow. The Soviet Union considered India as its most reliable partner in international affairs. Both the leaders Gorbachev and Rajiv Gandhi underlined to expand their bilateral relations not only for the benefit of the two peoples but also for the mankind as a whole. For strengthening peace and security in Asia first and then all over the world both the statesmen agreed to work on a number of issues. The Soviet Union looked enthusiastically the role of India in the entire history for preserving peace and the new Soviet leader Gorbachev had strived to take the Soviets to a state free from all types of tensions, suspicion and fear. He assured the Indians that his country would like to work actively alongwith India and would work for deepening Indo-Soviet ties. Rajiv Gandhi in that euphoric atmosphere assured the Soviet leader about India's unchanged foreign policy approach, i.e., the policy of non-alignment and assured to work for peace and disarmament. Thus the bilateral relations between India and the USSR improved and the atmosphere of cordiality and mutual understanding continued to grow further.

On the other hand, US perception of and India's anti-imperialist policies demonstrated their non-charitable relations, though both sides claimed it to be quite satisfactory. The fundamental reason is that both of them dealt Pakistan differently. India's earnest hope to dissuade Pakistan from engaging in a military competition could not bring tangible results. The Unites States had been longing for mutual reconciliation and so it urged both India and Pakistan to come to the 'negotiation table', but failed to make significant achievement. It was also realised that India's military lead over Pakistan and its desire for preponderant strength which was undoubtedly expensive and wasteful, prevented it to use the opportunities at its hand. The Stockholm example could not cast much influence on Indo-Pakistani bilateral relations. Neither of them was ready to sacrifice its requirements for military technology. A zone of peace was on the verge of transformation, transferring it into a zone of conflict. More importantly, the SAARC also could not modify itself in recognition of the realities of the situation.

TABLE-I

US FOREIGN MILITARY AID TO PAKISTAN
(in US $ Millon)

Year	TOTAL AID TO ALL COUNTRIES	AID TO PAKISTAN	% OF TOTAL AID
1981	3,244	–	–
1982	4,195	1	0.02
1983	5,599	261	4.66
1984	6486	301	4.6
1985	5801	326	5.61
1986	5839	312	5.34
1987	5102	314	6.15
1988	4831	261	5.40
1989	4828	231	4.78
1990	4893	230	4.70
1991	5894	337	5.72
1992	7198	384	5.33
1993	8146	228	2.80

Source: USAID: New Delhi, Annual, Various issues

TABLE-II

THE LEADING IMPORTERS OF MAJOR WEAPONS, 1985-89
(in US $ Million)

Importers	1985	1986	1987	1988	1989	1985-89
India	1,876	3,688	4,585	3,383	3,819	17,351
Afghanistan	82	611	687	939	2,289	4,608
Pakistan	675	616	467	467	694	2,919
Others (Third World countries)	5,753	5,026	4,601	4,012	3,893	23,267
USSR	497	473	497	483	359	2,309
Yugoslovia	103	103	234	748	450	1,638
Others (Industrial World)	2,615	1,903	2,116	2,335	2,589	11,558
Total :	11,601	12,420	13,237	12,367	14,093	63,692

Sopurce: SIPRI data base

TABLE III

SIGNIFICANT US MILITARY AID 1979-88 ($ Million)

	1979		1984		1985		1986		1987		1988	
	loan	Grant	loan	Grant	loan	Grant	loan	Grant	loan	Grant	loan	Grant
NATO	435.0	113.0	1530.0	200.6	1440.0	295.3	1266.0	281.7	625.9	402.4	649.5	275.4
S. KOREA	225.0	13.4	230.0	1.8	230.0	2.0	162.7	1.8	-	2.0	-	1.7
PAKISTAN	-	0.5	300.0	0.8	325.0	1.0	311.0	0.9	312.5	1.1	230.0	30.8
PHILIPPINES	15.6	16.1	50.0	1.5	15.0	27.2	14.3	90.6	-	152.6	-	127.6
THILAND	30.0	2.1	94.0	7.2	95.0	7.3	80.5	7.0	-	52.3	23.5	22.2
INDONESIA	32.0	2.8	45.0	2.4	32.5	1.7	19.1	1.9	-	12.1	4.0	1.8
MIDDLE EAST	4379.5	1346.7	2350.8	1449.7	188.0	2725.3	117.3	3088.5	12.0	3226.2	12.0	3210.4
AFRICA	21.2	3.0	27.4	46.5	10.0	71.2	-	62.9	3.0	28.4	-	18.1
LATIN AMERICA	27.5	3.0	66.5	294.9	25.0	243.8	7.6	226.3	-	215.1	-	142.1

Source : Military Balance, 1988-89.

TABLE-IV

TRENDS IN DEFENCE EXPENDITURE OF INDIA
(in $ billions)

Year	Defence expenditure	GDP	Defence expenditure GDP (%)	Per capital defence expenditure
1986	8.35	206.42	4.04	10.6
1987	9.30	259.11	3.59	11.6
1988	9.58	284.62	3.37	11.8
1989	8.94	279.80	3.19	10.8
1990	9.00	303.29	2.98	10.6
1991	6.53	252.55	2.68	7.61
1992	6.09	243.63	2.50P	7.10
1993	6.19	253.85 +200.00	2.44	7.21
1994	6.37	264.74	2.36	7.45
1995	6.54	271.63	2.47	7.53

Source : Asian Strategic Review, Various issues

TABLE-V

TOP TEN RECEIPIENTS OF ARMS DURING 1985-1992

Countires (Rank-wise)	**Deiveries Value in $ million)**
Saudi Arbia	52,000
Iraq	27,000
India	19,300
Afghanistan	15,100
Iran	13,500
Cuba	10,500
Vietnam	9,500
Syria	9,100
Anoola	8,500
Egypt	8,500

Source : Asian Strategic Review, 1992-93.

Table VI

Pakistan's Defence Expenditure (Rs. Million)

Year	DE	%income of DE over	GDP(fc)	DE as % of GDP	DE as % of Fed Government Expenditure
1978-79	10,302	06.48	177,844	05.79	34.50
1979-80	12,655	22.84	210,253	06.02	33.35
1980-81	15,300	20.90	247;029	06.19	33.01
1981-82	18,631	21.77	289,788	06.43	36.45
1982-83	23,224	24.65	327,909	07.08	39.31
1983-84	26,798	15.39	375,782	07.13	35.31
1984-85	31,794	18.64	435,015	07.31	35.30
1985-86	34,763	09.34	489,376	07.10	34.75
1986-87	38,619	11.09	545,888	07.61	36.94
1987-88	47,105	21.97	618,036	07.61	34.51
1988-89	51,053	8.38	596,300	08.56	32.63
1989-90	57,926	13.46	759,349	07.62	33.43
1990-91	63,598	09.79	887,807	07.16	34.63
1991-92	76,956	21.00	1024,529	07.51	38.67
1992-93	87,430	13.61	1153,517	07.58	37.20
1993-94	89,103	01.94	1308,470(E)	06.81(E)	34.54(E)

E - Estimated

Source : Strategic Analysis, November 1993

CHAPTER IV

Militarisation of Indian Ocean and Superpower's Indulgence

The Indian Ocean covers an area of nearly 30 lakh square miles, and surrounded by the continents of Asia, Africa and Australia. The ocean is circumscribed by India, Bangladesh, Burma, Pakistan to the north, Africa, Madagascar to the west, Indonesia and Australia to the east and the cold Antarctica to the south. Besides it has many islands and archipelagoes like Carayos, Rodrigues, Amsterdam islands and Chagos archipelago. The Persian Gulf and Red Sea are the gulfs of the Indian ocean.

The importance of the Indian Ocean is multidimensional, of which economic importance is vital. So, which was once considered as a neglected area, enfolded by major powers of the world acute tension cropped up gradually. It was as early as 1622 A.D. the British established its supremacy over the Persian Gulf and gradually they expanded their supremacy upto the Indian Ocean by the turn of the nineteenth century. Britain's supremacy prevailed till the end of the Second World War when her economy paralysed and her national strength protrasted. So Britain was compelled to withdraw from the Indian sub-continent. In such a situation a power vacuum was created in the Indian Ocean and the powers like China, USA, USSR and Japan rushed into the region. To India, the Indian Ocean was vital to her progress that time. Due to the untapped mineral, oil reserves and many natural resources which the Indian Ocean possessed, India showed her keen interest for her alternative sources of energy. The hinterland states like Nepal and Afghanistan had also vital economic stakes in the Indian Ocean. So they, too, could not remain impassive when the great powers started deploying arms in the Indian Ocean. Ignoring the interests of the littoral countries the United States and the Soviet Union started intensifying their arms build-up.

The US started developing her interest in the Indian Ocean following the handling of the security of Iran in 1947. The main contention of USA's policy was to contain communism in the region. Towards the close of the seventies it decided to expand the Diego Garcia base. The Carter Administration was reluctant in demilitarisation of the Indian Ocean. The Soviet Union on the other hand was quite silent till 1955. When it came closer to the littoral states and when started to moving to Ethiopia, her interest in the Indian Ocean grew. The British, French, Chinese and the Japanese interest in the Indian Ocean was not that much sensitive compared to the Super Powers. Their main underlying motivating factor was economy. Preserving national security being the important aspect of a country's foreign policy, the Government of India opposed all kinds of naval build up in the Indian Ocean by both the US and the USSR. It embarked upon massive campaign in the United Nations and other international fora. India's first step towards disarmament was to establish a Zone of Peace. The non-aligned countries continued to press their demand in non-aligned conferences. The security of the Indian Ocean was very much linked to the peace and security in the region and mainly in India. K.M.Panniker rightly pointed out, "while to other countries, the Indian Ocean was only one of the important oceanic areas, to India it was the vital sea. Her lifelines are concentrated in that area. Her future is dependent on the freedom of that vast water surface. No industrial development, no stable political structure is possible for her unless the Indian Ocean is free and her own shores fully protected."[1]

There were changes in administration in 1980 both in India and the United States. President Ronald Reagan came out victorious in the United States and Indira Gandhi's return to power raised hope expecting a change in their bilateral relations. It was believed that Indo-American relations would suffer a set back which was cordial during Carter-Desai era. Needless to say, the fear and suspicion that concerned the critics was the American hostile attitude towards India. One of the major sources of tension between India and the US was the American strategy in the Indian Ocean. The American military build up in the Indian Ocean was a potent danger for India's security and integrity. The US Government however assured not to violate the declaration of 1971 about the Indian Ocean. Ignoring its assurance the US started looking upon its naval and air bases in the Indian Ocean and even increased military build up. Her main contention was that it would

1. Panniker, K.M., *India and the Indian Ocean: An Essay on the Influence of Sea Power on Indian History* (Bombay: 1971), p.85.

preserve balance of power in the Indian Ocean area due to Soviet Union's expansion and influences. It must be remembered that whatever may be the US perception, her chief component of such a step was to take USA's position to a world's policeman. Thus ignoring India's repeated and consistent efforts to declare Indian Ocean as a permanent zone of peace, the US intensified its naval presence and improved its strategic position.

Indira Gandhi realised the gravity of the situation and growing threat to the non-aligned countries. Addressing the opening session of the Commonwealth Heads of Government at New Delhi in September 1980, she remarked, "The ocean has brought conquerors to India in the past. To day we find it churning the danger. The frantically increasing pace of militarisation in the Indian Ocean makes the 3,500 miles of our coastline more vulnerable. We must raise our voice against the last bastions of colonialism and racism."[2] But Washington had persistently opposed every peace promoting and trust generation initiative by the Soviet Union, India and others, like making Indian Ocean a zone of peace, Security plans for Europe and Asia, keeping the space free of military confrontations etc.[3] It were their vital interests which brought military powers to the forefront of policy considerations. "US vital interests in this region were; first, the preservation of western access to Persian Gulf oil resources, and second, the preservation and improvement where possible of a local geopolitical balance that minimizes of crisis to war, especially nuclear war".[4]

Since the beginning of the eighties the US had been holding regular military exercises in the Indian Ocean, particularly in the Diego Garcia which was unlawfully occupied by Britain. The US took steps to ensure that if situation compels it would deploy military force both in quantity and quality. The American move was a clear manifestation of violating UN declaration of making Indian Ocean a zone of peace. It was not only directed against the communist influence but also against the non-aligned littoral states. The chief aim of Reagan Administration was to develop the old bases as the foundation had already been established. The critics apprehended that any India strategy to diminish American movement in the Indian Ocean would

2. Bhargava, M.L., *Indian Ocean Strategy through the ages* (New Delhi: Reliance,1990), p.273.

3. Kaul, B.N., *India and Superpowers* (New Delhi: Pulse Publishers, 1989), p.108.

4. Kakkar, A.N.,(ed.), *Indian Ocean (Proceedings of an International Seminar)* (Allahabad: New Book House, 1987), p.57.

be met with stiff opposition from the US quarters. It would be resulted in the form of economic and military embargo which India could not afford. Indian advocacy of handing over Diego Garcia to Mauritius was supported by the littoral countries but it was thought that such a step of India would give further setback to the bilateral relations between the US and India. So India was not in a position to exert positive influence on USA to refrain her from its Indian Ocean policy. However, both India and the US had a bigger scope for drawing closer to each other. It was largely dependent on Indo-Soviet relations on the one hand and US-Soviet relations on the other. The US and the USSR being ideologically dissimilar, cordial bilateral relationship between them was an impossible task. Secondly, the US did not look the Indo-Soviet growing relationship with favour. On the other hand the US was taking steps to prevent India coming closer to the Soviet Union. From Indian point of view, the Indian government also did not want to put aside all their differences and to develop cordiality with the US at the cost of the USSR. So the mutual distrust and skepticism between India and the US continued as before. The Indo-Soviet relations on the other hand found no barrier to expand. Both the countries came closer to each other and shared experiences on major international issues. "Prime Minister Indira Gandhi and Alexei Kosygin expressed confidence that cooperation between the two countries would continue to develop further. Indian Prime Minister Indira Gandhi highly appreciated Soviet Union's important contribution to India's efforts to create a developed infrastructure".[5]

An essential prerequisite for peace in our region was the implementation of the 1971 UN declaration aiming at establishing a zone of peace in the Indian Ocean. The Indian government had actively participated in the meetings of the littoral and hinterland countries concerning the militarisation of the Indian Ocean. It was a matter of regret that despite the efforts of the concerned nations the great powers went on increasing military exercises in the region. "The AICC(I) urged the government to continue its struggle and to extend full support to the proposal for implementing 1971 UN declaration".[6] Indira Gandhi, the Congress Party President, was also equally worried about the developments in the Indian Ocean. She remarked that "the big powers were setting up new bases as a result of which new

5. *Times of India* (New Delhi), February 3,1980.

6. Zaidi, A.M.(ed.), *The Annual Register of Indian Political Parties, 1980,* op. cit., p.121.

problems were cropping up for India as well as for other developing countries".[7] So the existing efforts should be redoubled to ensure that the UN conference on the Indian Ocean is convened.[8]

The interests of different countries in the world are interdependent and they can progress mainly on the basis of mutual cooperation. In order to save the region from increasing superpower rivalry, their attempts to upgrade Diego Garcia base and efforts to establish new ones, it was necessary to promote the spirit of mutual cooperation and trust among the littoral states. No doubt, it was India's duty to set an example of good neighbourliness with the adjoining smaller countries. It was also desirable that our neighbours should increasingly realise that the lasting friendship could be achieved only on the basis of mutuality and reciprocity. The Bharatiya Janata Party reiterated "to strive for independence of peoples, the inviolability of sovereignty and territory of nations, dismantling of all foreign bases. In its view, only by sincerely adhering to the principle of genuine non-alignment, India would be able to contribute its mite towards freedom, peace and progress in the world".[9] "So the growing tension in the region could be solved if all the naval powers involved in the region and the states bordering the Indian Ocean chalk out a programme to terminate all bases, military installations and weapons of mass destruction. As the international laws seemed inadequate to meet the genuine aspiration of the littoral states, they must wake up to the threat of neo-colonialism endangering the life of the people off the shores of the Indian Ocean."[10]

The Indian Ocean was becoming an increasingly dangerous seat of international tension. The non-aligned countries were trying to raise world public opinion in favour of a Zone of Peace. "The Soviet Union was a firm believer of the idea of turning the Indian Ocean into a zone of peace. The Soviet government was even ready to work actively in that direction together with other states concerned."[11] In a seminar of Indian Ocean, External Affairs Minister P.V. Narasimha Rao stated, "if the Indian Ocean is made a zone of peace, it would contribute

7. Zaidi, A.M., *The Story of Congress Pilgrimage(1970-85), Report of the General Secretaries,* Session no. 76- 77,p.284.

8. *Selected speeches and writings of Indira Gandhi,* Vol.V, op. cit., p.391

9. *National Executive Meeting of the BJP,*New Delhi, September 5,1980. see *Miscellaneous Party Resolutions* of the BJP,Delhi, pp.3-4.

10. *Foreign Affairs Record,* vol. XXVI(12), December 1980. p.295.

11. *Ibid.,* p.273.

significantly to reduce international tension and in eliminating the problems that had arisen among the littoral countries."[12]

The international scene was not so grim before as it was in Reagan-Gandhi era. The United States now decided to increase its hold in Asia, particularly in the Indian subcontinent. As Iran was out of US influence, America turned her attention to Pakistan. The economic aid and military assistance to Pakistan brought fresh tension between India and Pakistan and indirectly it affected, Indo-American relations. No doubt, Pakistan was in need of massive aid for her economic advancement and it readily accepted US offer. It gave fresh fillip to Indo-Pakistani relations but at the same time created new problems for India. India tried her best to desist US from inviting another Indo-Pakistan war. It resisted the efforts of Pakistan disturbing peaceful and congenial climate of the subcontinent. It was quite natural for USA for seeking bases for its navy and air force in Pakistan. But some of the Western powers joined in the US efforts of rearmament of Pakistan which was believed as a step to aggravate tension. The United States was setting up electronic surveillance stations in Karachi and Peshwar to keep control over the Indian Ocean. The supply of British frigates, Sea Wolf Missiles and Plassey Radar homing and reconnaissance systems by the United King dom and French Mirage-5 fighters to Pakistan was criticised. The US action was condemned in the United Nations. But Reagan Administration staked its claim on the ground that it wanted to bring parity between India and Pakistan to avoid any sort of entanglement. "In fulfillment of Reagan's strategic consensus the US administration had made inputs in the region which had heightened the tensions. The modernisation and nuclearisation of the Diego Garcia, the intensification of the US military presence in the Indian Ocean led to the corresponding intensification of the Russians and other presences and the overt and covert backing to the selected South Asian countries aggravated the tension in the region. The scenario that had developed induced fear in India that it was sought to be encircled on all sides,"[13] It was also noted that in the Indian Ocean, Soviet Union had superiority in submarines over the US, every American ship in the Indian Ocean was shadowed by a Russian ship or sub-marine."[14] "Diego Garcia was a pre-eminent link in the chain of American bases girdling the earth round the equator. To India, as

12. *Organiser*, vol. XXXII(32), December 28,1980, p.9.

13. *India and the International Scene*, AICC Publication, Op. Cit., p.4.

14. *Organiser* February 22,1981, p.15.

the principal Indian Ocean country, the American move came as a direct nationalist challenge."[15] The Indian Ocean was no longer an ocean of lesser importance, but it had became an area of direct confrontation between the Super Powers. In this situation, Indira Gandhi addressing at the non-aligned foreign ministers' conference "called the big powers to de-escalate belligerent rhetoric, to reduce presences in the Indian Ocean and to resume the earnest search for understanding and peace".[16] "Looking at the pandemonity of the Indian Ocean, the Bharatiya Janata Party urged the government to take steps to prevent further deterioration of the situation and to find out options so that preservation of peace in the area is not threatened".[17] The Indian Ocean was in turmoil after it acquired central strategic significance to the Super Powers. According to the BJP "the protection of our EEZ and our islands outpasts, protection of the situation arisen from Super Powers rivalry acquired new relevance".[18] "The probability of sparks off superpowers conflict emitting from the Indian Ocean grew into a conflagration that endangered the physical existence of many littoral states of the Indian Ocean. So, a collective and organised efforts of the littoral states was urgently required to foil the expansionist designs of the superpowers in the Indian Ocean".[19] "The Indian attention was focussed in the main on five aspects of the Indian Ocean developments. One, the high profile US naval presence built rapidly in the Indian Ocean waters and specially Diego Garcia and to a considerable lesser extent, the Soviet naval presence; Second, the near-indefinite postponement mainly as a result of US opposition, of the conference convened by the United Nations to declare the Indian Ocean as a zone of peace; Third, the US search for and acquisition of base facilities in several countries on the Indian Ocean littoral; Fourth, the transfer of a substantial quantity of US arms including F-16 aircraft to Pakistan and reported Pakistan willingness to give the US base facilities in certain contingencies; and Fifth, threats posed by these developments to India's security, its sovereignty over its territorial water and the economic zone".[20]

15. *Organiser,* 1 March 1981, p.7.
16. *Selected speeches and writings of Indira Gandhi,* vol.V, op.cit., p.505.
17. *Rajya Sabha Debates,* Vol.C XVII, No.18, 11 March 1981, cols.303-04.
18. *Resolution Passed by the BJP in the National Council Session,* Cochin, 25th to 27th April 1981, p.23.
19. *Organiser,* 2 August 1981, p.14.
20. Gupta, B.S., "Indian Perceptions of Great Power Presence in Indian Ocean", in A.N. Kakkar (ed.), *op.cit.,* p.98.

Increasing numbers of American fleet alarmed the coastal states of the Indian Ocean. The non-aligned countries took up the issue in their meetings. It was believed that the US was virtually transforming the Indian Ocean into an American Ocean. They, therefore, urged the United States to refrain from its activities of controlling the straits linking it with the other oceans. The imperial ambition of the US was to use the natural resources the Ocean possessed. Thus the non-aligned countries wholeheartedly supported the efforts of the coastal states to keep US action at bay lest their security would be jeopardised. The Soviet Union strongly supported India's interest of declaring the region as a Zone of Peace. The US policy in the Indian Ocean was to weaken "the unity among the developing and non-aligned nations of the region by souring the wind of militarism where the basic precept was that lending oneself to big powers gambits by affording facilities on their territory was anathema".[21] The creation of sub-regional groupings under the guise of mutual arrangements exclusive of the big powers was intended to help it reap the whirlwind by way of intensified conflicts within the non-aligned group over within the non-aligned group over dilution of its precepts.[22] The Prime Minister Indira Gandhi expressed serious concern over the unfortunate developments in India's neighbourhood which otherwise threatened in bringing cold war to South Asia. Supply of sophisticated arms, nuclear weapons and aircraft to Pakistan created consternation among the adjoining nations of the Indian Ocean. Indira Gandhi argued that "India was earnestly trying to prevent the cold war in the Indian Sub-continent".[23] She remarked, "The Indian Ocean had ceased to be an area of friendship. The unanimous voice of the littoral states went unheard and unheeded. The increase in the naval presence of outside powers in the Indian Ocean dramatically increased in the wake of developments in Iran and Afghanistan. This escalated tensions in our area, did pose a potential threat to the stability of all the littoral states... The focus of the cold war had shifted from Europe to the Indian Ocean littoral."[24]

The AICC expressed apprehension on the militarisation of the Indian Ocean by the Super Powers who overlooked the interests of the littoral states and the resolution of the United Nations. The United

21. *Patriot* (New Delhi), 4 May 1981.
22. *Ibid.*
23. *Hindustan Time* (New Delhi), 29 September 1981.
24. *Selected speeches and writings of Indira Gandhi, Vol.IV* (New Delhi: Publication Division, Ministry of Information and Broadcasting, Government of India,1985), pp.198-203.

States was proceeding in militarising Diego Garcia and even persevering the threat of using the Rapid Deployment Force in the Indian Ocean. "The AICC called upon the superpowers to vacate their military presence from the Indian Ocean".[25] In this crucial juncture, "India needed a comprehensive Oceanic strategy, not to challenge the superpowers but to secure the minimum naval capability for self-defence in the era of armed peace".[26] Mr. Yuli M. Vorontsov, the Russian ambassador expressed the Soviet Union's desire to withdraw its naval forces from the Indian Ocean provided the US also agreed to remove its strike forces from the region".[27] He assured that the "Soviet naval detachment in the Indian Ocean was not aimed at any shore but was a preventive measure against possible US attack. Soviet Vice-President Imashev Sattar took the opportunity to mention that the friendship between the two nations was a force which stood in opposition to the aggressive forces of imperialism and restrained their actions diverted against peace and the freedom and independence of the people".[28] The USSR was eager to resume bilateral talks with the US on the limitation and reduction of military activities in the Indian Ocean". "It stood for the relaxation of tension, for removing the threat of war, for broadening peaceful cooperation throughout the world".[29]

The growth of Soviet maritime power after attaining parity in the nuclear weapons with the United States brought her close to the Indian Ocean problem. The Soviet Union also thought of deploying her merchant fleet, as it had its strategic interests in the Indian Ocean. However, the USSR did not pose any threat either to US or to the littoral states. Thus, the American perception about the Soviet navy's role was wrong. Though the Soviets had an eye on the Indian Ocean and the Soviet navy paid a number of visits to the countries adjacent to Indian Ocean. It was nothing but a gesture of good will visit. The Soviet Union had no bases like the United States nor it was supplying military arms and equipments to any country to further her aims like the US-Pakistan ties. To the contrary it had a Treaty of Friendship and Cooperation with India. On that ground the USSR had every right to

25. Zaidi,A.M., *Annual Register of Indian Political Parties, 1981*, op. cit.,p.607.

26. Misra, B.R., "US Strategy in the Indian Ocean: India's Perception and response", *Asia Pacific Community*, Vol.18, Fall 1982, pp.77-78.

27. *Organiser*, 29 August 1982, p.1.

28. *Ibid.*, p.13.

29. Brezhnev's speech at Kremlin in the dinner in honour of Indira Gandhi, *Foreign Affairs Record*, Vol. XXVIII, No.9, September 1982, pp. 227-229.

extend military aid to India due to security threat to India on account of US-Pakistan movements. Off and on Soviet naval ships had passed through the Indian Ocean escorting cargo ships or for exploring oceanographic experiments. So the Soviet Union won the confidence of India and other peace-loving and anti-imperialist nations. In a complete contrast to the US policy, the Soviet Union had always extended her support to Indian proposal in converting Indian Ocean into a zone of peace and dismantling of foreign bases in the Ocean's perimeter. It also opposed to American attempt to develop Diego Garcia into a full-fledged military base. These steps of the Russian government were highly eulogised in the non-aligned circle. As early as 1964 the USSR had supported the Afro-Asian countries of establishing a denuclearised zone in the Indian Ocean region.

The joint Indo-Soviet communique in 1980 showed enthusiasm for setting up a peace zone in the Indian Ocean. In subsequent years, the two sides called on an early implementation of UN declaration on the Indian Ocean and appealed to all powers, who were deploying their weapons, to refrain form aggravating the situation in that region. They also demanded dismantling of all foreign naval bases in the area and supported the proposal concerning the restoration of sovereignty of Diego Garcia and Chagos archipelago to Mauritius. The Soviet side demanded earliest convening of international conference in establishing a peace zone in the Indian Ocean. The Soviet Union showed enthusiasm to hold talks with the United States regarding the Indian Ocean. Also it appealed to all the maritime users of the Indian Ocean to abstain from establishing new bases and to come forward to hold negotiations so that the interests of all could be served. It offered proposals, to those who had permanent naval bases in the Indian Ocean, for international negotiations in reducing military exercises, combating terrorism on the seas and in the air. The non-littoral states who were not involved in the issue were also urged to participate to formulate a policy to avoid complex situation of the Indian Ocean. This is clear that the Soviet initiatives were upto satisfaction of the littoral states who were against increased up naval and military presence in the Indian Ocean.

On January 1, 1983 the United States set up a new regional command called CENTCOM comprising of states of South-West Asia and North East Africa. The task of CENTCOM was to act in coherence and to maintain communication among the pro-Western nations of the region so that the American participation in the Indian Ocean problems would be facilitated. The Rapid Deployment Force (RDF) was the central element of the CENTCOM. With the deployment of RDF the United States was on the verge of building a strong base for storing arms and equipments in case of any conflict related to the Indian Ocean. It provided considerable impetus to the imperialists in their air and naval transport facilities. The goal of the RDF was primarily aimed to check Soviet intrusion into the Ocean. However it also intended to prevent any kind of instability that might bring danger to us interests in the Indian Ocean. India's policy was to see that the Indian Ocean littoral states are protected from influences of the Super Powers. "It is only in such an atmosphere of non-interference they could play their right ful role in discouraging superpower rivalries in the Indian Ocean region".[30] "As the principal country in on its shores India had vital stakes in keeping the Indian Ocean an area of peace —from military bases, nuclear weapons and big powers rivalry. With India's security environment expected to become increasingly vulnerable to manoeuvrability by the big powers to seeking to extend their influence, it was planned to set up a National Council on security which would impart added emphasis to the defence factor in foreign policy."[31] "The assertion that the US had a right to interfere in the Asian countries because of its strategic interests, the way it was acquiring military bases in Asia and Africa, stationing of a permanent RDF for the purpose of intervention, building up of the Diego Garcia base with nuclear installations and other such developments made it clear in no uncertain terms that the US did not mind turning Asia into a major theatre of war. On the other hand, Soviet Union always supported for a peace zone in the Indian Ocean. So the Soviet-Indian relations reached a high degree of stability. In this sense, it would not be incorrect to describe Indira Gandhi as the noble architect of Indo-Soviet friendship in the post-Nehru period. The fact is that the maturing of Soviet-Indian relations had been a continuous process because the ties had their roots in socio-economic realities."[32]

The cold war between the Super Powers created unfavourable developments in our region, the deterioration of the situation over the question of Indian Ocean being one of them. To protect the interest of the littoral states and to keep the Ocean free form the US battle ground, "the NAM has to play a major role, the non-aligned nations

30. *Hindu* (Madras), 9 February 1982.
31. *National Herald*(New Delhi), 30 May 1982.
32. Chopra, V.D. *India and the socialist world* (New Delhi:Allied, 1983),pp.101-08.

should show exemplary solidarity in realising the goal".[33] It is noteworthy to state that the nuclearisation of the Indian Ocean and Super Powers' rivalry in this ocean was a matter of deep concern to the BJP. "The BJP expected that the Colombo conference would be able to make progress towards a resolution on the problem".[34]

India was the largest country in the Indian Ocean region with a long coastline of 5000 kilometers "whose western flank on the Arabian Sea is an integral part of the defence environment of the South, South West and West Asia covering the Gulf and the East African belt and whose eastern flank has the proximity to the chain of states in South and South-East Asia. India's own security and stability, as well as its essential trade and commerce is dependent on maritime traffic. In this perspective the escalation of arms race with the formation of RDF and expansion of Diego Garcia was regarded as a serious threat to India's national plans, its dreams of a better future and longing for a good-neighbourly relations."[35] So the basic conflicts in American and Indian objectives remained. After a change in American administration the divergences between them settled to some extent but not disappeared. India could not able to restrain US military posture beside offering peaceful proposals. India also could not show her potential in international forums. Over this tumult state of affairs the AICC(I) "expressed its concern over the delay in convening the conferences for declaring the Indian Ocean a zone of peace, in pursuance of the UN resolution adopted in 1971. This delay caused great disquiet in the littoral countries of the Indian Ocean."[36] The then Prime Minister Indira Gandhi was also equally critical of the prevailing situastion. She was concerned about the proceeds of the Super Powers into the region. In her address at the Commonwealth Heads of Government meeting, she stated that "the region bristled with the fleets, bases and new command structures of outside powers. Nuclear arms inducted in the name of security of others endangered the countries of the region. Many of the littoral and hinterland states were sucked into these power games."[37]

33. Damodaran, A.K.,"Non-alignment and India's Foreign Policy", *Indian and Foreign Review,* Vol. 20, No. 15, 15 May 1983, pp 7-9.

34. *Resolutions of the BJP, Fourth National Council Session,* New Delhi, April 15-17, 1983, p.4.

35. Khan, R.,"Fallout on India: US-Pakistan-China Axis", *World Focus,* Vol.4, August 1983, pp.34-35.

36. *Resolution passed in the AICC meeting* held on 20th and 21st October, 1983, Bombay, p.21.

37. *Selected speeches and writings of Indira Gandhi,* vol.V op.cit.,p. 439.

The non-aligned countries were very hopeful on their efforts and expected that they could change the minds of Super Powers. "In the wake of the UN report some military disengagements took place which were encouraging. The US evacuated Asmara and Bahrin and Russia quitted Berbera. This relinquishment of controls by the big powers was, however, not the result of international pressure in the UN but was the result of their own compulsions and interests. But the debate on the Indian Ocean as a zone of peace was leisurely and repetitive. The matter had never been considered particularly urgent. It seemed that the peace zone idea was caught up in the contest between the developed and the developing countries, between the North and the South, that is, the same sort of division that split the world in almost every major sphere of activity."[38] "Particularly, the peace zone concept had two dimensions; one, that of the regional states whose immediate concern was security and economic survival. Their vision of world peace did not transcend the regional barriers because they were not developed enough to have a global view of the problem. While the other dimension was that the regional peace was a step towards the global peace. In that case, the peace zone concept became subservient to the latter. Therefore, the concept of peace zone in the Indian Ocean was believed to be the inseparable from the global peace and unrealizable till the global peace is established."[39] On the other hand the motive of transforming the Indian Ocean into a zone of tension originated in two basic issues. "First, the geo-strategic importance and geo-political imperatives of the region; and second, the superpower rivalry or competition in the region influenced the geo-strategic factors in favour of their individual interests. The direct struggle and competition between the superpowers related to political, economic and military activities in the race for the right to impose one's will on the other."[40]

The Carter Administration had directed its military strategy towards North-East Asia. For sometimes the Reagan Administration continued to look towards North-East Asian countries. But in the first half of the eighties Japan's military preparedness put the South-East Asian countries under constant danger. The US administration now felt

38. Chopra,M.K., *India and the Indian Ocean: New Horizons* (New Delhi: Sterling, 1982), pp.148-49.

39. Majeed, Akhtar(ed.), *Indian Ocean: Conflict and Regional* Cooperation (New Delhi: ABC Publishing House, 1986), p.143.

40. Singh, Jasjit, "Indian Ocean: Geopolitics and Super power rivalry-I", *Mainstream,* vol.XXIII, No.9, 27 October 1984, pp.8-9.

that it became necessary to shift attention towards Indonesia, Malaysia and other South-East Asian countries to hold control over the Indian Ocean. The SEATO group was critical about Russian and Japanese interests in the Indian Ocean which coincided with the U.S. interests. So the Reagan Administration shifted its military strategy to South-East Asia. The US also showed its willingness to sell fighters and missiles to the SEATO group. Thailand and Singapore were keen to possess F-5E fighters and air-to-air and surface-to-air missiles. It was reported that USA was ready to extend military credit sales to Thailand and invited Bangkok for joint air and naval exercises with the US seventh fleet. The US capital became active in Indonesia and Malaysia leading to large investments in mining, suger, rubber etc.. It was observed that once the US dollar was penetrating into South-East Asia at a faster rate than any region. Thus the new policy of the US in the Indian Ocean was clearly visible. The USA saught to control all spheres those were vital to US interests.

Australia occupied a an important place in American strategy in the Indian Ocean. The islands like cacos and others which were of immense value for US naval and air exercises, were under Australian jurisdiction. So US thought of an integral chain between Australia, New Zealand and USA and thus tried to strengthen ANZUS. In this complex situation the non-aligned states clearly saw the danger that would come by the ANZUS. They had one option before them, i.e. , to persuade Australia to desist from helping the US in discharging naval and air exercises. So they appealed to both Australia and New Zealand to extend their help in making the Indian Ocean a Zone of Peace. They observed that the real aim of US policy was to dominate the region: Politically and militarily, so that it could use it to its advantage. So the militarisation of Indian Ocean was solely due to US actions and movements in the area. However, the ruling elites of USA assured that both the US and the USSR had equal responsibility in the process of militarisation of Indian Ocean. Of course, it cannot be denied that escalation of arms and nuclear race in the Indian Ocean was due to the movements of both US and USSR. But to treat the Soviet Union at par with the US would be a mistake. Off and on, the Soviet Union took steps in the effort of making the Indian Ocean a zone of peace. The USSR had never taken part in the militarisation process like the US. The Soviet Union had not increased her naval presence in the Indian Ocean when the US presence was at alarming rate. So the growing US involvement was not at all related to the USSR'S action. It had no relevance with the Soviet's intervention. It can be stated that it was a plea for the imperialists to make access to the Ocean and to dominate the strategically and economically important area.

The mounting Super Powers' rivalry in the Indian Ocean was taken seriously by the opposition political parties. "The BJP criticised the Indira Gandhi government for its failure in obtaining universal endorsement for the proposal of holding an international conference of declaring Indian Ocean a zone of peace".[41] Satish Aggarwal, the BJP M.P., wanted to know what steps government had taken to meet the situation. Replying to his question, A.A.Rahim said that "government had continued to take necessary steps required to safeguard the country's security interests. The government has also continuing its efforts in cooperation with other non-aligned states, for the full implementation of the 1971 UN resolution on the Indian Ocean as a zone of peace."[42] "By conviction, by historical and political necessity India had always believed in peaceful co-existence. There was equal respect, equal opportunity for all powers, big or small, to exploit the gifts of the Indian Ocean".[43] Kalyan Roy, the BJP MP, participating in a debate on Indian Ocean viewed that the naval forces of big powers posed threat in real sense. In his view, as far as Indian Ocean's impact on the national security was concerned "every global and regional imbalance and conflict should have nexus with our national concerns and our security considerations. What we need is conceptual clarity, efficiency and finesse in the practice of diplomacy because security and diplomacy are like Siamese twins. Indian Ocean was not important to us merely because Diego Garcia was there or the Soviet Union had linkages with Syria or North Yemen, but this was reducing our national interest to an absurd debate, like a debate about and between superpowers. At the same time we must also recognise the importance of the Seven Degree channel, we must recognise that we had an existing dispute with Bangladesh on New Moore Island. We have 319 islands in the Andaman and Nicobaar group and we have 18 islands in the Lakshadweep and Minicoy group. So protection of our territory is the Indian Navy's first task. Our trade in the region is quite high but the government failed to safeguard India's trade interests."[44]

41. *Presidential Address by A.B. Vajpayee*, Fifth National Council Session, 1984, op. cit., p.9.

42. *Lok Sabha Debates*, vol.XLIV(6), 7th series, Fourteenth Session, 1 March 1984, Cols.236-37.

43. *Hindu* (Madras), 29 May 1984.

44. *Rajya Sabha Debates*, vol.CXXXI, No.16, 13 August 1984, Cols. 295-301.

The US administration was not concerned to the Indian appeal and went on stockpiling arms at an increasing rate. The US involvement in the Indian Ocean had many reasons behind it. However other interests were less important than "containment of Soviet Union and earlier of China and over the past decade protection of the vital lanes of the Indian Ocean. In pursuit of these interests, the US established an erratic strategic tie with Pakistan that from its inception affected the nature and course of Indo-US relations, with the larger strategic environment of the Indian Ocean, the United States and India shared the ultimate goal of ensuring open sea lanes and access to gulf oil, the independence of the littoral states and their freedom from external interference and the avoidance of the great power confrontation."[45]

The security environment of India in 1985 was complex and tense. There were multiple threats to us. China's modernistion programmes, acquisition of sophisticated weaponry by Pakistan and Soviet occupation of Afghanistan were few among them. Pakistan's navy was also looking for procuring sophisticated hardware. Above all, the military exercises in the Indian Ocean caused anxiety to the Indian government. The quest for security was utmost importance to Government of India and so it insisted on the obedience to the declaration of the Indian Ocean as a zone of peace. It appealed to the neighbouring and other littoral countries of the Indian Ocean to pursue independent course of action instead of following imperialists' manoeuvres. The path to save the region from destabilisation and terrorism caused by the imperialists intrusion was the need of the hair and SAARC was mooted.

What disturbed the Indian political scene was Washington's plan to build launching site for medium and intercontinental missiles. With this, US intervention in the Indian Ocean greatly increased. Apart from Diego Garcia, the US Government was interested to link Philippines into it strategic drive in the region. Even the US went on destabilising Philippine's Marcos Government as the island was of utmost importance to protude military power into the Indian Ocean. The American ruling circle put every effort to keep their striking power in the oceanic area. The Indian government squarely condemned the US action and appealed other states of the region to use their power to turn the Ocean into a Zone of Peace. Addressing a joint session of the two houses of the Congress Rajiv Gandhi expressed India's apprehensions about the establishment of military bases in different parts of the world. He said

45. Hardgrave, R.L., "Why India Matters: The Challenge to American Policy in South Asia," *Asian Affairs*, vol.II, No.1,Spring 1984, pp.45-49.

that "the people were directly affected by the militarisation of the Indian Ocean and the inflow of increasing sophisticated arms into our vicinity".[46] The US concentrations in the Indian Ocean increased in the mid of the eighties. The US-Pakistan understandings were ideal strategy for the American government under which Pakistan agreed to US desire in naval activities a port services along Pakistan's coast. The Makran coast provided certain key facilities to US navy. A road network from Karachi to Makran coast provided supply lines to US deployment force. This constituted a further US intrusion into the Indian Ocean. It gave the US opportunity to get accurate information regarding Russian's or other power's deployment of warships by applying techniques of monitoring and reconnaissance through its satellites orbiting around the Indian Ocean. The American government justified her secret understanding with Pakistan on the ground that due to Soviet presence in Afghanistan it was enviable to keep the balance of power and so US cannot accept the concept of peace zone. However, Australia and Japan took American action not conducive for preserving congeniality in the Indian Ocean. Australia had deep interest in Cocos and Christmas islands and the Australian government condemned US concentration of arms in this region. Japan also realised that unless the Super Powers are out of Indian Ocean it would not help the littoral states in preserving peace and security. Indian government appreciated the Japanese attitude of supporting the peace zone concept. Infact, increasing militarisation of the Indian Ocean was not safe for the security of adjoining nations of the Indian Ocean. The critics argued that as the US administration was not ready to hold any talk regarding the Indian Ocean it was desirable for India to mobilise for world public opinion to check US actions. Side by side the Indian naval strength must be strengthened and upgraded to meet any threat from the Anglo-American bloc. It was realised that submarine launching and self-reliance in defence production alone could save India from the US-Pakistan alliance. Apart from this, "by broadening the institutional framework of cooperation, scope of cooperation among themselves can be ensured. The SAARC framework was a good beginning in this direction. A council for Indian Ocean Regional Cooperation may be set up in pursuance of the objective of widening the scope of cooperation. A working group may also be set up to examine seriously the causes of destabilisation and frequent regime changes in the Indian Ocean region and to suggest remedies for this

46. *The Times of India* (New Delhi), 14 January 1985.

potential problem which had been the most potent divisive factor and a bane of the Indian Ocean region."[47] As far as Soviet Union was concerned, it had always advocated peace and security in Asia and also supported Peace Zone Concept. The Soviet Union had repeatedly showed its readiness to resume talks with the US in this regard and also showed her desire for an international conference on this issue. "The USSR proposed that all states whose ships were using the waters of the Indian ocean should retrain from any action which aggravates the situation in this region, specifically the states in question should not send large naval formations and should not hold military exercises".[48] To the contrary, US had not shown her interest either to support USSR or to India. "So to persuade the US to check it from further militarisation of the Indian Ocean, India would need to remove suspicions about the nature of its military relations with the Soviet Union".[49]

Looking at the grave situation the Prime Minister Rajiv Gandhi remarked, "Fifteen years ago, the United Nations declared the Indian Ocean a zone of peace. Fifteen years later the Ocean had been transformed into a theatre of heightened tension and potential conflict. It is outside powers who were polluting the waters of the Indian Ocean with warships and nuclear submarines, erecting new command structures and establishing naval bases. It was essential to save Indian Ocean from the depredations of those whose military presence detracted from our security."[50] He added, "the confrontation between the two superpowers should not migrate to third world countries. The superpowers confrontation should be confined to their limited theatres and not appeared to the regions such as Indian Ocean which has traditionally been a peaceful non-confrontational area".[51] Thus it had been observed that militarisation of Indian Ocean was the only product of Super Powers rivalry. The critics say that the regional divergencies are also responsible for aggravating the worsened situation. They allege that though the big powers involvement was mainly motivated by global concerns, the regional confrontation mainly induced them to march ahead with sophisticated weapons. Whatever may be the causes of the Super Powers involvement in the Indian Ocean, it definitely created a different atmosphere in the sub-continent. If we cannot lay the sole responsibility on USA, yet it must be admitted that " the real aim of

47. Poulose, " India and the Indian Ocean:Changing Strategic Perspectives," *Asia Pacific Community*, vol. 29, summer 1985, pp.136-39.

48. *Pravda* (Moscow), May 20, 1985.

49. Mukherjee, D., ''Indian Ocean: Key Aspects", ***Mainstream***, vol. XXIII, No.43, 22 June 1985, p.9.

the US policy in the region was to establish military and political domination of this strategically important area rich in manpower and natural resources and to use it against the socialist world and the upcoming forces of national liberation".[52] The Indian Ocean which was regarded as a peaceful ocean once upon a time "was the most troubled spot of the world. As estimated by Ruth Iegar Sivard, of the 14 identified battlefields of 1989, 7 were Indian Ocean states. So the detente was yet to be translated into reality in the context of Indian Ocean states".[53]

Now the attention of economic exploitation being concentrated in the Indian subcontinent and in the Indian Ocean, military presence of Super Powers was not surprising. But it was real that any collusion between the two Super Powers to dominate the Indian Ocean region would bring all hazards to third world countries. It would destroy their economic and political unity just for supporting one of the contestants. It was therefore urged that the countries of the region should not divert their attention to the aggressive designs of the Super Powers. India rightly expressed her concernn over the growing militarisation of the Indian Ocean in the United Nations and in various international conferences. The proxy war between the two Super Powers was going to disturb stability and peace in the region and would bring catastrophe of a nuclear war. The American military build up in the region hardly justified Russian intervention in Afghanistan or its presence in the Indian Ocean. The aim of the US Government was not to interfere with the trade routes of India but it directly affected India's economic interests as it checked India's shipping and exploitation of natural resources from the sea bed. Thus Diego Garcia proved to be a guarantee to protect US interests—both political and economic. It is well known that fishing provides a major source of foreign exchange earnings. Mainly the eastern coast provides more than two-third of fishing benefits. So any foreign fishing trawlers in that area constitutes

50. *Statement on Foreign Policy of India, Prime Minister Rajiv Gandhi*, (New Delhi: Publication Division, Ministry of External Affairs, Government of India, 1987), pp.11-12.

51. Rajiv Gandhi's address at National Defence College, on October 8, 1985, see *Statements of Foreign Policy, Prime Minister Rajiv Gandhi* (New Delhi: Publication Division, Ministry of External Affairs, Government of India, 1986), p.13.

52. Bhatia, Vinod (ed.), *op. cit.*, p. 78.

53. Singh, Jasjit (ed.), *Indo -US Relations in a changing* world (New Delhi: Lancer International, 1992), p. 145.

a grave threat to our national security. Poaching in the EEZ by foreign trawlers is a national concern to India. India's more than eighty percent trade depends on maritime routes. Being surrounded by waters, oceanic wealth and its exploitation had much bearing on India's economic development. The Indian government had also entered into joint shipping ventures with the neighbouring countries to strengthen its trade facilities. Throughout the eighties, therefore, the Government of India was pre-occupied with the problems of navigation, territorial jurisdiction and exploitation of resources. So the government restricted the entry of foreign ships in its 12 nautical miles territorial waters. The main thrust of India's ocean policy remained full utilisation of living and non-living resources of the Indian Ocean. It was also believed that after achieving deep sea capability India would save her import bill which would reduce her dependence on foreign countries.

Throughout the eighties, therefore, the undersea exploitation of natural resources was an important question. The growing militarisation and the entry of warships in the Indian Ocean reduced the chances of optimal utilisation of sea resources. The critics argued that the Government of India should be careful of the entry of foreign powers and their deployment of any kind of armaments. The weapons, nuclear or conventional, on the ocean floor should be objected tooth and nail. The available resources in the ocean would substitute exhausted natural resources of the world. So any kind of mass destruction weapon would destroy the purpose of peaceful exploration of Sea resources for the economic benefit.

The foreign policy of India was attacked by the critics on many grounds. It was believed that Rajiv Gandhi failed to develop good relations with either of the SuperPowers. Therefore, the problem of Indian Ocean could not be solved immediately. "Rajiv had failed to build more stable and mature relations with the Soviet Union in a bid to mollify USA. Though the relationship between India and the USA was better than it was during Mrs. Gandhi's era".[54] The Soviet Union had one of the largest fleet in the Indian Ocean. With its bases in Ethiopia, South Yemen and Vietnam, the Soviet Union showed promptness in increasing her naval strength in the Indian Ocean. The Soviet naval exercise coupled with USA created fear and suspicion among the Indians. It was urged that the "Government of India should take the matter into consideration and to raise world public opinion against such military build up".[55] "Historically, the external powers who

54. *Organiser,* vol. 37, No. 28, 24 November 1985, p.4.

55. *Ibid.,* vol. 37, No.29, 1 December 1985, pp.13-14..

deployed navies in the India Ocean came to acquire political and economic control over most of the littoral countries. It was because the economic, technology and military capabilities of the most of the littoral were such that they were susceptible to pressures from powerful external powers. If India seemed to react rather strongly to the United States than to the Soviet Union, was caused by the unduly strident tone of the US statements".[56]

Therefore, it was urged that the Government of India should enter into agreement with the neighbouring countries not to provide any facility to the superpowers for military purposes. The United Nations was believed to be a deterrence to persuade the Super Powers in this regard. Moreover, it was the effective foreign policy and diplomacy which could restrain Super Powers military installations. Since India's neighbours were under the influence of Super Powers, a careful handling of the situation was only way out. By wakening world public opinion against Super Powers activities the Indian Ocean can be turned into a zone of peace. On this account, India should not discriminate between the US and the USSR. No doubt, much success could not achieve but the Government of India should continue its efforts for establishing a security zone around India.

The Soviet leader Mikhail Gorbachev during his visit in November 1986 showed Soviet Union's desire to consolidate military and political stability in the Indian Ocean. He showed USSR's willingness to hold multilateral talks with all countries connected to the Indian Ocean to guarantee the security of shipping lanes. He said that "the USSR was prepared to enter into negotiations with the US and other non-coastal countries having their warships in the Indian Ocean on a permanent basis in order to substantially reduce the strength and activity of the naval forces there; to hold negotiations with the United States and the Asian countries to develop confidence-building measures specially for Asia and the adjacent areas of the Indian Ocean".[57] "The growing role of Soviet-Indian cooperation in the whole system of international relations was determined by the consistently peaceful nature of the foreign policies of the world's first socialist state and of the largest non-aligned country, and by their positive approach to the pressing problems of our time. The goal of comprehensively strengthening the cooperation was particularly urgent because of the tension

56. *Holiday* (Dacca), 13 December 1985.

57. Vladimirov, Leonid P., *The Soviet-Indian Phenomenon* (New Delhi: Allied, 1989), p.71.

caused by the aggressive course of US imperialist forces. It was noted that the Soviet-Indian friendship was developing and strengthening dynamically and it was an important factor of peace and stability".[58] The Soviet Union highly valued India's efforts to restore peace and security in the Indian sub-continent.

The US bases in the Indian Ocean were strengthened further not only to check the Russian influence but they provided US to use sea lanes for maritime trade and also USA got the advantage of demonstrating its maritime power. "These bases permitted extensive use of air power to stall a ground war, it permitted the American forces to be near the desired area of influence and put an amphibious force ashore, if required. Importantly, these bases permitted ship repair, refueling and rest areas for vast nuclear propelled, nuclear deterrence submarine force, deployed by the US in the Indian Ocean. All the bases came in very handy to the US led MNF. It enabled the deployment of over 600,000 troops, huge naval fleet, amphibious forces and very large air force of MNF. Thus Diego Garcia and all other US bases remained active till the end of the eighties and posed security threats to India".[59] On the other hand "the presence of the Soviets in the Indian Ocean had been prepared by a long-standing policy of obtaining maritime bases. They enjoyed extensive facilities in certain parts of Iraq and Yemen. They also had anchorage facilities in Red sea, Hodeida and Singapore. But unlike the western powers, the Soviets had no extra-territorial enclave which they could develop as a naval base and strategic position".[60]

The US base at Trincomalee created genuine concern for India. The Indian government accounted the Sri Lankan government for allowing USA to enter into Sri Lankan territory when the demilitarisation process of the Indian Ocean was in progress. The Sri Lankan government officially denounced the charge but the Indian government raised the problem in various international fora. The Pakistani government was persuaded likewise not to come under the influence of the US. It was argued that sufficient good will and cooperation among the South Asian countries would prevent them from being economically exploited. This would also help them to use their energies and resources for their own national development and national security.

58. Mikhin, V., Indo-Soviet-Treaty: Fifteen years (New Delhi: Sterling, 1986), pp. 50-51.

59. Nanda, *R., National Security;: Perspective, Policy and Planning* (New Delhi: Lancer Books, 1991), pp.178-79.

60. Vas, E.A., *The Search for Security: Controlling Conflict and Terrorism* (Dehradun: Natraj Publishers, 1989), pp.214-15.

The technical and scientific progress of the region could improve their economic backwardness instead of playing as satellites to the big powers, diagonally opposite to each other.

The cardinal principle of India's Ocean Policy was based on peaceful approach which opposed military installations of big powers in the Indian Ocean. In the United Nations, in the non-aligned conferences and particularly in the Foreign Minister conferences, the Government of India raised her voice against the militarisation of the Indian Ocean. However, nothing worthwhile came out due to the indifference of the US. The big powers armada in the Indian Ocean and their search for new bases continued as before. So the long cherished peace zone concept had become almost obsolete. The reason was improper handling of the issue by the littoral states and their mutual antagonism and rivalry confined their efforts to regional conferences only. A few of them were playing a double standard suited to their domestic needs and interests. Thus they were divided into two ideological camps. Some of them had aggravated the situation. Even those who were regarded as pro-American allowed their port facilities to the US Government by which the later went on stockpiling arms and ammunitions in the Indian Ocean. In totality of situation, India's Ocean Policy was under a sever test. Lack of unity, social and cultural diversity and mutual suspicion led to the intervention of big powers. At that time India had to look to the Soviet Union for her security. But neither India allowed Russian bases in her maritime waters nor the USSR compelled India to do so. Rather the Soviet Union urged the littoral countries to act together and appealed not to allow their bases to be used by big powers for security reasons. At the political level the uphill task was to forge unity among the Indian Ocean littoral countries. As for example, India's soft corner towards Soviet Union created problem to develop cordial relations with Pakistan. Thus it was essential for both India and Pakistan to rise above mutual antagonism and to try for uplifting the standard of living of the people in the sub-continent. The regional cooperation was considered a substitute for preventing Super Powers entry into the region. The major stumbling bloc before the countries of South Asia was their economic backwardness. So for economic upliftment they had to seek aid from the developed countries. The formation of economic community in the Indian sub-continent could solve the problem and by initiating technical and scientific co-operation, closer identity among themselves could be achieved. The notion that they could not survive without foreign aid had negative impact with it. The big powers this way making their intrusion to the Indian Ocean.

Much was dependent on the attitude of the US and its role towards Pakistan. No doubt no nation can neglect her national interest. Though arming of Pakistan or militarization of the Indian Ocean coincided American national interests, it is beyond doubt that peace and security were of same importance to the littoral states. So any negotiation which fulfils the interests of both sides should be implemented under the UN supervision. It would be effective if regional economic power like Japan and China support the littoral countries. The Soviet government was also persuaded to withdraw its military exercises from the Indian Ocean coastal states. It was believed that in the absence of Soviet support the Indian goal of establishing peace zone could not be achieved. It is noteworthy to say that considering Indian anxiety over the Indian Ocean, the then Soviet President Gorbachev showed his willingness to support the Indian move. In his address at the joint session of the Parliament, he said that the Soviet Union was prepared: "at any time to begin with the United States and other non-littoral states which had naval vessels on a permanent basis in the Indian Ocean, negotiations on substantially reducing the size and activities of naval forces there, to hold negotiations with the United States and the Asian countries concerned on confidence-building measures in the military field related to Asia and the adjacent waters of the Indian and Pacific Oceans—:- "to take part in multilateral negotiations involving all states which were maritime users of the Indian Ocean—:- "to take part in working out a long overdue multilateral agreement on the safety of air traffic over the Indian Ocean."[61] Moreover, "the Soviet Union considered that the entire world community and the United Nations Organisation should be a regulator of joint efforts to the benefit of peace. The collective common sense of the world community would make it possible to defuse the tension in the Indian Ocean, to embark on the path of an interested and truly democratic dialogue on concerted measures to turn the Indian Ocean into a zone of peace."[62]

President Rene of Seychelles and Indian President Zail Singh in their joint address pleaded for early concerning of the international conference on the Indian Ocean. "They regretted that due to the strident posture of some great powers early convening of the conference was delayed. The US government was not interested in the Zone

61. Singh, Darshan (ed.), *Soviet Foreign Policy Documents, 1986* (New Delhi: Sterling, 1988), pp. 483.

62. *Pravda* (Moscow), 10 October 1987.

of Peace idea inspite of strenuous efforts by the non-aligned countries. The visit of US seventh fleet in March 1986 headed by USS Enterprise to Karachi created suspicion among the littoral countries".[63] Not only Seychelles but also other littoral had equal responsibility in that effort. "The non aligned movement had also great accountability in striving to enlarge the area of peace by staying out of military alliances. In this effort, it must be noted that the states belonging to military alliances also supported for disarmament effort".[64] "The foreign naval presence in the Indian Ocean and passage of nuclear weapons had come more from the allies of the United States. Inspite of political pressure to undermine US perceptions of the regional schemes of things, India had not endorsed the US presence or its self-appointed role as protector of maritime shipping in the Gulf".[65] And to get rid of imperialist pressures conferences and declarations were not sufficient. Because they are going for economic assistance, the imperialists have an upper hand. So it seems that the countries of the Indian Ocean requires radical transformation of their economic structure. "Logically, development should be of a non-capitalist type. It may lead to mobilisation of men power and natural resources. At the same time structural transformation was needed for high rate of growth and political viability. With a structural transformation in the Socio-economic set-up, a radical change in the path of development might result in a peaceful order."[66] "The better option for India was to strive to dispel mutual distrust and suspicions, forge closer ties and promote good neighbourly relations with countries on its ocean flanks, keeping in view the strategic calculations of outside powers and the emerging threat perceptions. India's approach to different neighbours should be such that peace and security in the region is established and intrusion of extra-regional forces is avoided. The country's foreign policy should be more pragmatic and flexible and initiative should be taken to promote cordial relations."[67]

With the demise of the Soviet Union and end of Super Power rivalry, a new geo-strategic environment has come into being. Thus,

63. *Deccan Herald* (Bangalore), 24 April 1986.
64. *Times of India* (New Delhi), 30 January 1987.
65. *Patriot* (New Delhi), 1 June 1988.
66. Bandopadhyay, J., " Problems and prospects of Peace and Development in the Indian Ocean Area," *Asian Studies*, vol.6(1), January-March 1988, pp.3-5.
67. Anand, J.P., "India's Indian Ocean Neighbours", *Strategic Anaylsis*, vol.12, No.2, May 1989, pp. 147-64.

the necessity to deploy naval forces and Sea-Launched Ballistic Missiles [SLBM] in the Indian Ocean has become unnecessary. Secondly, the absence of super power rivalry will reduce the possibility of direct intervention by a direct power in land conflicts in the region. Thirdly, there will continue to be major disputes that may result in unilateral interventions by regional powers. These need to be challenged through established processes of the UN or through regional organizations. The nuclearization of the region is now a reality. Prevention of nuclear proliferation, therefore, no longer applies and cannot be implemented. So the question now is of managing the present state of nuclear weapon capability, and simultaneously along the path of total nuclear weapons elimination. The recent events highlighted the importance of the UN as a peace keeping authority.[68] The International Institute for Strategic Studies, London, has reported that Russia is considerably cutting down its expenses on the construction of warships and submarines. In due course, the US may curtail the activities of its naval fleet in the Indian ocean, partly due to less urgent strategic requirements and partly due to domestic economic compulsions. China is expanding its armed forces, particularly its navy and is trying to acquire new bases in the Indian ocean. China is also trying to purchase modern submarines and warships from Russia in order to update its fleet. The only balancer against a mighty expanding China in the Indian Ocean can be the US. India should, therefore, welcome the preserve of the US Naval fleet in the Indian ocean and Indo-US naval cooperation should become a normal feature in Indo-US relations. It also should be in the over-all interest of the US not to allow China to expand its influence in the Indian ocean beyond a certain level.[69] "While considering the threats to India's security the possible interests of China and the great powers are an important determinant. The US global strategic interests make it imperative for it to maintain a visible presence here. The Indian Ocean and its literal region provides the US intervention capability in the region apart from securing the area for its strategic minerals...." ....In this environment that nations have to coexist in peace and harmony. Given the circumstances of the present difficulties that India finds itself besieged with, it is all the more necessary for her to ensure good neighbourly relations

68. *Times of India,* November 12, 1992, says Maj. General D. Benerjee.

69. *Tribune* (Chandigarh), 28 December 1992, Says Maj-General Rajender Nath (Retd).

so that it is able to optimize its meager resources".[70] "A cooperative Indo-US naval relationship can ensure peace and security in the Indian Ocean; such a development also could restrain Chinese access to this very oceans".[71] "Perestroika brought a substantial change in the Soviet Policies towards Indian Ocean and the Third World. With Perestroika in full swing, Moscow was totally occupied in setting its house in order, and reformulating its domestic as well as foreign policies. The only alternative to this desperate situation will probably be that the Indian Ocean states settle the existing differences among themselves and increase cooperation in as many issue-areas as possible. Perhaps, the creation of new regional organizations like the Organization of Petroleum Exporting Countries [OPEC] to function as castles of "raw material exporting countries" would, on the one hand, strengthen the position of Indian ocean status vis-a-vis the North and, on the other, would help them manage and allocate their resources more fruitfully. Moreover, increased cooperation in the fields of trade and technology among the Indian Ocean states would, [i] reduce their dependence on the North, [ii] enhance their bargaining power vis-a-vis the North; [iii] prevent the outflow of financial resources; [iv] reduce the burden of their indebtedness; [v] increase their political maneuverability and self-confidence, thus, paving the way for emerging as a well-knit monolith in the emerging world order".[72] "India is a peninsular country controlling the Indian ocean region. So America wants a friendly India for smooth traffic in sea-routes. Also it is the only sea-faring nation which can keep an eye on the expanding Chinese Submarine Force there with Indian navy".[73]

"India must base its external relations on strict reciprocity. India wants good relations with every country of the world. India would like to develop cooperative relations with all the countries of the world. India does not want to interfere in the internal affairs of any country and it expects other countries to accord the same treatment to India. The Narasimha Rao Government has not been successful in safeguarding in India's vital interests in the international arena. The impression

70. Sood, S.D., "South Asia : Security Perspective", *Strategic Analysis*, XV(12), March 1993, pp. 1225-38.

71. Subramaniam, R.R., "India, the US and Russia in a changing world order", *Ibid.*, pp. 1239-50.

72. Moosri, S.S., "Indian Ocean in the Emerging world order : The super power factr", *Strategic Analysis*, Vol. 16(10), January 1994, pp. 1323-46.

73. *Organiser*, 19 January 1992.

is that the Rao Government is dithering and drifting internationally as it is domestically. Whatever the situation may be, the striking point is the contrasting attitude of the two countries; the USA and Russia".[74] "The Indian Ocean is progressively becoming attractive for not only Western fleets to maintain permanent presence, but also for China which has started acquiring permanent bases. Our navy, hence, needs the size as well as the reach not only to protect the immediate borders, but to keep the sea lanes open".[75]

The American strategy in the Indian Ocean was altogether different from that of the USSR. The US had always sought to dominate the region and to keep the countries of the Indian Ocean region economically and militarily dependent. This was perhaps the major benefit it had achieved in its South Asian Policy. On the other hand the Soviet Union, even if in parity with the US in terms of military and economic, viewed the US strategy detrimental to the independence of countries of the region and so it tried to help them what ever way it could. Thus the rivalry between the Super Powers in case of the Indian Ocean as in elsewhere was not due to their economic and military power, but because they were two different systems, two different path in the ideological perspective. So it would be a wrong approach if both the Super Powers ambition and strategies are equated. If the Soviet Union now or then marched with her warships into the Indian Ocean, importantly it strived for the creation of peace zone in the Indian Ocean. The USSR's movement was nothing but to counter the imperialist forces, the outside intervention in the Indian Ocean. And the US, to the contrary, had always tried to prevent a peace zone coming into existence. Thus the difference of Super Powers on the Indian Ocean problem was nothing but the antagonism between the forces of socialism and the forces of imperialism-capitalism. This in turn caused problem to the Indian Ocean region. Both the Super Powers tried to prove that they were right in their actions.

India could not depend either on the US or the USSR. In case it depends on the USSR it would be disastrous as the Russian government would not come with immediate cessation of hostility because it would have international repercussions upto the magnitude of Third World War. Nor India could depend on China. The growing Chinese

74. *National Executive Meeting of the BJP*, Bhubaneswar, 7 November 1992, pp. 11-13.

75. *Presidential Address* by L.K. Advani, Planary Session of the BJP, 10-12 November 1995, Bombay, p.12.

nuclear capability was itself a matter of concern. Besides China had one G-class submarine with missile launching tubes and it has ability to introduce much superior in naval or military capability to counter the US threat. Thus it was such a time which increased big powers domination over the region for their politico-economic benefits. So India for her own security and stability opposed all kinds of foreign powers' presence. It demanded complete withdrawal of all foreign bases and strived for establishing a Zone of Peace. In this effort she was well supported by the littoral states. It is surprising enough why the militarisation continued even after the UN declaration supporting India's stand of a Zone of Peace? It can be stated that it was nothing but the lack of willing cooperation of a number of states adjacent to the Indian Ocean. The growing intra-regional rivalries and lack of enthusiasm prompted foreign powers to intrude into the Ocean and the Zone of Peace has been turned to a 'Zone of Conflict'.

CHAPTER V

India's Economic Diplomacy

The international system emerged in post Second World War is identified by division of the world into three camps, with different ideologies and political and economic programmes. The Western bloc who believed in private enterprises and followed capitalist path of development came to be known as the 'First World'. Secondly, the Soviet Union and other East Europe countries guided by communist ideology and believed in socialist path of development denominated as the 'Second World'. Thirdly, the developing countries who did not believe in both policies and pursued a different path designated as the 'Third World'. Economic under development was the dominant feature of Third World countries. On the other hand, the first and second world countries had a very high per capita income and were economically much developed. While the developed countries kept on strengthening their economy, the economic condition of the developing countries worsened further. Therefore, on many occasions the underdeveloped countries were urged to take up the principle of free trade and free capital movements.

The developed countries of the West were looking for markets in Third World countries. Due to their acute balance of payment situation the Third World provided a golden opportunity and they started offering concessional aid to many underdeveloped states. As a result, many of them came under the influence of capitalist or Socialist countries. Some of them also realised that instead of aligning themselves to either Super Powers, it would serve their purpose if they could choose a different path. The policy of non-alignment, therefore, came to be an ideal approach for them. The argument behind opting for such a policy was that they could get economic aid without being acting as proxy to the donor states. India is forerunner of the policy of non-alignment and many Afro-Asian countries started choosing it later. The irony of the fact that inspite of their independent course of action the Third World countries remained poor and underdeveloped. The slow growth of industries, the mortality rate and malnutrition continued to strike the poor Afro-Asian nations. The policies framed in the light of the situation could not meet their demands. The critics say that it is because of their failure in maximising financial and social returns they could not able to develop their economy.

The Indian model of economy did not give considerable impetus to the technological development, balance of payment situation, income distribution and employment opportunities. Dissatisfaction with the result of development efforts the Indian government faced vehement criticism. It was believed that the poor growth of GNP, slow growth of industries and many other factors put Indian economy in problem. The major question that implicated was the poor social, political and economic development. Though it was believed that the colonial history of India put herself in dwindling economy, it must be remembered that many colonial countries have surpassed India who once upon a time were at the same level of economic development,e.g., Singapore and South Korea. Even the GNP of Pakistan is higher than India. With so much potential and vast reserves of natural resources India is still regarded as an underdeveloped state.

The major question before the Government of India was how to develop economic condition of India. So the Indian government was looking forward a rapid industrial development. It was believed that with substantial technological, engineering and management base, India could progress rapidly. It was realised that without overall development, without the development of both public and private sectors, the infrastructure development could not be attained. Though, the importance of public sector did not subsidise much, the growth of private sectors had begun in the industrialisation process. Alongwith the industrial development, agricultural development was equally important to get maximum return and to realise it India had to go for eeconomic aid from the developed countries. India was the sixth largest borrower in the world in 1980. India's debt service ratio was at 25 percent, nearly as much as Philippines. The Soviet Union had taken a very special role for economic development of India. "The real economic security of India was growing because cooperation with the Soviet Union strengthened its position in the face of economic aggression on the part of the imperial west".[1]

The principal aim of import policy is import substitution which has been sought to be achieved through rules and regulations set by

1. Banerjee, B.N., *op. cit.*, pp.33-55.

the government time to time. A country generally encourages export rather than uncontrolled import. The developing countries usually prefer strict import control to avoid foreign exchange difficulty. Inspite of that they are suffering from the foreign exchange difficulty. It is not unwise to borrow money to keep the pace of development process for a developing country. But it is suggested that export income of the country should be promoted so that the interest on foreign exchange is not beyond control. Excess import must be regulated and resources inside the country should be utilised to produce goods to meet the requirements of people and the products should be sold abroad to earn foreign exchange. If this is done then the debts incurred through import can be checked and the standard of living can also be raised. The Indian government is certainly not against export promotion principles. "So the thrust of India's foreign economic policy over the years had been to limit the imports to meet priority needs, at the same time to step up the level of development imports beyond the level of export income, to borrow money to cover the import deficit, and thus to enhance the economy's capacity to meet rising domestic requirements and at the same time to augment export income to service foreign loans and increase the nation's purchasing powers".[2]

In the early eighties the Indo-American trade relations had received a set-back. Over the question of countervailing duties on certain US imports of Indian goods both India and the US differed. The United states stood to raise the countervailing duties from 2.5 percent to 20 percent which India opposed. "The overall duty clearly became prohibitly high and effectively ruled out Indian exports to the U.S. market and importantly the total benefit likely to flow to the United states in terms of employment and income in the affected industries was considered to be afflicted".[3] Moreover, with the announcement of the US special trade representative Governor Reuben Askew, "the US would not recognise the applicability of the multilateral trade negotiation agreement to India, the Indo-American trade relations suffered a setback".[4] Also, India's economy had been deteriorated due to the inability and inefficiency of the Indian government. Thus, the BJP argued that "to maintain the health of the economy, to the problems

2. Adiseshiah, M.S., *India's International Economic Relations :The Present and the Perspective* (New Delhi: Lancer Publishers, 1990), pp.12-14.

3. *The Economic Times* (New Delhi), 6 August 1980.

4. *The Indian Express* (New Delhi), 27 August 1980.

of growth, inflation, unemployment and balance of payments immediate attention was not paid by the government. There was no sign to improving industrial production. The government also failed in maintaining adequate supplies of power and materials. The National Executive of the BJP took the opportunity to warn the nation of the grim situation on the economic front which was in its view a direct result of mismanagement and incompetence of the congress government".[5] Moreover, the Government of India had secured a large amount of credits from different sources which amounted to $1600 million in six months. "The BJP saw no reason to go for more and more loans but to refuse it even if offered. In its opinion, the world financial institutions had a vested interest in offering us credits and influencing our policies".[6] "The declared purpose of aid is generally not in keeping with the real needs of the aid-receiving countries, rather it promotes state controlled economies and grandoise projects and leads to a perverted structure of elite-oriented system of production leaving the majorities of the people altogether out of considerations. The most serious effect of the aid is that the whole economy becomes captive to foreign capital and technology so that it has to depend on more and more imports of foreign capital goods at ever higher costs."[7] The Bharatiya Janata Party believed that we must adapt Western technology to match our own requirements and this way we can move towards an industrialisation process. "The party was committed itself to achieving economic goals enunciated in the Directive Principles of the Constitution. A system based on decentralised economy, integral humanism and Gandhian Socialism could ensure the basic requirements of bread, freedom and equality."[8] The BJP stressed that "a good economy always results in good foreign exchange reserves. During the Janata years, the reserves went up by Rs. 2350 crores and in 1980 the reserves stood at Rs. 5200 crores but it continued to come down as much as Rs. 600 crores per year. So the nation's wealth was being squandered."[9] Importantly, there was negative trade balance with USA which stood at–580.7 million US dollar (see Table 9).

5. Economic Resolution adopted by the National Executive of the BJP, see A.M. Zaidi(ed.), *Annual Register of Indian Political Parties*, 1980 (New Delhi : S.Chand & Co.,1981), pp.633-35.

6. *Organiser*, 6th July 1980, p.3.

7. *Ibid.*, 27th July 1980, p.7.

8. *National Executive Meeting of the BJP* at Hyderabad on October 26, 1980, See A.M.Zaidi,n.5, pp.659-60.

9. See Text of *Presidential Address by A.B.Vajpayee*, 28th-30th December 1980, op. cit., p.26.

With the increasing demand of Less Developing Countries (LDCs) for a New International Economic Order and at the instance of the United Nations an independent commission was set up under the chairmanship of Willy Brandt. The Brandt commission recommended in favour of Third World countries. In accordance with the Brandt commission report an international summit was organised at Cancun, Mexico. The developing nations demanded that the world financial institutions should operate under the guidance of the UN and also there should be massive transfer of resources. But the United states did not support it. So differences cropped up. The Western industrialised countries contended that the UN should not be given ultimate power of controlling world financial institutions. In this stage, the developing countries could not achieve their target as the financial institutions were being operated by financial aid of capitalist countries. In subsequent years the economic situation of the developing countries deteriorated further. So, India strived for a new economic system and strongly supported for a NIEO and a total reformation of international financial and monetary system. But for her technological and industrial development India was in need of massive economic aid and also transfer of scientific know-how. So the Indian policy makers felt that unless there is a change in the decision-making process in the international fora the demand of the LDCs could not be accomplished. India had played significant role in this regard. In the non-aligned summits Indian delegates consistently raised the question of the North-South economic cooperation. India has also emphasised the need of greater economic cooperation among the developing countries. Self-reliance was given top priority to meet the economic threats of the West. Development in agriculture and proper utilisation of vast natural resources would be an effective step to bargain with the developed countries. So India pleaded for collective effort among the South Asian countries to explore the facilities they had. As Mrs. Gandhi observed, "through political freedom the Government of India hoped to achieve economic advance. The economic dimension of the policy of non-alignment was not less important than political. Looking at the worsening economic situation, Mrs.Gandhi strongly urged for global negotiation for a NIEO. At the same time she highlighted importance of South-South cooperation and collective self-reliance to reduce the vulnerability to the actions of developed countries."[10] "The

10. Inaugural speech of Mrs. Gandhi at the Non-Aligned conference of the Foreign Ministers in New Delhi on 9th February 1981. See *Selected Speeches and Writings of Indira Gandhi, vol.V, op. cit.*, pp. 505-06.

inequalities and disequilibriums in the economic and social structures of the world, the glaring imbalances between demographic pressures and access to material and technological resources were the matter of concern. The Indian Prime Minister appealed that global well-being would be illusory unless the aspirations of developing countries were reflected in the management of the international economy and in the decisions of international negotiations."[11] The AICC (I) was of the firm opinion that India should recapture its old capacity for peace initiatives as during the decades of Jawaharlal Nehru regime and for promoting the cause of a just economic order free from exploitation of one nation over another.[12]

There was positive aspects of Indo-American relations in 1981. There was also steady improvement in their bilateral economic cooperation. High-technology transfer continued despite earlier misgivings. Indian policy makers were also keen to substantiate economic cooperation with the United states. At the same time Indo-Soviet economic relations improved. The flourishing relations between India and the USSR indicated the continuing relevance of Indo-Soviet friendship. Several reasons were responsible for the growing relations between India and Russia. Indian market was a source of benefit to Soviet economy. On the other hand, India received Soviet sophisticated manufactured products at cheap rates. So trade continued to be expanded. The visits of Soviet Parliamentarians, military leaders on different occasions testified the importance of India to the Soviet Union. During Mrs. Gandhi's reign India was the largest recipient of Soviet aid among the South Asian countries. This economic aid also reduced India's dependence on the Western countries. Importantly, there was also no guarantee of dependability on the US due to its changing policy towards India. On the other hand, the Soviet aid provided powerful impetus to the development and modernisation of Bokaro and Bhilai steel plant. The quality of the products also improved a lot. In addition to it the technical assistance provided the development of mining and coal industries in India. These plants were of great economic importance to India. In the field of ferrous and non-ferrous metallurgy India made phenomenal progress as a result of

11. Indira Gandhi's Keynote address at the commemorative meeting to mark the twentieth anniversary of the first summit conference of non-aligned countries in New Delhi on 11 February 1981, *Ibid.*, p.509.

12. *Resolutions passed by the AICC(I)* in New Delhi on 27-28 February 1981, see A.M.Zaidi, *Annual Register of Indian Political Parties*, 1981, *op. cit.*, p.620.

massive Soviet assistance. The Bharat Aluminium Company, BALCO, also established with the Soviet assistance. The growing demand of aluminium this way fulfilled to some extent. It is important to note that the Soviet aid helped in developing the production of nickel based industries. So the Soviet aid carried out an important role in making India self-sufficient in industrial out-put. India being rich in natural resources Indian Scientist were not able to extract it. In this connection also the Soviet scientific and technical assistance rendered valuable aide in exploiting rich reserves.

Power development attained much importance to Indian agriculture and industry. It was felt that only the significant progress in power engineering could fulfil Indian demand on power. The Indo-Soviet joint efforts in building up India's power generation capability increased the amplitude of their faith and cooperation. In this field, no doubt India was dependent on the Western help, but Soviet-Indian cooperation helped India in setting up thermal and hydro-power stations. The Neyvelli power generation center, Bhakra hydro power station, Hirakud in Orissa and Korba in M.P. are outstanding instances of Indo-Soviet cooperation. Due to Indo-Soviet joint efforts India could able to achieve self-reliance in electric power engineering. It is also important to note that after establishing numerous hydro and thermal power stations, the Soviet Union also extended her invaluable aid to upgrade and to produce qualitative products out of the established plants. Thus the elaborate cooperation programmes in the vital sectors of power, mining, metallurgy and many others were marked as the furthering of the Indo-Soviet friendship. India's policy of accelerating the process of development and attaining self-sufficiency was clearly due to the Soviet aid and the Indo-Soviet friendship firmly consolidated the durable friendship they had established in 1971. So their bilateral relations were maintained by mutuality of interests without contradicting their individual policy formulation in international field.

International relations are influenced by the domestic policies of nations. Likewise the bilateral relations between two countries are affected by their national interests. If there is convergence of their national interests their relations may be sold smooth and if there is clash then their relations are not good. "This depends on number of factors — geographical and geo-political situations: Social, economic and political strength of the countries and their perception of world

policy of self-reliance mitigated against the economic systems of the U.S. and other industrialised capitalist countries."[13] "The India's spokesmen highlighted the widening gap with the U.S. and urged a more favourable treatment to our exports. With unemployment running high in the United States, there was resistance to providing easier access to Indian goods. Efforts to step up export were often frustrated through the impositions of quantitative and qualitative restrictions."[14] On the other hand the USSR wanted to strengthen the economy of India for benefit of peace and stability in the world. It was pointed out by the observers that "the volume of loan extended by the USSR to India was as modest as compared to the large assistance of the western aid. The Soviet loan as well as Soviet assistance were directed to the most needy sectors of the Indian economy. At the time of energy crisis the Soviet assistance was directed towards the development of power industry."[15] On the other hand, once economic link is established with the West, it invited multinational corporations to Indian market. While the government was taking up economic liberalisation, it certainly aimed at improvement of economic standard of the country. But penetration of multinationals hampered economic growth. "The MNCs hampered the growth of independent economics and postponed much needed social change. They were primarily economic entities, but their influence often extended in numerous ways into the political areas affecting the political processes. So it was a challenge to the sovereignty of the host government through the MNCs. Because of abundant supply of cheap labour, the MNCs also exploited labour and thereby enhanced their profits".[16] "According to the Reserve Bank of India, India's foreign trade during 1980-81 showed a deficit of Rs.5,813 crores which was larger by Rs.3,364 crores then the level of Rs.2,449 crores recorded during 1979-80. The deficit of foreign trade widened substantially particularly in respect of the trade with the ESCAP, the ECM and North America. The value of imports had gone up very high. As against an increase of 13.1% in 1978-79, it increased by 32.4% and 39% in 1979-80 and 1980-81 respectively. The petroleum products cost in 1979-80 was Rs. 3267.08 crores which went up by Rs.5,586.87

13. "Indo-US Relations: What Reagan should not Do", *Link*, vol.23, no.23, 18 January 1981, p.9.

14. "Economic cooperation with the United States", *Southern Economist*, vol. 20, No.5, 1 July 1981, p.4.

15. Korneev, Victor L., "Indo-Soviet Relations: Expanding Economic Ties", *Commerce*, vol.143, No.3665, 12 September 1981, p.462.

16. *Organiser*, 21 June 1981, pp.8-9.

or 44.9% increase from the previous year. On the other hand the non-petroleum products which was 63.8% of total imports fell down to 58.6% in the first six months of 1981. India's exports in 1981-82 were placed at Rs. 7,781 crores showing an increase of Rs. 1,070 crores or 15.9 percent increase over 1980-81. India's overall exports in first nine months of 1981 amounted to Rs.5,317.04 crores reflecting an increase of about 15.2 per cent over Rs.4,613.47 crores in the corresponding period of 1980. Imports, on the other hand, was about Rs.9,426.15 crores during April-December 1981 showed an increase of 11.9 per cent over the figure of Rs.8,420.23 crores in the same period of 1980. The deficit for foreign trade for April-December 1981 was Rs. 4,109.11 crores as compared to the provisional deficit figure of Rs.3.806.76 crores in 1980."[17] An overall estimate showed that the balance of payments situations of India in 1981 was under trial. May be there several reasons for deteriorated BOP situation, but massive import put India under the blackmail of industrialised countries. The oil imports further worsened the economic situation of the country. To meet the challenge India sought financial aid from external institutional finances, like the IMF.

Increase in oil prices pushed up India's oil bill in 1980 and 1981. For that reason Government of India entered into an agreement with the IMF whereby an amount of SDR $ 5 billion was made available. With this the Government of India surrendered economic sovereignty to the IMF. As the 'Organiser' a weekly journal in its editorial under captioned 'Selling India', noted that "given our vast material, human and moral resources there was no reason why India went for borrowing from IMF. If there was any problem, the solution was by better management and not more and more unmanageable debts which would worsen the economic situation further".[18] In such a totality of seeking huge loan from the IMF, India had deviated from its declared policy of self-reliance. External borrowing of India had already reached the figure of Rs. 16,000 crores and any further borrowing from the IMF or world Bank would deteriorate conomic scenario further. So the BJP opposed the IMF loan and disapproved the acceptance of IMF loan having strings which was detrimental to national interest. In its view "it reflected the inability of the ruler to manage the national economy and not the necessity of the nation. The party was not opposed to foreign credits on concessional terms but such conditions would not

17. Sharma, S.R., *Indian Foreign Policy : Annual Survey*, 1981 (New Delhi: Sterling, 1985), pp.197-201.

18. *Organiser*, 1 November 1981.

be at the alter of nation's basic policies and the policy of economic self-reliance. The party believed that the solution to our economic problems did not lie in financial credit from abroad but in giving boost to domestic production, exports and internal mobilisation of resources and their efficient use through campaign of developmental credits and incentives and if policies are so modified that the workers could release their creative energies than it would push the wheel of economic development".[19]

In the financial year of 1981-82 The Government of India had got permission to borrow as much as Rs.1100 crores from world financial institutions. "Many companies had been forced to turn to the parallel economy to get capital at 24 per cent or more. Industry — both public and private — was hard hit. They had no money to pay for their essential requirements. The Bharatiya Janata Party viewed the situation not conducive to India's economic situation. The party alleged the government of surrendering to foreign economic imperialism, tilted its foreign policy towards one superpower and its economic policy towards another. The IMF loan is a foreign usury that would dampen India's economic capability".[20] It would be apt to understand that there was nothing harmful in the IMF borrowing as Indira Gandhi told in Rajya Sabha on the IMF loan controversy. She said that "the government aimed at self-reliance. It was also committed to build up indigenous capacity in production and progress towards self-reliance. As India needed to increase export to check the external borrowing, similarly IMF loan was an inescapable necessity to achieve more rapid growth in industry and investment. In any case she assured in the Upper House of India that even if India accepted assistance from the IMF, it would not hamper India's declared national policy and there was going to be no reversal of India's policy of using the loan to develop country's indigenous capacity and self-reliance".[21] There was hue and cry that the IMF loan would harness our economic objectives and was not a solution to India's economic problems. But "it was presumed that the loan would help India in strengthening the supply management moderated to demand pattern as well. The IMF loan could become a stand- by and India's capability to withstand any translational pressures would remain intact. Further, the government

19. *Resolution passed by National executive of the BJP, New Delhi,* December 4-6, 1981, pp.3-7.

20. *National Executive Meeting of the BJP at Bhubaneswar* on February 12 to 14, 1982, pp.24-27.

21. *Selected speeches and writings of Indira Gandhi,* vol.V, op. cit., p.279.

would put the loan into highly productive purposes under secret monitoring. This would also arrest the balance of payments malasie."[22] "The total foreign aid authorised till the end of February 1982 was Rs. 28653.78 crores of which the IDA shared Rs.7775.70 crores or 27.14 per cent share in total aid. Though over years, the Indian economy had become progressively self-reliant, foreign aid had an important role at the margin. It contained to provide to meet import needs of the economy."[23] In this connection the Soviet economic aid was quite impressive which continued to grow at a rapid rate without much crises and recessions. The Soviet Union had always showed willingness for expanding economic and technical cooperation with India. In the field of industry, science, technology and others the Soviet Union never hesitated to extend fruitful and beneficial cooperation with India. The Soviet people had been highly appreciated the economic cooperation between India and the USSR. "The Soviet-Indian economic relations were certainly correctly planned and long-term cooperation and such an approach throughout the world could ensure the balance development of all branches of the national economies of partner countries and also could yield greatest economic effect".[24]

Though there were Zigs and Zags, the Indo-Soviet friendship flourished and economic cooperation between the two countries enlarged. There are many factors responsible for deep-seated friendship and cooperation between India and the USSR of which two factors seem important. " First, the material transformation of India was the basic agenda of the ruling classes but this was not their sole concern. Second, the material transformation of India was linked with the strengthening of national sovereignty and not by the opening of India to imperialism. In achieving these two inter-related goals, the Indian ruling classes looked positively towards the Soviet Union. Further, the patriotic masses of India would not have allowed the Indian ruling classes to convert the country to neo-colonial penetration and exploitation".[25] "Trade relations between India and USA also started growing in 1982. It was expected to bloom due to growing technical collaboration between the Indian firms and the US firms. India was display-

22. Verma, Srikant (ed.), *Seven Hundred Days (An Appraisal)*, op. cit., pp.23-24.

23. Speech of Finance Minister, Shri Pranab Mukherjee. See *Lok Sabha Debates*, vol. XXV, No.16, Seventh Series, Eight Session, 12 March 1982, cols. 80-84.

24. *Izvestia* (Moscow), 3 June 1982.

25. Bhambhri, C.P., "Indo-Soviet Economic Cooperation", in Vinod Bhatia (ed.), *op. cit.*, p.169.

ing an increasing interest in collaborations between US high-technology firms and Indian enterprises".[26] Besides, the most significant visit of Prime Minister Indira Gandhi to Washington on 28th July helped further to set an atmosphere of cordiality between two countries. "Later on 31st August both countries signed agreements in New Delhi by which the US agreed projects of a total Rs. 78.2 crores, out of which Rs. 66.6 crores as a loan and Rs.11.6 crores, as grants".[27] In a sequel to the talks between Indira Gandhi and Ronald Reagan a number of projects were also identified. "On 20th of September, Prime Minister Indira Gandhi visited Soviet Union when both the leaders agreed to expand their bilateral economic relations and the Indian Prime Minister made a reference to a liberal terms on which Soviet assistance was extended to India".[28] The Soviet Union had decided to double its trade turnover with India by 1986. "The trade turnover between the two countries had touched a record of Rs.3000 crores in 1981-82".[29] The Soviet Union also indicated its desire of enlarging cooperation with private sectors in India. The Indian businessmen also heartily welcome Soviet willingness. They were anxious to import sophisticated technology in chemical, machine-building, metal working, paper industry and in many other fields to strengthen the industrialisation process of India. "The Soviet Union now emerged as India's leading trading partner of India and accounted for 97.5 percent of India's exports of chromed tanned leather, 96.8 percent of woolen knitwear, 83 percent of drugs and medicines and cosmetics and detergents, 76 percent of Mica, 69 percent of pepper, 65 percent of cashew, 45 percent of Coffee and 42 percent of tobacco".[30] "More interestingly the Soviet Union was ready to assist Indian manufacturers to patent and sell their products and inventions in the USSR. It is also showed readiness to cooperate with Indian organisations to select Soviet inventions for commercial manufacture and marketing in India".[31] Simultaneously, technnical, scientific and other foreign collaborations with the US made sweeping progress in 1982. The main objective of foreign economic policy of India was "an attempt towards a reconciliation

26. *The Economic Times* (New Delhi), 14 July 1982.
27. Satish Kumar (ed.), *Yearbook on India's Foreign Policy, 1982-83* (New Delhi : Sage, 1985, pp.43-45.
28. *Ibid.* pp.40-41.
29. *The Times of India* (New Delhi), 31 October 1982.
30. *Ibid.*, 3 November 1982.
31. *The Economic Times* (New Delhi), 5 November 1982.

between self-reliant national economic development and inter-dependent global reality. Such a balance between internal and external sources of development was difficult to achieve but India's foreign policy makers accepted this as a challenge".[32] Talking about self-reliant objective of the Indian government, Shri P.V.Narasimha Rao, External Affairs Minister said that, " building up of self-reliance internally and maintenance of an independent policy externally had been the twin objectives of the Government of India. Side by side with the development of a rural economy, the government was striving to build a modern industrial infrastructure. Foreign collaborations and technical cooperation, no doubt, provided impetus to India's development, but both operated within the framework of India's national priorities determined by an integrated planning process".[33]

The seventh Non-Aligned Summit was held in New Delhi under the chairmanship of India. The meeting was concerned about the economic situation of developing countries, particularly the non-aligned countries. The fact was that the debt burden on these countries was mounting on an unprecedented scale. The US financial aid also reduced to lowest level. The trade relation with the Socialist countries was also not satisfactory. It was believed that the economic problems of developing countries could be solved if the industrialised countries of both the West and the East help to rectify in the existing economic order. The Summit was realistic in the sense that all members agreed to launch global negotiations than striving for NIEO only. To get share in the decision-making process in the international monetary institutions, strategies were underway. It was clarified that cooperation between developed and developing countries should be linked together. Inspite of their request and appeal the attitude of the developed countries did not mark any change. To operationalise their demands, therefore, they mooted an Action Programme for Economic Cooperation and Coordination. The regional and inter-regional cooperation was give priority of all. There was also prolonged discussion on the economic recovery of the worst affected African countries.

The Indian Prime Minister remarked that the non-aligned movement had stood firm for a total restructuring of international economic relations. The member countries of the movement demanded for equality in the operation of international financial institutions. They

32. Bhambhri, C.P., "USA and India: Conflict and Convergence", *Mainstream*, 17 July 1982, p.7.

33. *Foreign Affairs Record,* October 1982, pp.261-69.

stressed in establishing a NIEO based on equality and justice. The non-aligned countries unanimously agreed to follow Action Plan and prepared to raise the question of NIEO in all international conferences. It must not be forgotten that the developed countries were also facing acute economic crisis that time. "So the requirement was for a world-wide conference that would suggest comprehensive reforms of the international monetary and financial system which was inadequate and inequitable".[34] In the words of Indira Gandhi, "... certain international financial institutions were set up, problems were not looked at in their totality nor was the changing world political situation taken into account. These institutions were meant primarily to promote the interests of advanced countries, many developing countries were not independent and so their legitimate interests went unrepresented... the more lasting solution is to restructure global financial trading systems so that the preoccupation of powerful nations with their immediate domestic issues does not damage the poor or override their long-term interest".[35]

Voice was raised about the balance of payments situation of Third World countries and apathetic attitude of the North to provide sanctions at concessional terms, but the imperialist countries did not pay any heed to those demands. So the economic scenario of the developing countries presented a curious spectacle. In case of India, the foreign exchange position was a matter of serious concern. Many political parties expressed their grave concern over country's economic situation. There was industrial recession and the ideal of self-reliance was virtually written-off. That was the stage when Soviet Union extended help to India, political and economic. The economic contribution of the USSR, however, administered incalculable usefulness. Our friendship with the Soviet Union which had been a cornerstone of our foreign policy was acclaimed by the political parties. The Bharitya Janata Party also highly appreciated Soviet contribution. In the words of Ram Jethmalani, "We can not behave like ungrateful people and take no notice or not give enough consideration to the fact that even from the West we have received economic assistance which far exceeds in its proportions, in its magnitude, the assistance which we have received from the Soviet bloc".[36] Both India and Soviet union

34. *Selected speeches and writings of Indira Gandhi*, vol.V. *op. cit.*, pp.388-89.
35. *Ibid.*, pp.397-99.
36. *Lok Sabha Debates*, vol. XXXVI (21), Seventh Series, Eleventh Session, 24 March 1983, Col.391.

looked for strong bond of relationship between them and stood for peace and mutual co-existence. It is not surprising why India and USSR came closer to each other. " India is a poor country and its first priority is to invest resources in economic development and any preparation for war on the part of India drains away her resources for economic development. Similarly, the Soviet Union was determined to show that socialism could bring prosperity. Moreover, India is a newly liberated country and so in contradiction with imperialism. The Soviet Union was also in basic contradiction with imperialism".[37] Having these common approaches it was natural for India and the USSR to be comfortable partners. The Soviet Union also highly valued the role of the NAM for a more equitable world order. India in no way ungrateful to the Soviet Union. The Bhartiya Janata Party recollected the days when Soviet Union stood for India. But the party was not satisfied with the working of the NAM. So it urged the non-aligned countries to demonstrate action in the most vital issues facing the world. "Deteriorating economic conditions in the world threatened the political stability of developing countries. So the BJP urged the members of the NAM to make the beginning towards it by working for South Asian Regional Cooperation for trade and commerce leading towards a South Asian common market".[38]

Of course, India purchased a large number of goods from the Soviet Union beginning from military aircraft to tanks and other items. But it could not make much head way in encouraging the Soviet Union to enlarge cooperation to a wide scale. "Several industrial units were lying paralyzed as the Soviet Union slowed down placing anticipated orders, e.g., some hosiery units in Ludhiana were badly affected".[39] "Trade is really all about selling and buying and therefore we must not politicise trade. We must trade with any kind of dewy eyed sentimentality. The difficulties arose in Indo-Soviet trade precisely because we had a tendency to view the whole question of Indo-Soviet trade in a kind of political isolation. It was also an undeniable fact that the machinery we needed, we could not buy it from the West at prices we could afford, therefore, our trade life with the Soviet Union started with machinery. It was abundantly satisfactory for the initial

37. Bhambhri, C.P., "Perspective on Soviet contribution to India in Defence efforts", in Vinod Bhatia (ed.) *Indo- Soviet Relations : Problems and Prospects* (New Delhi:Panchsheel, 1984), pp.42-43.

38. *Resolution passed at the Fourth National Council Session* of the BJP in New Delhi on April 15-17, 1983, pp.2-5.

39. *Organiser*, 27 March-2nd April, 1983, p.1.

requirement for which it was meant. But switching of to Western technology was not motivated by politics nor by sentimentality but purely by the country's requirements".[40] "India's attachment to the United States had also not been entirely emotional. The US was a primary sources of economic assistance and technology inspite of difference and ideologically the Indian elite was more in tune with American, than Soviet thinking".[41] If India was not interested to America's policies, yet in a mid-way of fully developed society the country needed Western technology to grow at a faster scale, at least faster than they could with Soviet technology.

The foreign investment policy of the Indian government was based on the principles evolved by India's first Prime Minister Jawaharlal Nehru. In April 1949 he stated, "The stress on the need to regulate, in the national interest, the scope and the manner of foreign capital arose from past association of foreign capital and control with foreign domination of the economy of the country. But circumstances today are quite different. The object of our regulation should, therefore, be the utilisation of foreign capital in a manner most advantageous to the country. Indian capitals need to be supplemented by foreign capital, not only because our national savings will not be enough for the rapid development of the country on the scale we wish, but also because in many cases, scientific, technical and industrial knowledge and capital equipment can best be secured, alongwith foreign capital".[42] Table 6 shows about Soviet-USA investment in India in the eighties. Out of total Rs.12740.18 million in 1980-90, the US had a percentage share of 25.32 compared to USSR's 1.36%. It represents that the Indian investment policy inside the country had a favourable trend towards USA. The USSR's ivestment was negligible till 1986 and afterwards the Soviet Union showed interest in investment in Indian market, whereas USA's investment though insignificant till 1984, after that it dominated the Indian scene. The reason being Rajiv Gandhi's assumption of power showed soft corner towards the US technology and Indo-American relations started improving.

Since independence many foreign companies have been attracted to collaborate with Indian businessmen. In a Span of five years (1980-

40. *Rajya Sabha Debates*, vol. CXXVI, no.8, 5 may 1983, cols. 220-21.
41. Nihal Singh, S., "Can the US and India be real friends", *Asian Survey*, vol.23, no.9, September 1983, p.1020.
42. Vakil, Arun, C., "Indo-US Economic Relations", in P.M. Kamath (ed.), *Indo-US Relations : Dynamics of change* (New Delhi : South Asia, 1987), p.134.

84), the Indian government had approved 2930 foreign collaborations, one-fifth of which were with the United States. The majority of the US investments in India was in the technical sector covering chemical and allied products, machinery and transport, and other manufacturing industries. Of the 602 collaborations approved with the US between 1980-84, 476 or 79 per cent tie-ups were technical in nature.(see Table V). So the foreign collaborations in the first half of the eighties occupied a peerless position in India's industrial, technical, scientific and commercial development. In the same period (1981-84) the Indo-Soviet foreign collaboration was insignificant. Out of total nine collaborations approved with the USSR all were technical in nature. (see Table VIII).

The foreign aid was essential for India for its conomic development. So India received aid from the Western countries as well as from the Socialist countries. But "the foreign aid-givers had shed a lot of tears for India's poverty. It had been maintained by the aid-givers that they were cooperating with India to fight backwardness. In reality, foreign aid for development had led to the building of capitalism in India and it had accentuated serious inequalities in the urban and rural sectors of the Indian social life. The foreign aid, whether from the socialist countries of the East or West, had strengthened the exploitative character of Indian society".[43] "Therefore, the Congress(I) reiterated its strong commitment to the building of a self-reliant economy on the basis of modern science and technology. It was believed that only an independent economy, invulnerable to outside pressures could safeguard our political independence. The Congress (I) was convinced that the reorientation of investment priorities in industrial and infrastructure sectors must be attuned to the key objectives of productivity, maintenance and modernisation. The AICC (I) noted with concern the contributed deterioration of the international climate for aid. The hardening terms of trade, the intensification of protectionist measures and high interest rates had imposed greater burden on the LDCs. It believed that the Non-Aligned Movement under the leadership of Indira Gandhi could help to find a solution".[44] The Bharatiya Janata Party was also equally critical of the policies of the foreign aid-givers and their economic policies towards India. At the same time the party criticised economic policies of the Indian government "Multinationals

43. Bhambhri, C.P., *The Foreign Policy of India* (New Delhi: Sterling, 1987), p.104.

44. *Resolutions passed* in the AICC Meeting held on 20th- 21st October 1983, Bombay, pp.24-32.

were being allowed to increase their presence in India. The Indian market had been flooded with imported electronic-ware showing a distinguishing lack of faith in our engineering competence. The BJP warned the government to change the economic policy or else it would drain on additional resources including trained man-power as well as foreign exchange".[45] The trade deficit with the USSR was Rs.1490 million in 1982 rose to Rs.(-) 2780 million in 1983, a total deficit of Rs. 4270 million in one year. (Table 1). According to the BJP " It was due to the vested interests in imports of non-essential items which squandered away our scarce foreign exchange. The import and export management had resulted in an unprecedented trade deficit thereby making the balance of payments position more precarious".[46] "The total amount of India's external debt that had to be repaid in U.S. dollars stood at 11093 million as on 31st December, 1983. This excluded the outstanding IBRD loans of about $1193 million which was supposed to be repaid in a mix of currencies".[47] " The wholesale price Index which was 223 in January 1980 had crossed 344 mark in September 1984. The consumer price Index had also risen sharply. It had gone up from 360 in 1980 to 584 in 1984.

The foreign economic policy of the government was succumbed to pressure from several quarters. Despite increased imports of capital goods, intermediate products and other raw materials, industrial production became stagnant. Industrial sickness had become a common phenomenon in the country. Performance of the government in achieving self-reliance had been utterly bleak. Continued imports of basic items like rice, wheat, pulses made self-reliance a mockery. In this situation the BJP clearly observed that further economic development would be completely in jeopardy unless some quick recovery programme is not taken".[48] "Therefore the BJP announced to work for the establishment of a New International Economic Order and vowed to take initiative for trade and monetary reform and importantly North-South dialogue with emphasis on enhanced South-South coopera-

45. *Resolution passed by the National Executive Meeting* of the BJP, 21-23 October 1983 in Lucknow, p.16.

46. BJP National Executive Meeting, 4-5 January 1984 in Indore, See A.M.Zaidi (ed.), *The Annual Register of India Political Parties,1984* (Publication Division : Indian Institute of Applied Research, 1986), pp.64-65.

47. See *Lok Sabha Debates*, vol.XLV, No.13, Seventh Series, Fourteenth Session, 9th March 1984, cols.3-13.

48. *Resolutions adopted in BJP National Council* in Pune on 12th-14th October 1984, See A.M.Zaidi (ed.), n.49, pp.125-1228.

tion".[49] The Indian government also felt the necessity of early North-South and South-South cooperation. Mrs. Gandhi said, "Given the will for cooperation, there is no dearth of opportunities for organizing and broadening interdependence on the basis of mutual interests and benefits.... Interdependence is the rational of the dialogue and co-operation between North annd South".[50] She stressed on some points which would make international cooperation more efficacious: "Reversal of the present trend in the flow of assistance, particularly concessional assistance from developed to developing countries; reversing protectionist trends; provision of financial support for balance of payments problems in the transitional stage of oil importing from developing countries; and above all development of the solidarity and collective self-reliance of developing countries to reduce their vulnerability to pressures from and events in affluent countries".[51]

The economic hegemony of the Western countries combined with their exploitative nature enslaved the new nations of Asia and Africa. The price and fiscal system affected the economies of Third World countries. In fact, the economic and technological superiority of the Western countries put the developing countries dependent on the former colonial powers. The North-South dialogue had not taken off the ground. Inspite of concrete efforts made by some non-aligned countries the international debt situation was alarming. The call for NIEO was not taken seriously by the developed countries and thereby almost reached a temporary dead-end. So the pivotal concern of the non-aligned countries was to turn the economic hegemony in favour of Third World, to devise means for greater share in the international system and above all for a venture for collective self-reliance and the NIEO. They opposed the inequality and different forms of discrimination in the comity of nations and demanded equal participation in the solution of major economic problems. It must be stated that in this regard the Socialist countries specially the USSR supported the efforts of India and other non-aligned countries. It had always come against the existing mechanism of monopoly regulation of the West and advocated consistently the restructuring of international economic institutions. The cooperation of newly independent countries, including India, in international financial institutions and its speedy implementation which would ensure the removal of economic backwardness was always supported by the Socialist countries.

49. *Election Manifesto* of the BJP, General Election 1984, p.21.

50. *Selected speeches and writings of Indira Gandhi*, vol.V, Op. Cit., pp.342-44.

51. *Ibid.*, p.345.

The Soviet Union sharing common principles with India showed eagerness to expand the trade relations. So "the Indo-Soviet trade jumped from a mere 500 roubles in 1960 to 7200 roubles in 1984. This was possible due to the correct application of the rupee payment system and modern trade dynamics. Soviet cooperation with India's Public Sector was picking fast. Russians were providing assistance for the Vishakhapatnam steel plant, the Vindhyachal Thermal Power Station and so on. The Soviet aided projects in India produced almost 40 percent of the country's cast iron and steel nearly 80 percent of metallurgical equipments, medicines and other projects".[52] The Indo-Soviet collaboration came in several forms to India—economic, military and political. Starting from Goa and Kashmir to supply of sophisticated weapons and the Soviet aid in transport, education, public health and in other key sectors embodies Indo-Soviet strong ties in international affairs. It must be noted that interests of India and the Soviet Union converged due to many reasons. No doubt, the USSR had political interests of alleviating India as a strong nation, both militarily and economically, yet the concerned problem was Pakistan's military alliance with the United States. Unlike the Indo-Soviet relations, the Indo-American bilateral relations had never been perceivable. Immediately after the assassination of Indira Gandhi the Indo-American relations slid down. India's stand on major international issues contradicted with that of USA. India's objection to Reagan's Star War programme affected their bilateral relations. However, it did not mean that India and America had no economic links. India was in need of US economic assistance for meeting humanitarian and strategic requirements. A large segment of Indian personnel were engaged in the industrial and other core sectors of the US. "India was interested in increased investments by American firms in Indian industry in order to raise technological levels of Indian manufacturing. Some American firms had entered India being attracted by India's potential. There was little evidence that India had lost its independence in dealing with potential or actual foreign investors. So it was desirable that the US government by its own programs and by its influence within multilateral economic institutions, such as the World Bank and the IMF supported the economic policies of the Indian government. Those policies sought to stimulate development in general and to encourage greater efficiency and flexibility within the industrial sector, whether

52. *The Hindustan Times* (New Delhi), 2 January 1985.

public or private".[53] So also "a number of initiatives had been taken on the American side to promote US investment and to reduce the threats of protectionist trends legislation passing through the legislation passing through the Congress. The number of approved joint ventures and technology transfer agreements was on the increase. For the fourth year in a row, the US had the largest number of collaboration agreements approved by the Indian government. Most of these were in the form of technology transfer and licensing agreements".[54]

So, the United States had also economic stakes in India. But the American corporations had no control in Indian market. So unwillingness of Indian government to provide opportunities to the US investors and reluctance of private sectors to allow comfortable investment opportunities marred bilateral relations between India and USA. The Indian government was looking for self-reliant economy and that is why the Indian leaders repeatedly expressed unwillingness to ingress American companies to Indian economy. "It was under Reagan that the US firmly abandoned multi-lateralism and increasingly resorted to bilateralism in matters of concessional aid, a play which gave ample opportunities to the Americans to twist arms of the poor countries. Thus India entered the phase of Indo-US relations during Reagan's second term with even increased misgivings about his policies towards Third World countries".[55] It may be said that the Indo-American relations was dominated by misgivings and ill-advised foreign policy approaches. The US interest of dominating South-Asia certainly contradicted Indian perceptions of an independent South Asia. The United States went on assisting Pakistan to keep its hold in the region both politically and economically. "This had been perceived by Indian policy makers as a design by the US to check India's role as a regional power and retarding its economic development, too, which caused non chalance in their bilateral relations".[56]

The Indo-American bilateral relations were not in fine form and the US investment policy had many ramifications for which US companies were not encouraged to enter into Indian market. So liberalisation of foreign investment had not taken seriously by the

53. Singh, Jasjit (ed.), *Asian Security : Old Paradigms and New Challenges* (New Delhi : Lancer International, 1991), pp.218-23.

54. *Hindustan Times* (New Delhi), 29 November 1984.

55. Viswam, S., "India and President Reagan", *Mainstream*, vol.XXIII, No.12, 1984, p.6 and p.48.

56. Sharma, S.K., "Indo-American Relations : why non chalance?" *Journal of Political Studies*, vol. XVIII, No.1, February 1985, pp.43-44.

Indian government. But ".....under international pressure applied by the IMF, the World Bank and other capitalist countries, India was opening its economy and liberalising the rules of foreign investment and import of technology. The export-led growth was ultimately linked with an invitation to imperialism in India because multinationals had excellent marketing network and they had to be invited to give a push to foreign trade. Thus, the advocacy of the new economic strategy for India became synonymous with the advocacy of invitation to foreign capital and technology in India. The advocates of Free Trade Zones in India were in effect acting as lobbyists for imperialism in India".[57] Thus, the economic challenges in the country were multi-folded. No doubt, absorption of modern technology and attempts to bring radical changes in the public and private sectors were certainly entertaining but the external economic environment was not helpful for India. There was unprecedented credit squeeze and concessional assistance by the developed countries. Therefore, the Government of India had been endeavouring for a New International Economic Order. The international financial institutions dominated by the developed countries were implementing policies that were clearly intended to reduce the growth potential of economics of the developing countries. India had always been in the forefront of the struggle for a restructuring of the international economic institutions and had called for a conference on money and finance for development with universal participations".[58]

In between 1980 and 1985, India received a total of $1412.6 million in terms of US economic assistance. In 1985 alone $179.8 million was sanctioned for India's economic development. So it is not that the American economic assistance had no bearing on India's development, but it considerably reduced from the previous year 1984 and subsequently it reduced to an ever low $ 126.2 million in 1989 which we shall discuss later. (see Table 7). On the other hand, the Soviet economic assistance in 1985 stood at $ 1200 million out of $ 2,390 million in total which amounts to more than half of that year. Indian trade with the USSR increased further in subsequent years. The fact is that the Soviet aid was concentrated in major industrial, metallurgy and related fields and aimed at long-term benefits. "The

57. Bhambhri. C.P., "Imperialism in India", *Social Scientist*, 141, February 1985, pp.39-41.

58. *Resolutions passed in the AICC(I) Meetings* held on 4th and 5th May 1985, Delhi, The AICC(I) publication, pp.22-23.

Soviet economic aid had been concentrated on developing the basic industries in the state sector. Whereas American aid was designed to bring India into the American sphere of influence, Soviet aid was designed to help it strengthen its economy and ultimately achieve real economic independence. It is often claimed by Soviet and Indian commentators that it was the Soviet willingness to provide aid which initially encouraged the Western countries to move in and then impelled them to offer better terms than they would otherwise have done in the absence of Soviet proposals".[59] The Soviet technical collaborations were exiguous in number compared to the US and concentrated on a few chosen sectors, particularly in energy, steel and metallurgy, power plants and heavy electrical equipment. As for example, throughout the eighties the Indo-USSR collaborations were technical in nature and in 1987 only financial-cum-technical collaboration emerged. Soviet percentage share was very less which was 0.648 (See Table 8) yet Moscow helped to set up industrial capacity in India. It is astonishing that why then there was no improvement in Indo-Soviet collaborations. Because " The Soviet projects contained the seeds of their own demise, for at maturity Soviet-assisted industries in India outgrew Soviet percentage and turned westwards for satisfaction of increasingly sophisticated technological needs".[60] As a result, in India's global imports the Soviet imports and exports stood at only 1509.5 million roubles and 1574.9 million roubles (See Table 2) compared to the American import and export $ 1641.9 million and $ 2478.3 million respectively in 1985 (See Table 4). The percentage of Soviet share was 2.2 in 1985 which was almost same since 1981 and after 1985 it started declining (Table 2), even though it is recognised that Indo-Soviet trade was improving day by day.

India's endeavour to achieve explicit economic independence and its role in world affairs for a just and durable economic system was treated with great sympathy by the USSR. " The economic ties between the USSR and India had helped India to solve major problems in India's progress, namely in the construction of the foundation of heavy industry, development of power, fuel complex and on other key sectors. Their bilateral relations, friendship and cooperation was playing a more important and beneficial role in the entire system of

59. Duncan, Peter S., *The Soviet Union and India* (London : Routledge, 1989), pp.69-73.

60. Thayer, Carlyle and Ramesh Thakur, *Soviet Relations with India and Vietnam* (London : MacMillan, 1992), pp.177-78.

international system".[61] "The Soviet Union expressed gratitude over economic ties between the USSR and India that had been instrumental in solving problems of major importance for India's progress, key problems of each specific historic period — whether the building of basic heavy industries or the development of the fuel and energy sector".[62] "The Soviet Union was doing everything possible to acquaint the Indian business circles of what it had to offer. Its active participation in Indian international exhibitions, the organisation of special Soviet exhibitions, seminars and symposia were all directed to achieve the objective. In 1985, almost a fifth of India's trade was with the USSR and it was growing at the rate of about 15 percent yearly, one of the highest rates of growth India had achieved with any country. It was a measuree of the dynamism of mutually beneficial nature of this trade".[63] " The United States also seemed to be pleased at Rajiv's liberalisation steps and it developed softness to the Indians and even to foreign private sectors. The US also geared up economic cooperation with India. So both the superpowers-USA and USSR -seemed to be vying with each other in helping Rajiv in building up 21st century India".[64] Thus " the Nehruvian model of friendship with the USSR that was pursued assiduously later provided a great deal of manoenvrability to Indian diplomacy. The Soviet Union also had few friendly countries in the entire region of Asia. It was fully convinced of the Indian friendship that did not undergo even when the Janata government came to power. On the other hand, even when there was a variance of Indo-American strategic perceptions, India had a remarkable degree of economic cooperation with the US. It seemed that the US was seeing a large potential in the Indian market"[65] and that was the reason why Indo-American relations in the early period of Rajiv Gandhi's era was developed without much divergencies. But the American loans for India created hue and cry in America. So the US again seemed as an unreliable economic partner. Beyond all questions "the main difficulty is that as long as India goes round with the begging bowl to America, as long as we do not set our own house in order–socially, economically, politically and otherwise–America will not respect or heed our voice. Similarly as long as America things or

61. *Pravda* (Moscow), 22 May 1985.

62. *Foreign Affairs Record,* May 1985, p.133.

63. *Financial Express* (Bombay), 23 May 1985.

64. *Organiser,* 9 June 1985, p.1.

65. Gujral, I.K." The Imperative of Nonalignment," *World Focus,* vol.6, No.7, July 1985, p.21.

behaves in a superior or dominating manner, as it long as does not accept the need for a New World Economic, cultural and communication order, it will not able to play its due role in world affairs-especially in the develcping countries".[66]

In such a totality the BJP considered any foreign loan inimical to India's development. In its view, "if the country is to escape endless dependence on foreign loans and knowhow and the strongholds of MNCs, we have to evolve a technology appropriate to our needs and resources. High technology which should be sought when essential is not an unmixed boon as was evidenced by the Bhopal gas tragedy".[67] In defiance of the resistance by the opposition political parties foreign collaboration proposals were approved by the central government in the area of colour T.V. picture tubes, one from M/s Punjab Display Devices Ltd. for collaboration with M/s Hitachi Ltd. Japan and the other from U.P. Electronics Corporation Ltd. Lucknow, for collaboration with "M/s Toshiba Corporation, Japan and M/s Mitsubishi Corporation Ltd. Japan. "Mr. C.Janga Reddy, the BJP M.P. in Lok Sabha renounced for such foreign collaborations".[68] With the changes in industrial policy, liberalisation of economy and relaxation of FERA, the multinationals were encouraged to set up their own companies independently or in collaboration with Indian companies. Thus the self-reliance drive of Indian economy was substituted with the ingress of foreign companies. The BJP alleged that "such a policy not only deviated to the principle of self-reliance but would also ultimately result in a big drain on our resources. It seemed to be an attempt to undermine country's self-confidence at the behest of multinationals who had shown their hostile attitude to India on many occasions".[69] "It was apparent that the ruling elites were reluctant to opt for self-reliant development. The only way to avoid such misadventures was to have planned cooperation among developing countries, preferably on a state-to-state basis, based on the needs, the potential and the resources of them".[70]

66. Kaul, T.N. "Indo-US Relations", *Man and Development,* vol.VII, No.3, September 1985, p.54.

67. *Resolutions passed in the National Executive Meeting* of the BJP, 19th to 21st July, 1985, Bhopal (M.P.), BJP Publication, pp.4-5.

68. *Lok Sabha Debates,* vol. XII, No.22, Eighth Series, Fourth Session, 18 December 1985, col.20.

69. Resolutions adopted by the BJP National Executive Meeting at Chandigarh, 3rd-5th January 1986, for de tails see A.M.Zaidi (ed.), *Annual register of Indian political parties, 1986,* Op. Cit., pp.42-43.

70. Dutt, R.C., "Self-Reliant Development and NAM", *Secular Democracy,* vol.XIX, No.8, August 1986, p.49.

The international economic scenario in the eighties was altogether different than that of the previous decades and so "the foreign economic relations of India during the 80s had posed qualitatively different issues that those in the previous decades of the 50s, 60s and 70s. The IMF loan had successfully imposed import liberalisation on India which would perpetuate adverse balance of trade... and with the failure of the developing countries to achieve any breakthrough either at UNCTAD or GATT, the situation for India looked rather difficult".[71] Under the prevailing international economic conditions in the eighties, India looked for a new strategy in its trade policy. The importance of export promotion policy was realised. So India started exporting manufactured items to other developing countries of Asia and Africa. Though international financial institutions also showed favour towards developing countries, the Western countries did not change their stance on rigid tariff system. So Indian desire of increasing trade activities with the Third World countries on manufactured commodities was aimed to bring huge foreign earnings. On the other hand, " the import policy was also in the line with the new orientations being given by the government to the broad economic framework since 1980-81. The export-import policy provide further impetus for exports by a number of incentives to make all possible savings in imports, to support the growth of indigenous industry and to maximise the utilisation of country's major resource endowments in manpower and agriculture. The process of import liberalisation had been carried during the Seventh Plan Period for achieving a higher growth rate in exports. Thus India's trade policy was oriented towards promotion of exports with the help of import substitution".[72]

India's trade balance in the eighties was negative. As a developing country the deficit budget and negative trade balance was not harmful to nation's development and progress. "However, there were some external and several internal factor holding back as a function of low domestic production and productivity, and others involving a somewhat wasteful use of imports, particularly those expected to meet consumption needs like cereals and edible oils, or intermediates like iron, steel and cement which could be produced within the country if there is less idle capacity in these lines of production. The factors holding back domestic production and exports include high and rising

71. Bhambhri, C.P., *Op. Cit.*, pp.137-38.
72. Rao, M.S., *Trends and Development of India's Foreign Trade* (Allahabad : Chugh Publications, 1991), p.218.

costs of production, outdated technology and wasteful use of scarce capital and in the case of exports, particularly the pressure of domestic demand, inadequate infrastructure, short supply of inputs and the maze of licences and controls which were a feature of country's administration".[73] The internal debt was nearing one lakh crore rupees in 1987. The BJP therefore "warned against this inexorable slide towards bankruptcy. On the foreign exchange front, the rapid deterioration in the position was reflected in the escalating debt servicing ratio which was estimated to touch 30 percent in 1987 as against 15.4 percent in 1985. The mounting foreign debt was estimated at the record level of Rs.30,000 crores. Thus that by discarding much on external resources the government was taking the road which had been taken by countries like Brazil, Mexico and Philippines. The BJP also witnessed with alarm the growing scale of invasion of our national economy by multinationals. In the process, some of our national units like Sindri Fertilisers were jettisoned. The deliberate and continuing sell-out of Indian industries to foreign interests was noxious for the nation. The BJP demanded immediate reversal of such policies in the name of modernisation, for real development comes within and can not be borrowed from out side. The real boost would come, the BJP stressed on its argument, only through a total mobilisation of national resources including farmers and workers. Therefore, the BJP called for some urgent steps : that the foreign collaborations should be permitted only in strategic and sophisticated line of production and policy of liberalisation of imports should be replaced by the policy of selective import liberalisation".[74] No doubt, "there should be close interaction between developed and developing countries but the developed nations should transfer the technology without much strings attached to it, without plundering economy of the Third World countries and with a reverse in protectionist trend policy".[75] Such a policy can alone eradicate poverty and can check negative trade balance and would herald a new economic environment.

India had been championing the causes of peace and harmony, and through the SAARC it tried to strengthen ties among the South Asian countries, which the Soviet Union warmly supported. The Indian

73. Adiseshiah, Malcolm S., *Role of Foreign Trade in Indian Economy* (Delhi ; Lancer International, 1986), p.20.
74. *Resolutions adopted by the National Executive* of the BJP in Vijayawada on January 2, 3 and 4, 1987, pp.14-17.
75. Speech of BJP M.P. Mr. Kalpanath Roy. vide *Rajya Sabha Debates*, vol. CXLII, No.9, 27 April 1987, cols. 253-54.

government appreciated Soviet Union's rapid economic growth and showed its willingness to raise economic standard of India on Soviet line. The USSR happily extended all possible help in bilateral trade and economic cooperation to accelerate social and economic development of India, modernisation of Indian industry and to raise standard of living. The USSR was also working in close cooperation to establish contracts and agreements with the Indian companies which yielded tremendous economic growth of India. "For years Soviet-Indian economic cooperation had been chiefly geared towards the basic industries of the Public Sector and while retaining this cooperation, Soviet organisations also sought to expand and intensify their ties with Indian companies of varying sizes".[76] "Institutional and Organisational arrangements under which trade being carried out had several advantages for India. The bilateral trade agreements had contributed to the rapid growth of India's foreign trade and India's exports to the USSR and East European Countries largely amounted to trade creation. Major advantages of Indo-Soviet trade were repayment through goods, growth of export of non-traditional items from India without any promotional expenditure, increased the bargaining power of India with the West and so on".[77]

Indo-Soviet economic relation was registering into a new phase of cooperation, though a number of internal and external changes were taking place in both countries. The Indo-Soviet trade stepped-up at a time when the Western countries were pursuing on discriminatory trade practices and creating constraints in India's trade with other countries. " On 6th June both countries signed a protocol incorporating several agreements relating to energy, power and metallurgy. Under an agreement signed on Oil and gas the Soviet Union agreed to deliver to the oil and Natural Gas Commission (ONGC) of India, the same month, the first of the three geo-physical computer systems of the model EC-1061. On 26th June in Moscow, again they signed a time-bound scientific and technological programme encompassing all major fields. The two countries also finalised a draft on integrated long term cooperation in contemporary science and technology. On 12th July, Indian Private Sector enterprises and a Soviet Organisation decided to set up a few joints ventures for the production of consumer goods. Later in November, a trade protocol was signed for 1988 which

76. Vladimirov, Leonid P., *The Soviet-Indian Phenomenon* (New Delhi : Allied, 1989), pp.75-94.

77. Agrawal, Ashok Kumar, *India's Trade and Economic coop eration with Developing and Socialist* Countries (New Delhi: Commonwealth Publishers, 1989), p.153.

envisaged a trade turn over of Rs.5,000 crores, 25 percent more than the anticipated turn over of Rs. 4000 crores in 1987".[78]

There was increase in trade between India and the USSR in 1986-90 as compared to 1981-85. This trend enlarged Soviet-Indian economic relations and testified Soviet economic commitment when India was in resource constraints. As Mr. Gandhi stated, " The friendship between India and the Soviet Union is deeply founded in our sharped vision of a world peace—. Our friendship is neither ephemeral nor a matter of mere convenience. It is a mutuality enriching relationship based on understanding and respect, equality and mutual benefit. It is a creative relationship".[79] There are several political and economic factors which motivated the Soviet Union to enlarge on friendly relations with India. " India provided significant quantities of certain raw and processed materials, some machinery and considerable consumer goods needed by the Soviet Union. Success in penetrating the Indian market with a wide range of goods also served as a key to Soviet penetration of other Third World markets. On the Indian side, too, the most important motive for relations with the Soviet Union was probably political— the perceived need for Soviet political support against India's adversaries[80] "Though there were lack of a Indian interest in Soviet manufactured goods, the relatively low level of Soviet technology available for exports, at the same time, however, both sides derived substantial benefits from their economic relationship and while the Soviet Union was not economic partner of choice for India, yet the Soviet Union offered very attractive terms on their bilateral trade and remained free to look for better deals elsewhere".[81]

"The Soviet-Indian trade was not a mere exchange of goods, but it had been linked with India's planning, industrial and agricultural development. It was also based on rupee-payment system which enabled India to buy goods for rupees at a time when it had only limited foreign exchange reserves. It also helped India to keep its debt profile within manageable limits and to reduce exchange

78. Satish Kumar (ed.), *Yearbook on India's Foreign Policy, 1987-88* (New Delhi : Sage, 1988), pp.58-60.

79. *Statement on Foreign Policy of Prime Minister Rajiv Gandhi* (New Delhi : Publication Division, Ministry of External Affairs, April 1988),p.12.

80. Mukerjee, Dilip, "Indo-Soviet Economic Ties", *Problems of communism*, vol. XXXVI, No.1, January-February 1987, pp.13-14.

81. Thornton, Thomas R., "Gorbachev's Courtship of India : India and the Soviet Union", *Round table*, 304, October 1987, p.462.

instability".[82] " The friendship and cooperation between India and the USSR did not come into existence from nothing. Neither did they stem from momentary considerations. The steadily developing Soviet-Indian relations were based on a historical and spiritual affinity of the two great nations which was pre-determined by the objective course of mankind's social development. Their bilateral relations accelerated social and economic development of the Soviet Union and modernisation of India's economy".[83] Rajiv Gandhi, the then Prime Minister of India narrated the Indo-Soviet relations in these words, " Our relations with the USSR have been traditionally close and warm. They are now expanding at an unprecedented pace, improving qualitatively to new levels. Special mention must be made of the new thrust in the increased trade and economic cooperation and more specially in the science and technology co-operation".[84]

Moreover, there had been pleasing progress in bilateral relations with the United States. The United States had acquired the position of largest trading partner of India. "Progress was particularly noticable and significant in economic cooperation and technology transfers. Their relations acquired a new momentum following Prime Minister's visit to the United States in the autumn of 1987".[85] On high technology transfer to India, the US showed eagerness. The steady progress in this regard can be seen in the approval of a super computer, Cray XMP-14. "The US was the most important source of direct foreign investment, joint venture collaboration and technology transfers. The areas included software, electronic components, automotive parts, intermediate and steel based equipment, consumer electronics and household appliances. According to an Indian Press report the US State Development cleared a proposal by the American aviation firm Northrop to transfer all the technology needed for the F-5 jet plane". [86] We can now ask the question why India was going in so many diverse aveas to

82. *The Patriot* (New Delhi), 29 November 1987.
83. Glebov, Ivan, "USSR and India : Cooperation in the interest of progress and peace", *International Affairs* (Moscow), February 1988, pp.26-32.
84. Speech of Rajiv Gandhi during debate in Parliament on Demand for Grants of Ministry of External Affairs on 20 April 1988, Vide *Statement on Foreign Policy of Prime Minister Rajiv Gandhi* (New Delhi : September 1988), Op. Cit., p.11.
85. *Resolutions passed in the AICC meeting* held on 23rd and 24th April 1988 at Maraimalai Nagar (Tamil Nadu), p.34.
86. Satish Kumar (ed.), *Yearbook on India's Foreign Policy*, 1989, Op. Cit., pp.61-62.

make herself more acceptable to the US? "Most obviously and importantly, the Prime Minister wanted hi-tech for India. Secondly, he wanted hi-tech in defence and wanted to purchase sophisticated weapons. And thirdly, he wanted recognition and support for India's role in South Asia".[87] The US appreci ated modernisation and liberalisation steps taken by the Indian government. There was substantial progress in trade and technology transfer and project were sanctioned for India. The Indian companies and US companies came to understanding to increase their level of collaborations. "The United States assured that rules and regulations would be made simpler for Indian exports to clear the US customs. India also assured the US that concerns of streamlining procedures to avoid delay were being given added attention. The two sides reiterated the commitment to further strangethen bilateral trade".[88] Thus it is clearly evident that US had been the largest trading partner of India and it had also substantial economic stake in India. "So the US always sought to see India stable, growing and with integrated economic entity to preserve and expand the advantageous position the US had".[89]

The Pepsi Cola Project created problems for Rajiv Gandhi government. The Pepsi Company was visualising to set up food processing and soft drink concentrate manufacturing units. The Pepsi project with an outlay of Rs. 22 crores was formally cleared in collaboration with Punjab Agro-Industrial Corporation (PAIC) and the Tatas where the Pepsico's share was 55 percent. " The BJP was opposed to the idea of allowing a multinational into very heart of India's agricultural economy. The party had always maintained that the Kisan has to be provided with opportunities and facilities for diversifying his sources of income. It was also opposed to processing of fruits and vegetables as the benefits go to the pocket of the foreigners. The party was of the view that the entry of the Pepsico would immediately turn the growing processed food industry in the corporative sector sick. It would cripple the existing corporatives causing incalculable harm to the small farmers. So the BJP warned the country against the steady erosion of

87. Hari Kumar, K.N.," Rajiv and the US: Trading non-alignment for hi-tech?" *Mainstream*, vol. XXVI, No.29, 30th April 1988, p.22.

88. *The Times of India* (New Delhi), 15 May 1988.

89. Rose, Douglas S., "A letter from the publishers", *Span*, vol.24, No.8, August 1988, p.2.

the nation's self-reliance".[90] There was also resentment and reaction in press over the import of ergot affected wheat from USA. The BJP deputy in Lok Sabha, Dr.A.K.Patel, raised the question on the floor of the House. "He requested the government for a high level inquiry into the matter".[91]

During the eighties India faced serious burden on external debt. There was also foreign exchange crisis. To get rid of these crises India had to deal with world financial institutions which aggravated the foreign exchange crisis. "The road followed by India in the eighties to overcome the challenges of economy were based on a package of policies. First, the government of India went in for a big loan from the IMF with conditionalities. India continued this approach and foreign debt of India upto 1988-89 was estimated at 53 billion US dollar. Second, the policies of liberalisation, the long-term fiscal policy, the growing financial and technological collaborations with foreign countries were the new thrust areas of the 80s to accelerate economic growth of the country. The consequences of the policies of the eighties were debt dependence and technological dependence of India on the industrialised countries of the West. According to the world Bank, the debt service ratio of India had risen from 8 percent in 1980 to an estimated 27 percent in 1988".[92] " So after the four decades of independence the Indian State had grown in size but not in competence. Both its size and its incompetence were dictated by its legacy from the past and the milieu in which it evolved. The constraints on the external market were acute. Of course, the growth of the urban salariate had enlarged the domestic market. But it was doubtful if it was capable of supporting the long production runs of most modern large-scale manufacturers. In any case the size of the middle class was very much a function of the size of the state".[93]

To add fuel to flame, the United States had named India alongwith

90. Resolutions passed by the National Executive Meeting of the BJP, Ahmedabad, 7 October 1988, Vide A.M. Zaidi, *Annual Register of Indian Political Parities, 1988* (Publication Department, Indian Institute of Applied political Research, 1990), pp.169-70.

91. *Lok Sabha Debates*, vol.XLV, No. 21, Eighth Series, 12th Session, 13 December 1988, cols. 24-25.

92. Bhambhri, C.P., " The United States of America and India", in M.Rasgotra, V.D. Chopra and K.P. Misra (eds.), *India's Foreign Policy in the Nineties* (New Delhi: Patriot, 1990), p.122.

93. Guha, Ashok, (ed.), *Economic Liberalization, Industrial Structure and Growth in India* (Delhi : Oxford universi ty Press, 1990), p.48.

Japan and Brazil in the Unfair Trade Practices under section "Super 301" of the US Trade Act. "The US contention was that India's policy of linking imports to the exports obligations was not conducive to America's interests. Another issue which had become a major irritant to the U.S. policy makers was India's policy stipulated foreign equity upto 40 percent and there were also restrictions on the use of local raw materials. Such an attitude of the US demonstrated its imperialist drive of establishing its own economic sovereignty over India"[94] and to weaken India's economic independence and self-reliance. "A nation's economy is as strong as its currency and when the currency deteriorates it brings down not only economy but also subvert the country's democratic polity and security. The deficits which led India to foreign borrowings and low foreign exchange reserve made the nation bankrupt and depreciated the value of rupee".[95] So, "the Bharatiya Janata Party pleaded for self-reliance and to keep multinationals out of the field of consumer industries. The Party regarded self-reliance as an overriding component in our external economic relations, including the import of technolology and capital".[96] "Self-reliance cannot be attained merely by reducing imports. Self-reliance does not mean insular economy. Self-reliance means accepting the challenge of making Indian industry competitive and the Indian rupee convertible in the international market. Self-reliance means a self-confident economy...as conceived by Pandit Nehru, "means an economy which can meet all the import requirements through exports. To achieve such a level of exports four types of adjustments are necessary in today's world: reduction in excess domestic demand, enhanced competitiveness, freeing the economy from unnecessary regulation, and capability for self-enforcement".[97] "Indira Gandhi relentlessly pursued the social and economic strategy of Pandit Jawaharlal Nehru. She brought about the Green Revolution...the INC renews its total commitment to Indira Gandhi's war on poverty. Rajiv Gandhi creatively updated the Nehruvian model. He began the process of restoring Indian industry to meet the challenges facing us in the emerging intensely competitive world economy. He bequeathed to his successor a vibrant economy with the highest growth rate ever recorded in Indian history, inflation in single

94. *Organiser,* 18 June 1989, p.6.
95. *Resolutions Adopted by the National Executive Meeting* of the BJP in Bombay on September 23-24, 1989, pp.4-5.
96. *Election Manifesto of the BJP,* Lok Sabha Election 1989, p.18.
97. Text of Resolution Adopted at the 79th Plenary Session of the INC, Tirupati. *Op. Cit.,* p. 40.

digit, industrial growth in double-digits and exports booming at an annual average of 17% in dollar terms for four consecutive years. Throughout this period, India's creditworthiness in capital markets of the world remained high".[98] "In an egalitarian society, the aim of the economic policy has to be growth with social justice. Over the years, there has been a dynamic crystallization of economic policies of the INC. When the Congress Government came to power under the leadership of P.V.N. Rao in June 1991, the country was undergoing a severe balance of payments crisis. "Industrial growth rate turned negative from May 1991 onwards, while the inflation rate increased from 9.1% in 1989-90 to over 12% in 1990-91. Inspite of heavy taxation, the resources of the exchequer were in bad shape as characterized by mounting fiscal and budgetary deficit. The immediate task before the Government was to stabilize the balance of payments position. Bold steps were taken to store up country's foreign exchange reserve, as a result, the reserves rose from $1.1 billion in June 1991 to $5.6 billion in March 1992. A major programme of economic reforms and structural adjustment was put through to encourage a spirit of enterprise and competitiveness in the country, to achieve a reasonable measure of macroeconomic stability in terms of the government's fiscal deficit. The AICC fully supports these policies of economic reforms. The fiscal deficit was brought down from 8.4% of GDP in 1990-91 to 6.5% in 1991-92 and 5% in 1992-93. The reduction in the fiscal deficit has helped to reduce inflation rate, which came down from 17% in August 1991 to 6.8% in March 1993. The AICC endorses Government's commitment to bring in further reform of the capital market to ensure transparency in transactions and dealings and to strengthen investors protection"[99]. "From the 1980s, imbalances have developed in mutual trade, especially since 1985, largely because of India's difficulty in diversifying imports from the Soviet Union. For the first time since January 1991, all production in the Soviet Union has ceased to be regulated through central planning. According to available figures industrial production fell in January by 4.3% as compared to January 1990. This is considered the biggest drop in a year. Production of coal and oil has declined by 8.9% and output of rolled ferrous metals by 5%. Output of timber industry has fallen by 3% from 1990 and paper by 5%''.[100]

98. *Ibid.*, p. 41.

99. *AICC Meeting,* Surajkund, Faridabad, 27-28 May 1993, pp. 2-7.

100. *National Herald* (New Delhi), 2 July 1991.

"The economy is in shambles. The trade deficit has reached an all time high. The mounting foreign debt, the sky rocketing high prices, the galloping inflation and a rapidly growing unemployment have pushed India to the brink of an impending economic crisis".[101] "The BJP resolves to launch countrywide agitation against unabated price rise and other anti-people economic policies and measures of the Congress Government of the law and order situation. The party views this as a conscious and deliberate effort by some elements within the country, aided and abetted by foreign forces, to subvert the unity, integrity and stability of the country".[102] "At the regional level, India is less affected by the developments in the Slavic states. Because their foreign policies are dominated by the consideration to get more and more Western aid and technological know how. Thus, they are more inclined towards building a relationship with the developed world than with the developing societies. Though they are inclined towards the West, Indo-Russian relations find no impediments. India represents the best possible alternative to Russia".[103] "It is clearly manifested as India and Russia today 15 January finalized a new political treaty and signed memorandum of understanding on trade and supplies of defense and power generation equipment".[104] "Under agreed principles of bilateral trades signed in Moscow by the delegation, the value of Russian goods will be calculated on the basis of rupee-dollar rate. The invoicing will be in dollars but the payment will be in rupee during the period of transition".[105] "The Minister for Commerce, Mr Pranab Mukherjee and the Russian Minister of Foreign Economic Relations, Mr S. Yu Glazier, reached an agreement on repayment and counter-trade. The two sides also signed an agreement that with effect from January 1, 1993, the repayment of credit taken for procurement of machinery and equipment by Indian organizations, including payments against overdue liabilities, if any, will be made in Indian rupees directly into the special accounts of Russian organizations in commercial banks in India. The agreement relates to discussion between the two sides regarding the protocols on the deliveries of machinery and equipment from USSR to India on deferred payment terms, which were

101. *Political Pesolution adopted at the National Executive Meeting* of the BJP held on 26 May 1991, p. 17.

102. National Executive Meeting of the BJP, Thiruvanthapuram, *Op. Cit.*, p.10

103. Yadav, R.S., "Indo-US Relations, Problems and Prospects", *Monthly Public Opinion Survey*, XXX1X(2), November 1993, pp. 8-14.

104. *Hindustand Times* (New Delhi), 16 January 1992

105. *Financial Express* (New Delhi), 21 January 1992.

signed in 1981 and 1985".[106] "One of the major threats to any democratic system comes from economic inequality and under-development. Absence of a sound economic base weakens the very foundations of a society. Almost all developing countries in general and small countries in particular share the basic problem of restricted domestic markets, which makes them vulnerable to international economic influences. If all the small developing states come together on a common platform, they can go a long way in dealing with these problems. Developing countries, therefore, should work together to gain reciprocal trade benefits from the industrialized world".[107] "India cannot be and should not be, a carbon copy of any other country. India must liberalize, industrialize and modernize, but it must do so the Indian way. India has to become a light unto itself. We have to evolve our own model -- a model that will be integral, humanist, holistic, reconciling our own needs with the experience outside. Deriving inspiration from Yuga Purushas like Gandhiji and Deendayalji, we must proceed with economic progress encompassing the last man on the ladder of development".[108] "The BJP for liberalization with self-reliance, or to stress the swadeshi angle, self-reliance with liberalization. The BJP does not believe that the future of India can depend on the goodwill of foreigners, whether they are multinationals or foreign countries. It maintains that India must have a strong and self-reliant domestic economy, for without that we cannot have a competitive international economy. The countries which have acquired international clout today have been able to do so by carefully husbanding their home economy by keeping to lean budgets and maintaining a competitive edge in exports. The role of foreign capital in their economy has been very small. The BJP also favours this policy that the Multinational companies do not swamp our economy and are kept under control".[109] "The government's priorities are lop-sided. Instead of fostering more competition within the domestic market, the government is opening up the country to competition from foreign multinationals. It has been running after foreign capital instead of taking steps to improve the efficiency of Indian industry, including public

106. *Statesman* (New Delhi), 29 January 1993.

107. Vice-President S.D. Sharma inauguarated 11th conference from the members of small countries. Text of a Press Release issued in New Delhi in 21 September 1991. *Foreign Affairs Record*, XXXVII (9), September 1991, p. 170

108. *National Executive Meeting* of the BJP, Sarnath Varanasi, 13 March 1992, p.8

109. *Resolution adopted at the National Executive Meeting* of the BJP held in Bjopal, 22-24 August 1992, p.19.

sector units. It is also allowing indiscriminate imports, instead of reducing excise duties on home-made goods. The BJP warned the government against the looming economic disaster endangered by its anti-people economic policies. The party is determined to carry on the fight for the reversal of wrong government policies and the faulty implementation of some other policies".[110] "On trade front, on which the entire package is hinged, the failure is even more marked. The trade deficit in 1992-93 is expected to widen to $4.5 billion against $3.1 billion last year [1991-92]. The current account deficit, that is, including merchandise as well as other trade, will also increase to about $7 billion, only slightly less than the current account deficit in 1990-91. During the last two years, the foreign debt has swollen by about $10 billion a year just to keep going. The BJP has stressed the need for internal consolidation before proceeding with external liberalization, and this principle forms the basis of its Shadow or Alternative Budget. The cuts in customs duties in BJP's budget cover capital goods and raw materials only and do not extend to finished consumer goods. The government is doing exactly the opposite and will end up redisrupting Indian industry".[111] "The BJP calls for a thorough reexamination of the state of the economy in the light of our national interests, and for a national debate before it is too late, and before the increasingly panicky government plunges the nation into yet another massive crisis".[112] "In the last two decades we have embarked on a mindless increase in our foreign debt. This foreign debt will suck away whatever earnings we are getting from our exports. It will set in motion a further worsening of balance of payments leading to further devaluation of the currency. As foreign debt mounts, the cost of putting up project also shoots up. The country must rely on its own intrinsic strengths, not on loans from outsiders. The government must reduce the budget deficit. There should be a planned programme for debt reduction by not only cutting down drastically on borrowings -- by converting budget deficits into surpluses but also by liquidating existing debts. For the BJP, Swaraj and Swadeshi are indivisible. The main impulse for growth in India has to come from its own capital, its own very able entrepreneur, its own hardworking peasants and workers. That is why the BJP is opposed to unfettered entry of foreign

110. *National Executive Meeting* of the BJP, Bjubaneswar, 7 November 1992, pp. 7-8.

111. *Resolution adopted at the National Executive Meeting* of the BJP, Calcutta, 10 April 1993, p.8.

112. *Ibid.*, p. 10.

capital and multinationals, except in high-technology areas".[113] "The BJP believes that community participation and involvement is crucial to all programmes of development. Scientific monitoring is also essential for the success of our policy and programmes. Rapid economic development with full employment and reasonable stability in price-level... through `Swadeshi' and `Swavalambhan', judiciously combined with self-confidence".[114] "The BJP has warned the government several times to beware of the trap being laid by multi-nationals and their agents, to ensure countries like India into opening up their lucrative markets with grandiose talk about free trade".[115] "The primary purpose of any country's foreign policy is to promote its national interest -- to ensure its security, safeguard its sovereignty, contribute to its growth and prosperity, and generally enhance its stature, influence and role in the comity of nations. A country's foreign policy should also be able to serve the broader purpose or promoting peace, disarmament, and development and of establishing a stable, fair and equitable global economic order"[116]. "Though enthusiasm was lacking in the State Department for making mutually beneficial trade the centerpiece of relations, there has been a dramatic surge in American commercial interest in India. Since the reforms began in 1991, the US has emerged the largest single foreign investor in India, contributing more than 40% of total direct foreign investment approved. American exports in the first 11 months of 1993 increased by an impressive 38%, notwithstanding the overall stagnation in India's imports. India's exports registered a respectable 20% in the same period. The annual bilateral trade is approaching the level of $7,000 millions, with a surplus in favour of India"[117]. "Foreign Economic Relations Minister, Pyster Aven expressed his Government's will to normalize trade with India and assured the Indian ambassador that by the end of 1992, Russia would supply another two million tons of crude oil in addition to one million ton. Russia has also decided to supply another 3 million tons oil to India in 1993"[118]. "The Indian side also expressed

113. *Towards as Debt Free India,* BJP Publication, pp. 1-11.

114. *Humanistic Approach to Economic Development (A Swadeshi Alternative).* BJP Publication, 1992, pp. 52-53.

115. *Economic Resolution on Dunkel Draft,* National Executive Meeting of BJP held on 18-19 December 1993, New Delhi, p. 12.

116. Dubey, Muchkund, ''India's Foreign Policy in the Evolving Global Order'', *International Studies,* 30(2), April-June 1993, pp. 117-29.

117. *Hindu* (Madras), 3 February 1994.

118. *Patriot* (New Delhi), 4 October 1992.

interest in using Russian expertise and technical experts in Indian companies. The Confederation of Indian Industry [CII]in its discussions with the Committee for trade were able to list many consumer items or supply to Russia in keeping with the needs of the Russian market. Indian professional expertise and experience was offered to the Russian side. CII and the Russian Fund for Support of Economic Reforms agreed to finalize an agreement and joint programme for cooperation in these and other areas of mutual interest with a view to facilitating direct contact between Indian industries and their Russian counterparts in various regions"[119]. "History has emphasized that the greatest good can come from strengthening international cooperation. Interdependence becomes more and more real and compelling with every passing day. More than ever before, economic and ecological security have become matters that transcend rational boundaries"[120]. "India's firm commitment to integrate into global economy, outlined the economic liberalization process underway in India, the opportunities opened up for US high-tech companies in the Indian market and India's comparative advantages in the large number of highly skilled and qualified manpower. He explained the incentives being given by Govt. of India to attract foreign investment in electronics sector"[121]. "The BJP has already rejected the Dunkel Draft proposals relating to agriculture. It has asked the government to re-negotiate other parts of the Draft keeping our specific national interests in view. This is what most developing countries tried to do and many of them succeeded before they decided to approve the Draft. The Narasimha Rao government, on the other hand, succumbed completely to pressures from the US and EU and has accepted the Draft in toto and signed on the dotted line without any amendment or reservations. Under these circumstances, the BJP wholly disapprove of the Dunkel Draft and reject in toto"[122].

The General Agreement on Tariff and Trade [GATT] set up at the end of the Second World War, was originally part of an institutional arrangement to emerge from the Bretton Woods Conference, 1994. Free flow of trade being the best way for global economic prosperity,

119. *Foreign Affairs Record,* XXXiX(5), May 1993, p. 155.

120. Prime Minister's Address at 89th Inter Parliamentary Union Convference, New Delhi, 12 April 1993, *FAR,* p. 106.

121. P.R. Kumaramangalam's Speech at Silicon Companies (in Round Table Conference), *FAR,* p. 109.

122. *Text of Resolution adopted by the BJP,* National Executive Committee on 18 December 1993, New Delhi, p.12.

the US entered into bilateral agreements before the outbreak of Second World War with 29 countries to bring about mutual reduction of tariffs. Ultimately in 1947, the GATT was signed to be negotiated under the proposed International Trade Organization. Because GATT is a technical treaty, it aims at curbing unfair business practices, commodity agreements, largely areas of concern to Third World countries.

The key principle of the GATT is the reciprocity on which members negotiate tariffs. If one country lowers tariff on the export products of another country, the Most Favoured Nation [MFN] principle then require the same tariff on other GATT members. The NFN clause contains in Article 1 of Part I which entails equality of treatment to all contracting parties. The reason behind the MFN principle is to outlaw the discrimination and retaliation characterizing trade.

One hundred and nine countries are members today, majority are developing nations. A non-member nation can also be a part of the General Agreement if it is passed by a 2/3rd majority. Unlike the IMF and IBRD, in the GATT each member possesses one vote and nobody has a veto. Generally, decisions are taken through consensus formula instead of voting and any amendment of the rules needs two-third support of the present members on a particular day. The Dunkel Draft proposal seeks to widen the scope of the GATT and to create a Multilateral Trade Organization.

The main constituents of the proposed Agreement on TRIPs which will require modifications in the existing regime or patents in India are as follows:

[i] Scope

The basic requirement of the Dunkel proposal is that inventions in all branches of technology shall be patentable, whether products or processes, if they meet the three tests of being new, involving innovative steps and being capable of industrial applications. It has also been provided that micro-organisms will be patentable. In respect of plant varieties, there is a separate obligation to provide for protection by patents or by an effective sui-generis system, or by a combination of the two.

[ii] Duration

The duration of patents has been envisaged for a term of 20 years.

[iii] Compulsory Licensing

The rigorous conditions attached to compulsory licensing would rule out the grant of automatic licenses of right. Nor can compulsory license be given solely because the patented product is not being manufactured within the territory of the party granting the patent.

[iv] Burden of Proof

It has been provided that in regard to process patents, in certain circumstances, in an identical product when produced without the consent of the patent owner, shall in the absence of proof to the contrary, be deemed to have been obtained by the patented process[123].

CHANGES SOUGHT BY INDIA — ON TRIPs

"India is seeking —

[i] a textual change to make explicit the farmers' right to retain a part of his crop for his use as seen in subsequent crops;

[ii] a dilution of the provision/concerning patentability of micro-organisms;

[iii] additional flexibility in grant of compulsory licenses in case where it is feasible to work a patent in India, but it is not so worked;

[iv] elimination of the pipeline protection"[124].

INDIAN PROPOSALS

"Annex may be split into two parts- Part A and Part B. Part A would comprise of those products which are MFA items as defined in Article 12 of the MFA. Part B would comprise of non-MFA products.

Products in Part A only would be relevant for integration under Article 2 of the Agreements on Textiles and Clothing. However, products in both Parts A and B would be relevant for safeguard action under Article 7 of the Agreement.

Consequential changes to reflect these modifications in the Annex would have to be made in the relevant Articles of the Draft Agreement.

Raise the integration factors from the current figures of 16%, 17% and 18% in the three stages which would help in making

123. *The Uniguay Round of Multilateral Trade Negotiations-4, Backgound Paper*, AICC, June 1993, pp. 12-13.

124. *Ibid.*, pp. 18-19.

the integration process more uniformly spread. Raise substantially the growth factors for the quotas"[125].

"On the Trade-Related Aspects of Intellectual Property Rights [TRIPS], India's stand has been that sufficient flexibility must be provided in any multilateral agreement to take into account the developmental and technological needs and public policy objectives of developing countries. On Trade Related Investment Measures [TRIMS], India has taken the stand that investment measures are used to harmonize the interests of foreign investors with public policy objectives and priorities and the ability of Government to employ such measures should not be curbed. In respect of trade in services, India has made a conditional offer of market access in selected services sectors. In trade in Agriculture, it has been Government's stand that India will not make commitments in respect of governmental assistance to agriculture, which are not consistent with India's present stage of development. Government have clearly stated that India will not accept any changes in its national established. laws and policies which are not in the national interest"[126]. "The principled policy we adopted that agriculture should be brought within the discipline of GATT on three counts: Firstly, the developing countries have some advantage -- but they cannot enter into the market of the industrialized countries as they are highly subsidizing their agriculture. Secondly, it is a competition between the power of providing subsidies to the agricultural sector. We have demanded that we should have access to the markets of the developed countries and protection of our entry into the market of the developed countries in agricultural production. Thirdly, we would not have the right of market intervention -- procurement, stock and distribution. The tariff is reasonably high -- 100%, 150% and 300% so far as India is concerned. It is 100% in respect of primary products, 150% in respect of processed agricultural products and 300% in respect of edible oils. So, there is no question of accepting any obligation so far as India is concerned on import front"[127]. "The South as a whole has sufficient markets, technology and financial resources to make South-South cooperation and effective means for widening the development options for its economies. The South must build its

125. *Ibid.*, pp. 25-26.

126. *Foreign Affairs Record*, Vol. XXXVII(12), December 1991, India's Stand on Uniguary Round Issues, p. 234.

127. *Reply of Pranab Mukherjee to GATT Debate in Rajya Sabha*, AICC Publication, pp. 4-6.

capacity to sustain a fast pace of growth even if the Northern engine in low gear. South-South cooperation alone can give the developing countries a collective weight and countervailing power that cannot be ignored by the North"[128]. "Foreign companies are shifting their production to India because it means more profits. India joining GATT or not joining GATT will not make any difference to their cost calculus. Nowhere else not even in Communist China or the Soviet Union, the gap between what might have been achieved and what has actually been achieved is as great as India. This is not the fault of former colonial matters, or wicked Western capitalists, or the cruel hand of fate. It is largely India's own doing"[129]. "The agriculture was brought in the agenda because America was losing its share in agriculture. The European Community were also worried because they were large exporters of agricultural commodities. The buyers were some of the Third World nations, some of the African nations and some of the European nations. They thought that when exports from nations like India and China would grow, they would again lose their coveted sector of agriculture and so, agriculture should also be brought under the GATT. Then, about bio-technology... it will destroy the entire R&D of patents in bio-technology are granted, if the patent laws in India are changed to incorporate the patents of seeds and bio-technology. The investment rights have also been incorporated in the agenda. It is incorporated because of facilities to repatriate a large amount of profits. Even today, there are something like hundred foreign companies whose total equity capital is 141 lakhs. The sum total of the equity capitals of these companies would be Rs. 10 to 15 crores. Out of that they are repatriating profits to the tune of Rs.100 crores to their respective countries. If these companies will come with full protection for their investment and for repatriation of their profits, everything goes away, and the country will not only lose money, but will also lose control on compulsory licensing"[130]. "The BJP leaders favour the economic policy of the Congress Government though they have disagreement on certain aspect of the liberalization. It would invite foreign investors, especially in the field of high-technology and infrastructure. Besides, it lays emphasis on making the indigenous industry competitive and then slowly opening up the economy to

128. *Organiser*, 6 March 1994, pp. 10-11.

129. *Ibid.*, 20 March 1994, p. 15.

130. *Rajya Sabha Debates*, 6 December 1993, pp. 3-4.

international competition"[131]. "Considering the prevailing economic scenario, the Congress government lays emphasis on strong Indo-Russian trade ties. Engineering and consume goods, leather, tea, etc. have been identified as the thrust areas for strengthening bilateral trade between India and Russia. Moscow also emphasized the importance of direct contact between the private sectors of the two countries[132]. "India offered to take the lead in working out operational modalities to increase cooperation amongst countries of the Asia Pacific regions for sharing industrial information and technology. Kazakhstan, a CIS country with vast natural resources, offers vast prospects for setting up joint ventures with India to explore mineral resources and development of oil sector. Russia would purchase goods worth of Rs.3000 crores from India this year against the repayment of rouble credit by India. The 1993 agreement on debt repayment provided for export of Indian goods worth about Rs.3000 crore a year to Russia"[133].

But the BJP severely condemns the liberalisation and economic reforms being carried out by the Congress government. According to the party, "the deterioration of the country's political health in matched by steady worsening in the nation's economic condition. The last four years of so-called reforms have been terrible for the great majority of Indians. Prices have soared, poverty has increased, rupee has tumbled and national debt has climbed to unprecedented heights. In India no economic strategy can be deemed sound that aggravates the unemployment problem. BJP has always been in favour of a liberal economy but it must benefit the common man. No development model can succeed in India, certainly not a model imported from outside, unless it focusses on the needs and interests of the poorest of the poor land weakest of the weak[134].

"The current global economic scenario resulting from major discontinuities provides a level-playing field for industries in developing countries with respect to establish MNCs for the first time"[135], according to C.K. Prahlad. The rupee recorded an all time low of Rs.38.30 against US dollar in February 1996. "Upto the end of

131. *BJP Meets Indian Industry*, BJP Publication, 26-27 April 1993, New Delhi, pp. 3-17.

132. *Statesman* (New Delhi), 3 October 1995.

133. *Times of India* (New Delhi), 17 October 1995.

134. Presidential Address by L.K. Advani, BJP Plenary Session, 10-12 November 1995, Bombay, pp. 16-19.

135. *The Hindu* (Delhi), 6 February 1996.

December 1995, growth in exports have risen by 24.17% in US dollar terms. During the same period, imports have also risen by 29.27% and the trade deficit for December is only 199.82 million dollar as against 516.35 million dollar in November, 1995. Dr C. Rangarajan, RBI Governor, said, taking into account this trends on the capital account, the deficit on the current account is sustainable and manageable"[136]. Despite all challenges and problems created by reactionary forces, foreign investment in India was encouraged, as a result, "Allied Signal INC of the US plans to set up a facility in India for the manufacture amorphous metals which is used in amorphous metal distribution transformers [AMDTs]"[137]. "As part of its plan to link up with regional trading blocs in Asia, the European Union [EU] proposes to enter into a Memorandum of Understanding [MoU] with the SAARC. EU considers South Asia as an area of opportunity and it has a stake in the economic integration between India and Pakistan"[138]. The Indian Government expects "foreign direct investment [FDI] in India to total about 2 billion dollars in the financial year 1995-96"[139].

The real Soviet investment in India started in 1987. Table 6 gives a clear picture of it. We can assess from the table that the Soviet investment stood at an average of 1.34% in the eighties, because only in 1989 the Soviet investment raised to a significant level, even more than the USA (19.63%). However, the American percentage share dominated economic scene of India. Although figures fluctuated from one year to the next, it is clear that US investment percentage share in the eighties was remarkable, at an average of 25.32%. It is of no doubt that India received a low amount of grants and credits from the US as compared to Pakistan and Bangladesh. Table 10 gives a glimpse of how Pakistan, Bangladesh occupied importance in US interests that other South Asian countries.

India's trade relations with the Super Powers substantially differed throughout the eighties, because India's foreign trade with these two countries was determined by different reasons. In case of imports, the 80s witnessed a major proportion of India's imports flowing from the USA vis-a-vis those from the USSR. Inspite of the protectionist tendency of the United States, India's imports from the US turned out to be $ 15494.6 million in nine years (1980-1988) and export $

136. *Ibid.*

137. *Hindu* (New Delhi), 1 March 1996.

138. *Times of India* (New Delhi), 8 March 1996.

139. *Times of India* (New Delhi), 15 March 1996.

19317.7 million (Table 9) as compared to the USSR's imports and exports of Rs. 151875.4 million and Rs.Rs. 176240 million respectively. (Table 1 gives a clear vision of India's trade relations with the USSR). From these tables we have seen that India's exports has been very low in the early eighties, the reason being that of foreign exchange shortage and payment difficulties stood as a major hindrance in the growth of India's exports to both the Super Powers.

To sum up, the economic link between the Super Powers and India has been subjected to variegate explanations. The Americans considered India pro-soviet and anti-America, the Indian government time and again indicated that the economic and commercial ties were strong and friendly. We can state that there were much discrepencies and contradictions excepting rare instances of convergencies in their bilateral relations. But to categorise India pro-soviet would be a total misinterpretation of Indo-Soviet friendship. It is a fact that Moscow had helped India in trouble and stood with India on many occasions, even in international fora and both countries avoided any type of action that would threaten the basis of their friendship. But it would be incorrect to say that they had no stresses and strains in their history. In reality, whenever there was any difference, it was tactfully and diplomatically avoided. So both India and the USSR realised the mutual need of each and other, in contrast to the US. The Indo-American relations seemed to be marked by dismatched observations and understanding that affected their affable relations. Certainly they had lack of mutual need of each other.

TABLE I

INDIA'S TRADE BALANCE WITH USSR
(in Rs. Million)

Year	Exports to USSR	Imports from USSR	India's Balance of Trade
1980-81	10137.1	8295.4	+1841.7
1982	17.000	15,510	+1490
1983	13.590	16,370	-2780
1984	15,020	18,120	-3100
1985	21,980	19,390	+2990
1986	21,800	15,000	+6800
1987	21,100	20,900	+200
1988	24,750	24,800	-50
1989	41,000	29,000	+12000
TOTAL	176,240	151,875.4	

Source: DGCI & S., Calcutta.

TABLE II

VOLUME OF SOVIET TRADE WITH INDIA
(in million roubles)

Year	Soviet Import	Soviet Export	Total Trade Turnover	Soviet's Balance of Trade	% of Soviet Trade
1980	878.6	861.2	1739.8	-17.6	1.8
1981	1333.9	1064.1	2397.9	-269.7	2.2
1982	1473.8	1040.2	2514.0	-433.6	2.1
1983	1051.0	1271.6	2322.6	+220.6	1.8
1984	1272.0	1537.5	2809.5	+265.5	2.0
1985	1509.0	1574.9	3084.4	+65.4	2.2
1986	1233.6	957.7	2191.2	-275.8	1.7
1987	1072.6	1105.4	2178.0	+32.8	1.7
1988	1123.3	1128.7	2252.0	+5.4	1.7
1989	1770.6	1147.0	2917.6	+623.6	2.1
1990	1603.8	1176.3	2780.1	+427.5	1.2
1991	1458.3	1239.2	2697.5	+219.1	1.4
1992	1261.5	956.8	2218.3	+304.7	1.6
1993	1342.7	1042.1	2384.8	+300.6	1.9
1994	1379.0	1023.4	2402.4	+355.6	1.5
1995	1385.4	1136.7	2522.1	+248.7	1.7

SOURCE: O.E.A., Foreign Trade Statistics, various issues

TABLE III

AUTHORISATION OF EXTERNAL ASSISTANCE TO INDIA (Rs. crore)

USA	1980-81	1982-83	1983-84	1984-85	1985-86	1986-87	1987-88	1988-89	1989-90 (April-Sept.)
Loans	135.0	67.4	77.0	93.9	47.0	57.9	25.4	....	....
Grants	26.8	23.0	39.4	24.0	19.5	37.7	30.3	34.5	65.6

USA	1990-91	1991-92	1992-93	1993-94	1994-95
Loans	108.3	124.6	113.3	146.2	163.4
Grants	115.1	136.2	134.8	151.6	153.7

Sources : *Economic Survey*, various issues.

TABLE IV

INDO-AMERICAN TRADE (US$ MILLION)

Year	US Exports to India	US Imports from India	Total Trade Turnover	Merchandise Trade Balance
1980	1689.4	1097.6	2787.0	+591.8
1981	1747.4	1202.1	2949.6	+545.4
1982	1598.5	1403.8	3002.3	+194.7
1983	1827.8	2191.4	4019.2	-363.6
1984	1569.6	2551.5	4121.1	-981.9
1985	1641.9	2478.3	4120.2	-653.0
1986	1536.0	2464.6	4000.6	-747.0
1987	1463.7	2761.5	4225.2	-1069.4
1988	2497.9	3167.0	5664.9	-468.8
1989	2463.3	3550.9	6014.2	-851.1
1990	2486.0	3191.0	5667.0	-705.0
1991	2518.9	3451.4	5970.3	-932.5
1992	2637.2	3267.7	5904.9	630.5
1993	2681.5	3658.3	6339.8	976.8
1994	2729.1	3519.9	6249.0	790.8
1995	2978.3	3724.2	6702.5	-745.9

SOURCE : US Bureau of Census, Highlights of U.S. Export and Import Trade, Monthly, various issues.

TABLE V

INDO-USA COLLABORATION CASES

Year	Total Collaboration in India: All Countries	Total collaboration with the USA	Percentage share	Technical -cum- Financial	Technical
1980	526	125	23.76	19	106
1981	389	85	21.85	15	70
1982	590	110	18.64	24	86
1983	673	135	20.05	32	103
1984	752	147	19.54	36	111
1985	1024	197	19.23	66	131
1986	957	189	19.74	71	118
1987	853	196	22.97	57	139
1988	926	191	20.62	120	71
1989	605	127	20.99	93	34
1990	666	133	19.96	91	42
1991	951	177	18.61	52	125
1992	1520	332	21.84	155	177
1993	1476	298	20.19	153	145
1994	1648	317	19.24	214	103
1995	1826	401	21.97	276	125

SOURCE: Indian Investment Centre.

TABLE VI

US-USSR INVESTMENT IN INDIA (Rs. MILLION)

Year	Total foreign Investment: All Countries	US investment	Share	USSR Investment	Share
1980	89.24	21.69	24.30	0.00	00
1981	108.71	22.48	20.68	0.00	00
1982	628.06	50.33	08.01	0.00	00
1983	618.73	138.92	22.45	0.00	00
1984	1130.02	89.50	08.00	0.00	00
1985	1260.66	399.25	31.71	0.00	00
1986	1069.52	293.70	27.46	0.00	00
1987	1077.06	295.15	7.40	2.96	0.27
1988	2397.57	971.37	40.51	4.40	0.18
1989	3166.65	621.65	19.63	95.80	3.02
1990	1283.21	344.82	26.87	71.08	5.53
1991	5,166,94	1,748.92	33.85	86.19	1.67
1992	38,015.42	11,382.60	29.94	115.84	0.30
1993	88,617.97	34,729.78	39.19	19.48	0.02
1994	11,751.07	5,316.28	45.24	1,009.95	8.59
1995	12,624.09	6,428.46	50.92	1,248.04	9.89

SOURCE: Indian Investment Centre

TABLE VII

US-ECONOMIC ASSISTANCE IN INDIA
(US $ Million)

Fiscal Year	USA'S Amount Committed
1980	246.4
1981	299.5
1982	251.8
1983	219.8
1984	215.3
1985	179.8
1986	178.2
1987	126.9
1988	123.9
1989	126.2
1990	198.9
1991	202.5
1992	241.9
1993	231.3
1994	254.4
1995	264.2

SOURCE: USAID : New Delhi

TABLE VIII

INDO-SOVIET FOREIGN COLLABORATION

Year	Total Collaboration All Countries	Total Collaboration with USSR	Technical	Financial -cum- Technical	Percentage Share
1981	389	2	2	0	0.51
1982	590	2	2	0	0.33
1983	673	4	4	0	0.59
1984	752	1	1	0	0.13
1985	1024	4	4	0	0.39
1986	957	5	5	0	0.52
1987	853	6	4	2	0.70
1988	926	7	5	2	0.75
1989	605	9	5	4	1.48
1990	666	8	3	5	1.20
1991	951	12	6	6	1.26
1992	1520	27	5	22	1.78
1993	1476	9	2	7	0.61
1994	1503	12	3	9	0.79
1995	379	3	0	3	0.79

SOURCE: Indian Investment Centre

TABLE IX

INDO-AMERICAN TRADE (In US $ Million)

Year	India's Exports	India's Exports	Two Way Trade	Trade
1980	1097.6	1678.3	2775.9	-580.7
1981	1202.1	1734.4	2936.5	-532.3
1982	1403.8	1581.7	2985.5	-177.9
1983	2191.4	1812.6	4004.0	+378.8
1984 +1003.3	2551.4	1548.1	4099.5	
1985	2478.3	1641.9	4120.2	+836.4
1986	2464.6	1536.0	4006.6	+928.6
1987 +1297.8	2761.5	1463.7	4225.2	
1988	3167.0	2497.9	5664.9	+669.1
1989-90	3728.6	3552.9	7281.5	+175.7
1990-91	3996.3	4370.5	8366.9	-374.4
1991-92 +1903.7	6001.4	4097.7	10099.1	
1992-93	6421.7	5928.4	12350.1	+493.3
1994 (March)	438.1	521.9	959.8	+83.6

SOURCE: Us Department of Commerce, various issues.

TABLE X

US GOVERNMENT FOREIGN GRANTS AND CREDITS BY TYPE AND COUNTRY

(in $ Million)

Country	1980	1981	1982	1983	1984	1985	1986	1987	1988	1989	1990
India	168	215	89	74	84	42	36	64	138	69	-31
Pakistan	66	94	167	348	415	481	347	235	389	-388	522
Srilanka	55	32	49	63	84	90	65	40	43	43	72
Nepal	17	19	22	28	24	26	20	22	19	15	19
Afghanistan	4	-5	-1	-2	-4	-21	-3	29	30	76	57
Bangladesh	175	129	202	219	265	175	178	150	170	138	172

Sources : Statistical Abstracts of the United States, various issues.

TABLE XI

DISTRIBUTION OF INDIA'S FOREIGN TRADE WITH USSR AND USA COMPARED (In Rs. Crores)

Year	**Import (USSR)**	**Export (USSR)**	**Import (USA)**	**Export (USA)**
1979-80	822.3	638.1	926.1	805.7
1980-81	1013.7	1226.3	1618.6	743.3
1981-82	1136.9	1659.9	1419.7	919.6
1982-83	1413.2	1669.8	1426.5	928.3
1983-84	1645.6	1305.9	1841.9	1395.6
1984-85	1788.1	1879.6	1700.6	1765.8
1985-86	1677.5	2005.7	2063.7	1973.8
1986-87	1014.8	1867.2	1961.1	2331.7
1987-88	1278.9	1971.5	2025.0	2907.6
1988-89	1257.8	2609.4	3197.2	3735.9
TOTAL	13048.8	16833.4	181800.4	17507.3

SOURCE: Statistical Pocket Book of India and Statistical of India, various Issues.

CHAPTER VI

Conclusion

The Bharatiya Janata Party was born under fast changing circumstances when the Janata government could not fulfill its full term and the Congress Party was emanating with its powerful forces. The BJP was coming out with a programmes to provide stable government and strong alternative to the Congress Party. The BJP spotlighted the historic role of Indian politicians and thinkers and was determined to fulfill the aspirations of freedom fighters for a developed and independent India, free from the clutches of imperialist forces. The Party marked out Gandhian Socialism and intended to implement those set of norms and values which would helpful for social upliftment and in eradicating poverty and exploitation. The BJP was highly distasteful to the Congress way of functioning but showed its readiness to support the Congress Party in case it entertains the policies which are designed to help poor masses. It also extended its willingness to cooperate with other parties in arresting authoritarianism and anti-national programmes of the ruling party. Reviewing the many - folded crises in various walks of life, the BJP cherished consensual policies and programmes on major issues, national and international. It held the view that conflict and consensus are two inseparable parts of democracy and any kind of action contrary to it would spoil the sustenance of democratic ideas.

The Bharatiya Janata Party believed that people have no credibility in the opposition political parties. It is due to their inability to provide a stable alternative to the Congress Party. So the BJP urged all the opposition political parties to work in combination to prove their integrity. Second, the opposition political parties are not mass based political parties. In this case also the BJP encouraged all the opposition political parties to work at the grassroot level fighting for the people's cause. They can serve the cause of healthy democracy by concentrating their attention on people's need and working achieve it instead of fighting to capture power.

The Bharatiya Janata Party (BJP) was founded in 1980 and fought the general election in the same year. It was not quite impressive in the first election result as it secured only four seats. The party was founded to provide an effective opposition in India. In the whole period of Seventh Lok Sabha the BJP could wield much influence inside and outside the parliament. In the Eighth General Election, though the party could not capture much seats, however, it secured massive popular support. No doubt, sometimes its pronouncements seem to be subjected to the interests of the party and not based on larger and general interests. However, the entire thinking of the party did not contradict the interests of the nation as a whole. So our study makes an attempt to examine some aspects of the foreign policy of India as well as the response of the BJP. This attempt has involved a brief study of some important issues which dominated the foreign policy of India. We have attempted to delineate the role of BJP in moulding and influencing the foreign policy of India. On the whole, our study supposes that the role played by the opposition has considerable impact on India's Foreign Policy. As national politics the BJP has different stand so also in foreign policy. The party considers that by making India powerful in defence, in nuclear, and economic field, the nation can preserve and protect its unity and integrity. On the issues like nuclear and West Asian conflict (Arab-Israel), it's views are contrast to the views of the Indian government.

The cardinal principles of India's foreign policy is based on anti-racialism, anti-colonialism and anti-imperialism which is the denouement of past experience of Indian leaders. Against this background even after independence the Indian policy makers advanced the championed principles of India. The most mirthless situation in the global strategic environment was the stockpiling of nuclear and anti-human weapons in Third World countries. Such an unencumbered race of arms in the early fifties not only splotched the image of newly establish United Nations but also contaminated immaculate air of the whole world and blotted the Paris Peace Conference. The enormous loss of money after the unchecked arms race could have been used for the process of industrialisation of the industrialised countries, even if not after the economically backward states. So the antagonistic attitude of the Western imperialist countries in their official aid aggravated the worsened economic condition of Third World countries. In case of India, low per capita income, population explosion, stagnant industrial development made her hospitable to the capitalist countries. But it is not that India picked the policy of non-alignment to get more aid from the affluent West but the story has many reasons. Though such a policy brought her external economic assistance, both from USA and USSR, yet her volition of self-reliance and to avoid complete military alignment there was only one option of being non-aligned. So for a country like India with developing economy, it was desirable to avoid any conflict to keep herself out of military blocs and to pursue the policy of non-alignment further. Beyond doubt, India's policy of non-alignment acquires large scale support from Third World countries. Subsequently, many countries have joined in the non-aligned movement raising its membership from 29 in Bandung Conference to 108 in the Jakarta Summit.

Despite minor differences among the member states, by and large, they acted in unanimity whenever any major issue cropped up. They wanted peace and stability in their region to consolidate their newly independent states. After a long subjugation of the colonial powers, the non-aligned countries wished to remain free from the ongoing debate on armaments. They had to tackle the problems of poverty, hunger and disease and therefore avoided the antagonisms between the East and the West. Keeping away from the ideological groups they looked after their problems, and strived to strengthen their economy and minimised the involvement with the Super Powers. In such a totality, non-alignment gained momentum for the promotion of peace.

The Soviet view bolstered up the non-aligned movement being pursued by the Third World. The Soviet leaders highly valued the contributions of the movement in urging the developing countries to desist from the imperialist blackmail. It is, of course, true that the Soviet Union had interests behind such a support to the NAM. It is clear that the USSR was opposed to Western domination and their policies to bring Third World countries under their grip. So the USSR and the US had ideological differences on many international issues. But it would be illogical if we see the Soviet stand on this angle alone. The Soviet Union was a Socialist state and it wanted that the developing countries of the world should pursue their independent course of action. The fact is proved on the ground that the USSR provided economic, scientific and technological aid to the developing countries; e.g., India, but not like the West where the Western aid had always strings attached to aid. Besides, the Soviet aid was aimed at development of the developing economy and certainly it did not compel India to toe the Soviet line. Therefore, there was strong Indo-Soviet ties with least divergenes whereas the Indo-American bilateral ties was suspicious and was characterised as multicolored dissonant. The American policy makers did not support the non-aligned policy of India. On different occasions they were captious about India's links with the Soviet Union. They preconceived that India's close relations with the Soviet Union corroded the non-aligned status of India. Whatever may be the statement of the Western press, no body will disagree with it that the Indo-Soviet friendship was based on different grounds, it was a cooperation that founded on mutuality of interests. While the US adopted its old policies, the Soviet Union had never attempted to intervene in the foreign policy choices of India. So by cementing the bond of Indo-Soviet friendship, India not only availed many advantages but also kept intact her non-aligned status.

Taking Mrs. Gandhi's tenure as a whole, she started with bridging India's relation with the US, but in the process the Indo-American relations clashed with each other. The Indian government upheld its policy of non-alignment and guarded its independence in all international fora without being dictated by Super Powers directions. At the same time, the Indira government did not allow India's relations with USA or with USSR go unsymmetrical. So the guiding factor of the foreign policy of India was to maximise benefits, a matched game of politics but without getting bolted in their policies. So Nehru's doctrine of asserting India's place under the sun and to uphold non-alignment, was obviously India's chosen path in the eighties also. Thus it would be apt to state that India's foreign policy throughout the eighties was to construct a benign relations with the West and to retain the good will of the USSR. Of course, the critics view it in a different angle. This policy of winning friendship of both the Super Powers was to invite hostility with them. Besides it was tacked that with this stand of the government the policy of non-alignment would loose its strength. But in unhealthy situation of troubles on many fronts, adversaries all around, predominance of hostile elements inside and outside the country, India's option of reaping warm and benevolent relations with the great powers was the need of the hour.

In a changed international environment the role of the NAM was more challenging. The NAM which had so far been characterised as policy of the weak by the Western press, soon started gaining confidence and popularity. The emergence of detente in the eighties did not relinquish non-aligned movement. The critics argue that since there is end in cold war and bloc confrontation, there is no relevance of the movement. But it is foolish and illogical to give such a statement ignoring other factors and issues that the NAM had been fighting for. May be NAM was struggling for an end to colonialism, imperialism and racialism, but the end in racialism or colonialism does not make it redundant. The most challenging task before the NAM was economic. Third World countries were still groaning under poverty, illiteracy and multi-faceted socio-economic problems. The international financial institution were not favourable to the developing countries. There was existence of rigid tariff system unfavourable to the Third World Though it seemed that East-West division has ended, in true sense the division still existed. Thus the problems had multiplied and manifolded. It is much more challenging than before. The world is at crossroads, tensions are mounting. Inspite of the agreement between the two Super Powers to destroy their nuclear weapons, no concrete result has come out of it.

New states are getting their independence and are running with economic subjugation. India's role in this situation is widely recongnised. It should work relentlessly and move vigorously to achieve its objectives; a peaceful world free from tensions, a just and equitable economic order, and end of colonialism. The Indian government considered non-alignment as an elementary instrument to bring peace in the world. So it urges the South Asian nations to keep a vigilant eye on the imperialist moves whose aim is to distract them from that direction. The government of India also asked the neighbouring countries to give a better shape to the movement so that the imperialist force would not be able to break the NAM. In this direction an effective role of the non-aligned countries in the international fora is required, much more than before. The Indian stand is that keeping aloof from the imperialist camp and tightening the bond with the Socialist bloc, the non-aligned states could play effective role and they could preserve the main contents of the non-aligned movement. Here it is surprising to note the contradictory choices of the Indian government. While on the one hand it asks to avoid Western aid and the industrialised countries blackmail, on the other hand it does not find any fault in getting aligned with the Soviet Union. It remains as a mute question whether India should avoid USA alone, why not both the Super Power? The US had also offered invaluable aid when India was in need of it, as for example, aid of food-grains in the days of famine. So why did India always seek to avoid West not the Socialist Russia?

Arms aid by the Super Powers to India and her neighbours has created tension in the region. Due to Super Powers strategies to win their respective friends with their vitriolic military help, the years of relative peace turned out into frantic conflicts. The BJP welcomed all peace initiatives initiated by the USSR but was critical of her suspicious role of offering peace plans and not allowing itself to desist from arms race. If the hypocrisy implicit in stockpiling the war heads, there could be no hope of peace in the world. The key to regional security and stability in South Asia subjects to the warm relations between India and Pakistan. Though the conflicts are deep-rooted both states should endeavor to wipe out the shade of wide differences for larger interest. So what was urgently required was a reconciliation between India and Pakistan. As we have observed, there was lack of sufficient initiatives by both India and Pakistan that marred their bilateral relations. The critics give different opinions regarding deteriorated Indo-Pakistan relations. They say that the climate of mistrust and suspicion aggravated as a result of irreconcilable stands adopted by both countries, some day or other. Though both of them realised that only widespread people-to-people contact could ease the tension, their efforts failed once and again. All agreements, all peaceful drives and doctrines, be it Shimla or bilateral talks other than Shimla, turned out to be futile and the prospects of settlements of the basic problems remained as before. The opposition political parties blamed the Indian government for its failure of promoting a climate of good neighbourliness. But we should not forget Pakistan's actions in letting down all peace initiatives proposed by India and went on getting military aid from USA. So the chaotic situation that prevailed in the sub-continent alone encouraged the hostile forces to exploit not only India but also Pakistan.

The 'real causes' for their divergences were manifold. First, it was because Pakistan's subversive activities in Jammu and Kashmir and Punjab. Second, the role of the US to instigate local hostile forces to create terror in the country and above all, the third factor was the 'unwillingness of the rulers' of both countries to restore cordiality in their mutual dealings. The BJP holds the view that the national security is a primary responsibility of a state. Security of a nation is an integrated whole : an amalgam of the internal, the economic, the social, the political, the military and the diplomatic. The Indian diplomacy can assist in the protection of our national interest only if it is guided by a purposeful foreign policy. Therefore, the BJP urges the government to find a solution in the strategically sensitive areas.

With the solution of the Punjab problem and the US direction to solve the Jammu and Kashmir problem in the spirit of Shimla Declaration, one may be hopeful of solution to the Indo-Pakistani confrontation. It cannot be denied that friendly relations with the neighbouring countries are deemed of utmost importance and considered as the most effective antidote to the imperialist threats and to overcome sharpened confrontation among themselves. So the 'easiest solution to the problem of the sub-continent' is that the Government of India should stick to its policy of peace and non-alignment and should urge the Pakistani government to abjure its policy of military preparedness and creating hostility in the Indian border. Friendship with the neighbouring countries is of utmost importance to the BJP. The security threat can be wiped out by strengthening South Asian Association for Regional Cooperation (SAARC) and by strengthening relations among the South-Asian countries. The BJP evangelised for an all-embracing settlement of all outstanding matters with Pakistan.

There is little doubt about Moscow concern with the developments in India. Time and again it has shared its opinion with India about Anglo-Pakistani policies to harm Indian interest. Though Rajiv Gandhi assured the Soviet Union to continue the policies of his predecessors, slightest inclination toward US for technology and scientific knowledge created suspicion in the Soviet quarter. The inclination to the West was short-lived and the Indo-Soviet bilateral relations improved well. The Indo-American trade relation could not succeed well due to USA's uncompromising attitude towards India. As a result, the Indo-Soviet trade expanded towards the end of the eighties. India also received arms assistance from the Soviet Union. The Soviet Union's principal concern in South Asia had been to prevent the region from coming under the grip of the US. It was the Chinese factor also which encouraged the Soviet Union to come closer to India. The Chinese government aided Pakistan militarily and supported Pakistani nuclear programme. Towards the end of the eighties the international scenario changed altogether. Democracy revived in Pakistan. The newly elected Prime Minister Benazir Bhutto was more interested to develop cordial relations with India. It was felt that there is no end in the arms race and both India and Pakistan would not be benefited from attacking each other. They had numerous problems to tackle; economic, social and political. It was also realised that by spending their money after arms they will not be able to check their economic depressions. Besides, the world economy was also regressing. The Indian counter part also equally responded the Pakistani desire. The fact is that, with the end of cold war they were not eager to aggravate their relations. On the other hand, there was tremendous improvement in Sino-Indian relations. Collaborations on science, technology and other related fields between India and China was impulsive. Notably, the improvements in Sino-Soviet relations also helped to ease tension in South Asia. So the three nations India, China and USSR came closer to each other. These was high hope among the people that the cold war in South Asia will not last long.

The United States was skeptical about Soviet-Indian relations. The US suspected that if India received arms from the US it would leak the secrets of American arms to the Soviet Union which was its cold war rival. If at all it happens, it would hamper United States strategic concerns in South-Asia. So the US insisted on the General Security Military Information Agreement (GESOMIA) which the Indian government considered inimical to its interests. Thus they had different perspectives on arms agreements. The United States would have been a comfortable partner, had India sacrificed her Soviet links. But the Indian government cannot do it (if USA persist India on the same line today) even after the breakdown of Soviet Union. The reason is simple, on the ground that in the past whenever India showed her need to buy American arms there were always demurral from the American side. So one cannot be sure, if India goes to Washington instead of Moscow (now after the breakdown of USSR) the former may put more stringent terms as there is no USSR to fulfill Indian needs, It may also affect India's self-reliance in defence production like the nuclear fuel supply to Tarapore.

There is no longer Soviet threat to America's actions. It is trying to impose its interests and desire over all nations. Here it may be noted that in the nineties also the US is more concerned about Pakistan than China or Japan. USA has long-term interest in West Asia, economically and politically. So to get access to Saudi Arabia or Iraq or elsewhere in West Asia, Pakistan will alone give her needful leverage. So Washington does not want to please New Delhi at the cost of Islamabad. In case of arms supply to India, supposing that USA would not bring any hurdle in terms of contract or supply, it is certain that Pakistan will go out of Washington's hands as Pakistan can not see an armed India. So unless a broad political understanding comes into existence among the these nations, any sort of arms aid from the US in the nineties seems to be bleak.

In years to come, the casque of American policy will remain anti-communist and anti-nonalignment. The US would not see eye to eye with Moscow even if it is not a communist regime. Moreover, it will definitely keep on opposing nonaligned policy of India. So despite the desire of the Indian government in the nineties to build a more subtle relation with United States, it is hardly expected to give result in concrete terms. Therefore, what is required now is that the Government of India should not try to appease either USA or the imperialist forces of the West, by giving up its non aligned status. Only desirable step is that differences and discord that exists today should pass out of sight. The openness in our dealings should not dissipate at any cost. We must recongnise the deep roots we have with the erstwhile Soviet Union and should try to arrange it in a new form with all the countries those were part of Soviet Union once upon a time. Understanding the reasons for embroilment the government should adopt a more pliable, pragmatic and meritorious policy to build her image in the world. These is-no permanent foe in the international relations and a mature relationship around the world would facilitate for an efficacious role of India in the international forums.

In the eighties and now also, Indo-American relations have been a cluster of misunderstandings, allegations and counter-allegations, Though there are many reasons behind it, the nuclear issue is also one among them. The motive of the United States and its 'vital interests' in the South Asian region causes to reverse the process of detente. Thus, India's relation with the US is marked more of strain than cordiality. We have also seen that Indo-American divergences also causes discrepancy between India and Pakistan on nuclear issue. Both sides attack each other's nuclear programme. Even if both sides reiterates their positions and policies with candor time and again, differences on vital issues remain unresolved.

Regarding India's nuclear policy, there is no need of elaboration. India has always stood for peaceful use of nuclear energy. The hostile elements, no doubt, sketch the nuclear programmes non-conducive to create regional stability. But we cannot accept this view as India has never shown any type of aggression or violation of contracts that it is obliged to do. If there is any sort of discord between India and Pakistan and India and USA, it is due to the lack of mutuality of interests. If Pakistan goes for an atom bomb being assisted by one Super Power, there is no reason why India will not go for nuclear taking the help of other powers. Security of a nation depends not only how it is modernising its army or navy or how it is superior to other powers, but the attitude of the neighbours. 'When my neighbour is attacking me with a knife, it is folly on my part if I do not go for a knife and I shall alone be responsible for my destruction.'

In such a totality the critics argue that India should go nuclear. But it is not a question whether India should go nuclear or not. Because it will not bring tangible results. The question is how to save the region? A Patriotic citizen definitely seeks to see nation's glory, but should it be by acquiring biological and chemical weapons? And also compelling its neighbours to go on that line? When the world economy is worsening, world financial institutions are deficit of funds, should not we think in terms of global benefit? Should not we bother about the existence of our fellow-beings in our own country by providing economic benefits, eliminating poverty and illiteracy with the fund that we are spending on acquiring arms? While the world is moving towards nuclear disarmament, thanks to the peace initiatives of Gorbachev and largely by Soviet Union it would be insanity if we keep on arming ourselves. It is not a question whether disarmament efforts will succeed or fail. Even if it fails we should put every effort in it. Why should the developing countries like India and Pakistan will waste their resources in purchasing chemical weapons and next day going to the big powers for a loan? Disarmament process is in progress. The two Super Powers have agreed not to proliferate nuclear weapons to the non-possessing states. So there should be several talks between India and Pakistan to defer their nuclear programme. In this perspective, the role of non aligned movement as well as SAARC are more desirable. Though last non aligned summit held in Jakarta noted with concern about the developments in this regard, no concrete result came out. It is due to the irreconcilable stands taken by both India and Pakistan. It appears that the role of the great powers are also quite challenging in this issue. They should take up the 'regional issues' with consensual approach. It must be remembered that reduction of the nuclear arms should begin from the area where it is concentrated, not to speak of South Asia alone. The treaty to eliminate nuclear arms should bind all nations who are capable or incapable of producing nuclear weapons. A global nuclear weapons verification system can only ensure a peaceful and tension free world, or else mutual extermination is not far away. It should be borne in mind that unless we are able to usher in a non-violent, tension free world we cannot give a wide berth to certain military capability to guard our sovereignty and territorial integrity from Janus-faced military aggression.

The militarisation of Indian Ocean had raised eyebrows among the people of the sub-continent. The problem remained as a complex one and no settlement could make its way, because the talks held at the official level could not adopt a mutually accepted formula. Though there was 'climate for negotiations' to ease tension, the gesture of goodwill rejected by either of them. So the situation had developed to such a complexity that India and other littoral states were engulfed by the Super Powers confrontation. The critics viewed the situation altogether differently. To one section of the commentators the Indian Ocean militarization process has been so aggressive due to regional conflict, mainly the conflict between India and Pakistan. As the US took the Pakistani side, the USSR supported India in that case also. The Indo-Pakistani confron- tation was aggravating day by day and it seemed sometimes that there was no solution to the problem. When Pakistan was envious of being powerful in South Asia, it invited USA to intrude into their regional conflict. Gradually, USA strengthened its position in the Indian Ocean. Soviet Union supported India's call for a peace zone in the area in all international forums.

Another section of the critics view that the militarisation of the Indian Ocean is unconnected to the regional conflicts. It is rather the superpower rivalry to attack and counter-attack, to balance each other and the desire of thwarting the ambition of the other stimulated the intrusion of sophisticated weapons into the Ocean. They argue that India has also economic interest in the Indian Ocean. Though the Indian government has shown enough avidity in making the Indian Ocean a zone of peace, it should not allow the region to be turned into a superpowers' playground. For this, India should increase her naval capability and naval strength to meet the threat of the external powers.

It is true that instability of the region has been greatly contributed by the external powers' intervention. But it would be impalpable to state that India should fall into the line of the Super Powers. If India goes on increasing her naval strength, first, it will put heavy burden on her economy. A developing country like India cannot sacrifice her economy just to counter external powers. Moreover, it cannot acquire enough strength to counter USA or Russia. Second, it will pose more security threat to the littoral states. It is also true that in case of any Indo-Pakistani war the United States will not hesitate to use her maritime installment in the Indian Ocean. All this can be best tackled if India can raise world public opinion in favour of UN declaration, declaring 'Indian Ocean a Zone of Peace'. Moreover, it should take into confidence the neighbouring and littoral states. Political paramountcy would be more effective than the military build-up. Continuing the process of strengthening 'strategic awareness' against USA's increased military build-up it should keep faith in the United Nation's declarations. India, also, must emphasis the fact that due to geo-strategic realities the role of Pakistan is much more valid than Washington's actions. The coordinated and concerted efforts of the NAM can only put pressure on USA's maritime warfare.

After the disintegration of the USSR, it is not a point to discuss whether its maritime strength has decreased or not, but definitely it will pose security threat to India. Even the erstwhile USSR was not creating trouble to India. the movement of Russia in the Indian Ocean was actually on a much lower scale.

To day, we cannot think in terms of 'selective security safeguard' confined to a particular region. So the survival of humanity is also closely linked with all parts of the whole world. That is why India is against any intervention in the Indian Ocean. It must be correct to say that India stands upright and independent in this direction. The immediate and practical solution, therefore, rests on the role of United Nations also. To renew the efforts for equanimity is though complex, yet the requisite steps can constrict turbidity and can transmit pease aftermath.

Above all, India's Indian Ocean policy is quite peaceful and aim at establishing a Zone of Peace. It is not titled towards any power. But the problem continues. So the main question before the Indian policy makers is how to get rid of the tense situation within a shortest possible time? Quite clearly, it depends on the attitude of the powers involve in the area and the support of the littoral countries in India's endeavour of peace zone area. In other words, there should be mutuality of interests between the great powers those are employing fissiparous tactics in the Indian Ocean and the Indian Ocean littoral states to check out a mutually benefit programme to ensure that the security to the littoral nations does not place in a house of cards. An immediate halt to drift the atmosphere of congeniality and to prohibit the use or threat of use of nuclear weapons from the Indian Ocean is the paramount importance in the nineties.

On economic front that the Indo-Soviet friendship came in a big hand to hasten developmental process of India. Scientific and technological collaborations continued to assign a key role in the development of public and private sectors rendering the needs of India for a rapid all-round development. Bilateral collaborations on steel, metallurgy, energy and other fields helped India to lay the foundation of a modern industrial society. In the ultimate analysis if India has been able to achieve self-reliance and dynamic economy and an equitable economic condition in the country, the Soviet Union has made impressive contributions. To the contrary, the Western industrialised countries cannot be termed as comfortable partners to India. It is true that for sometimes the United State was the largest economic partner of India (in the early 80s). But overall analysis testifies that Indo-American relations were not considered gleeful. Therefore, India has agitated against the enfeeblement of North-South economic cooperation. The BJP remarks that it is vital for India to go for a comfortable North-South relations. The BJP stands for a foreign policy that would help in bringing a New International Economic Order. The party strongly supports India's endeavour in international conferences where India has raised the issue and clamors for a NIEO, where the exploitation of the rich over poor the South-Asian countries would be left out. To set sail an equitable world economic order and to get rid of maroon from the unjust treatment of the West, the Indian government appeals, the US and other Western developed countries should put into affect the Brandt Commission report. It is to be seen how soon India's requests are corporealised, because the West dominates the world financial institutions and it does not consider the Third World as a major force in its economic club.

The economic security and development are interconnected. Decelerated economic growth not only curbs economic development but also leads to involvement of a foreign power. It also retards self-reliant drive and liquidates established industrial resources. It is also suggested that the internal development of a country is related to economic independece. In case of Sri Lanka, the ethnic conflict prompted the US to provide all possible help only to keep Sri Lanka as an American hostage. Thus, external dependence is a multidimensional problem. It is well known that foreign debt problem often leads to dependence on foreign countries, who in the name of assistance captures economy of the receiving state. It is proposed that only economic confidence building measures can prevent a country to go to the doors of the aid giving nations. So building up of environment against imperialist countries should be the priority of a developing country.

Towards the end of the eighties and the early nineties India has faced serious foreign exchange crisis. The economists suggest that liberalisation of Indian economy and Privatisation of public sectors can earn tangible results. India is going through slow restructuring of economy and is looking for liberalisation. It is admitted that the strategy of the Indian government is essential to support its developing economy. But at the same time it is viewed that liberalisation would invite multinationals to wield their importance and the national industry will be jeopardised. Importantly, the MNCs make inroad to the national economy in such a way that sometimes they happen to influence the foreign policy of that country. That is why, the BJP strongly oppose the ruling party's policies of surrendering before multinationals and allowing themselves to leave India letting the Indians to suffer from the evils created by them, for instance the Union Carbide case. So, not only Indian but also major South Asian countries are under the grip of economic imperialism of the West. The Western industrialised countries, on the other hand, are not abjuring their economic expansion. In such a situation India's responsibility is to bring South Asian countries to a common economic platform for their common advantage as well as for whole Asia. The regional cooperation should have to be based on the interest of all nations of the region. The 'centre-piece' of the argument is that the natural and economic resources of each and every country should be made available not only to the concerned nation alone. In the initial phase of building modern independent industrialised economy, they may face serious economic problem and financial deficit which should be met by their mutual cooperation, i.e., the developed nations of the region should extend financial support to the developing countries of the sub-continent.

In the nineties, some remarkable progress have been seen all over the world. The Soviet Union is no more integrated. Pakistan is not getting American support. The Clinton administration has showed its desire to reduce aid to Pakistan both economically and militarily. India is becoming stronger with its second largest army strength in the world and massive stockpiling of arms with newly built and modernised weapons. The US is becoming friendly to India after the crumbling of the Soviet Union. So in this situation, it is expected that the security problem of South Asia would be settled. Though there are occasional divergences between India, Pakistan and India, USA it is hoped that the arms acquisition by the South Asian countries and arms supply by the US will soon end. We may state that mere words does not sound good, but to provide the means to obtain concrete results, measures should be taken so that the 'dangers of annihilation' subsidises and purpose of the sub-continent is fulfilled. The justifiability to exist and to allow others to exist should be encouraged repelling the logic of arms acquisition at the earliest.

To sum up, the nineties have ushered in a totally different international world than the earlier decades. The world is undergoing radical transformation, transferring the multi-polar world to a uni-polar world. The influence of the United States is seen everywhere starting from global disputes to regional conflicts, from world financial institutions to regional institutions. In this situation, the Bharatiya Janata Party has always stood for closer ties with the neighbouring countries of South-Asia so that they can properly tackle external pressures — political and economic. The importance of regional co-operation should be oriented to create a 'Common South-Asian Home' and to bind other willing nations in their bond to fight against the 'Menace of Imperialism'. The Government of India should retain its policy of peace and non-alignment and try to forge closer ties with the SAARC members. It is not important if they are united in case of a crisis or in case of an imperialist threat. The real strength lies how far they are able to band together on all issues overcoming their differences for along-term perspective, and if not, economic colonialism is not far off.

Bibliography

Party Documents and Reports:

Documents of Indian National Congress: (listed Chronologically):

All-India Congress Committee, *The Background of India's Foreign Policy* (Delhi : Indian National Congress Publication, 1952).

..............., *Resolutions passed at the Congress Working Committee,* New Delhi, August 7, 1977.

..............., *Resolutions adopted at the All-India Congress Committee Meeting,* New Delhi, April 21-22, 1979.,

India National Congress, *Election Manifesto,* 1980.

..............., *Resolutions passed in the All-India Congress Committee Meeting,* New Delhi, 6th-7th December, 1980.

..............., *Resolutions adopted by All-India Congress Committee,* New Delhi, February 27-28,1981.

..............., *Resolutions adopted by All-India Congress Committee,* Bombay, October 20,1981.

..............., *Resolutions passed by Indian National Congress,* Calcutta, December 20-22, 1983.

..............., *Resolutions passed in the AICC Meeting,* Bombay, October 20-21, 1983.

.............., *Resolutions passed at the 77th Plenary Session of the Indian National Congress,* Calcutta, December 28-30, 1983.

..............., Election Manifesto, 1984.

..............., *Resolutions passed in the AICC Meeting,* Delhi, May 4-5, 1985.

..............., *Inaugural speech by Congress President Shri Rajiv Gandhi and the Centenary Resolve at Congress Centenary Session,* Indira Nagar, Bombay, December 28, 1985.

..............., *Congress Jan Margdarshika* (Delhi: Akhil Bharatiya Congress, Committee, 1987)

..............., *Resolutions passed at Congress Working Committee,* New Delhi, December 26-27, 1987.

..............., Resolutions passed in the AICC Meeting, Maraimalai Nagar, Tamil Nadu, April 23rd and 24th, 1988.

..............., Resolutions passed in the AICC Meeting, New Delhi, November 4th and 5th, 1988.

..............., Election Manifesto, 1989.

..............., India and the International Scene, AICC(I) Publication.

..............., Self-Reliance in Defence, An AICC(I) Publication.

..............., A Brief History of Congress, An AICC(I) Publication.

..............., The Foreign Policy of the Indian National Congress, An AICC(I) publication.

..............., The Message of Tirupati, An AICC publication, 1992.

..............., Pradhan Mantriyon Ki Report (1980-1990), AICC(I) publication.

Documents of the Jana Sangh: (listed chronologically):

The Jana Sangh, Resolutions on Defence and External Affairs, Party Documents, Vol.3, Delhi, June 1952.

..............., Resolutions by the Central Working Committee, Delhi, December 20, 1953.

..............., Resolution passed by the All-India Sixth Session of the Jana Sangh, Ambala, April 5, 1958.

..............., Manifesto and programme as adopted by the Bhartiya Pratinidhi Sabha, Banglore, December, 1958.

..............., Resolutions adopted by the Bhartiya Pratinidhi Sabha and Bharatiya Karya Samiti, Poona, June 27-July 8, 1959.

..............., Resolutions passed by the All-India Working Committee, Rajahmundry, Andhra Pradesh, September 29- October 1, 1962.

..............., Presidential Address by Sri Raghu Vira at Tenth Session, Bhopal, Madhya Pradesh, December 29- 31, 1962.

..............., Resolutions passed at Emergent Working Committee Meeting, Bhopal, January 19th and 20th, 1963.

..............., Resolutions passed at the Bhartiya Pratinidhi Sabha Session and the Central Working Committee, Hyderabad, August 27-28, 1963.

..............., Resolutions adopted by the Working Commit tee, New Delhi, May 24th and 25th, 1964.

..............., Resolutions passed by the Bhartiya Pratinidhi Sabha and the Working Committee, Gwalior, August 11-15, 1964.

........................., Resolutions passed by the Bhartiya Karya Samiti. Patna, December 4-6, 1964.

........................., Principles and policies as adopted by the Bhartiya Pratinidhi Sabhha, Vijayawada, Andhra Pradesh, January 25th and 26th, 1965.

........................., Resolutions passed by the Bhartiya Karya Samiti,Jaipur, April 3rd and 4th, 1965.

........................., Resolutions passed by the Bhartiya Pratinidhi Sabha, August 17th and 18th, 1965.

........................., Resolutions passed by All-India Working Committee, Kanpur, January 15th and 16th, 1966.

........................., Resolutions passed at the Thirteenth Annual Session and All-India Working Committee, Jullundur, April 30-May 2,1966.

........................., Resolutions passed by the All-India Working Committee, Lucknow, July 12th and 13th, 1966.

........................., Resolutions passed by the All-India Central Council, Indore, September 7, 1968.

........................., Souvenir : Fifteenth Annual Session, Bombay, April 25-27, 1969.

........................., Presidential Address by Shri A.B. Vajpayee at The Bhartiya Pratinidhi Sabha Session, Chandigarh, July 18-19,1970.

........................., Resolutions passed by the Central Working Committee, Delhi, November 6, 1970.

........................., Jana-Deep Souvenir. Delhi, March 1971.

........................., Resolutions passed by the Central Working Committee, Delhi, August 13, 1971.

........................., Resolutions passed by the All-India Working Committee, Madras, October 9th and 10th, 1971.

........................., Resolutions adopted by the Bhartiya Pratinidhi Sabha, Ghaziabad, November 27-28, 1971.

........................., Resolutions adopted by All-India Working Committee, Bhopal, January 27-28, 1972

........................., Resolutions passed by the Bhartiya Pratinidhi Sabha Session, Bhagalpur, May 5-7, 1972.

........................., Resolutions passed by the Central Working Committee, Jaipur, November 18-19, 1972.

.........................., Resolutions on Defence and External Affairs, Party Documents, volume 3, New Delhi, 1973.

.........................., Resolutions passed in the Eighteenth All- India Session, Kanpur, February 9-11, 1973.

.........................., Resolutions passed at the Bhartiya Pratinidhi Sabha Session, Hubli, Karnataka, July 16-18, 1973.

.........................., Resolutions passed by the All-India Working Committee, Varanasi, January 5-6, 1974.

.........................., Resolutions passed by the All_India Working Committee, Ujjain, April 5-7, 1974.

Documents of the Bhartiya Janata Party: (listed chronologically)

Bhartiya Janata Party, Economic Resolutions Adopted by the National Executive, New Delhi, April 23, 1980.

.........................., Resolutions as adopted by the National Executive, Delhi, September 5, 1980.

.........................., Miscellaneous Party Resolutions, Hyderabad, October 25, 1980.

.........................., Resolutions as adopted by the National Executive, Hyderabad, October 26, 1980.

.........................., The only Alternative : Shri M.C. Chagla's Address at BJP Session, Samata Nagar, Bombay, December 29,1980.

.........................., Economic Policy Statement as approved at the First National Convention, Bombay, December 28th-30th,1980.

.........................., India at the Crossroads : Text of presidential Address at First National Convention, Samata Nagar, Bombay, December 28-30, 1980.

.........................., Resolutions on the Current International Situation and our foreign policy as adopted by the National Executive, Cochin, April 23, 1981.

.........................., Resolutions adopted in National Council Session, Cochin (Kerala), April 25th-27th, 1981.

.........................., Resolutions as adopted by the National Executive, Delhi, December 4th-6th, 1981.

.........................., Resolutions adopted at National Executive Meeting , Bhubaneswar, February 12th-14th, 1982.

.........................., Resolutions adopted at National Executive Meeting, Delhi, April 12-13, 1982.

.........................., A Report on Mini-General Election at National Council Session, Surat, June 4-6, 1982.

.........................., Resolutions adopted at National Executive Meeting, Bangalore (Karnataka), August 28-30, 1982.

.........................., Resolutions adopted by the National Executive Meeting, Vigyan Bhavan, New Delhi, April 13-14, 1983.

.........................., Resolutions Adopted in the Fourth National Council Session, New Delhi, April 15-17, 1983.

.........................., Resolutions adopted at National Executive Meeting, Lucknow, October 21-23, 1983.

.........................., Resolutions passed at the National Executive Meeting, Indore, January 4-5, 1984.

.........................., Resolutions adopted by National Executive Meeting, Indore, January 6-8, 1984.

.........................., Presidential Address by Shri A.B.Vajpayee at the Fifth National Council Session, Indore, January 6-8, 1984.

.........................., Constitution and Rules as amended by the National Council, Indore, January 7, 1984.

.........................., Resolutions adopted by the National Execu tive, Ahmedabad, March 31 and April 1-2, 1984.

.........................., Resolutions adopted in the National Council Session, Ekatmatanagar, Pune, October 12-14, 1984.

.........................., Election Manifesto, 1984.

.........................., Resolutions adopted by the National Executive Meeting, Bhopal, July 19-21, 1985.

.........................., Text of Resolutions adopted at National Executive Meeting, Gandhi Nagar, Gujrat, October 8-9, 1985.

.........................., Resolutions as adopted by National Executive Meeting, Gandhi Nagar, October 10, 1985.

.........................., National Study Camp, Gandhi Nagar, Gujrat, October 11-13, 1985.

.........................., Resolutions Adopted in National Executive Meeting, Chandigarh, January 3-5, 1986.

.........................., Presidential Address by L.K.Advani in the Plenary Session, New Delhi, May 9, 1986.

.........................., Resolutions as updated and approved by the Second Plenary Session, New Delhi, May 9-11, 1986.

.........................., National Executive Meeting, Gwalior, July 18, 1986.

.........................., Two years of Congress misrule : A charge sheet, As approved by National Executive, Jammu, October 19, 1986.

.........................., Presidential Address by Shri L.K.Advani at the Ninth National Council Session, Vijayawada, Andhra Pradesh, January 2-4, 1987.

.........................., Statement by Shri L.K.Advani, June 5, 1987.

.........................., Resolutions adopted at the National Executive Meeting, Rohtak, April 19, 1987.

.........................., Resolutions adopted at the National Executive Meeting, Jodhpur, Rajasthan, October 9-11, 1987.

.........................., The Tip of the Iceberg: The story of three scandals, 1987.

.........................., Resolutions adopted at the National Executive Meeting, Ernakulum, Kerala, January 1-3, 1988.

.........................., Presidential Address by L.K.Advani at the Fourth Plenary Session, Deen Dayal Dham, Agra, April 8, 1988.

.........................., Resolutions adopted at the National Executive Meeting, Jamshedpur, Bihar, July 1-3, 1988.

.........................., Resolutions Adopted in the National Executive Meeting, Ahmedabad, October 7, 1988.

.........................., National Executive Meeting, Bombay, Sep tember 23-24, 1989.

.........................., Presidential Address by L.K.Advani at the Eleventh National Council Session, Shanmukhananda Hall, Sion, Bombay, September 25, 1989.

.........................., Resolutions adopted at the National Execu tive Meeting , Palampur, Himachal Pradesh, June 9-11, 1989.

.........................., Resolutions adopted at the National Executive Meeting, Udaipur, Rajasthan, March 3-5, 1989.

.........................., Election Manifesto, 1989.

.........................., India Stands US, BJP prakashan.

.........................., Our Five commitments, BJP prakashan.

.........................., Expanding Horizons : B.J.P.'s First Decade, Calcutta, April 6, 1990.

Government Publications :

Government of India Publication: Congress Bulletin issued by the office of the AICC, No.5, July-August, 1950.

.........................., Congress Bulletin issued by the office of the AICC, January-February 1957.

.........................., Government of India, Annual Report 1964-65 (New Delhi : Publication Division, 1984).

.........................., The Tashkent Declaration, (New Delhi: Publication Division, 1966).

.........................., Annual Report (1981-82) (New Delhi : Gov- ernment of India , Publication Division, 1983).

.........................., Annual Report (1982-83) (New Delhi : Government of India, Publication Division, 1984).

.........................., Annual Report (1983-1984) (New Delhi : Government of India, Publication Division, 1985).

.........................., Annual Report (1984-85) (New Delhi :Govern ment of India, Publication Division, 1986.

.........................., Annual Report (1985-86) (New Delhi : Government of India, Publication Division, 1987).

.........................., Annual Report (1986-87) (New Delhi : Government of India, Publication Division, 1988).

.........................., Annual Report (1987-88) (New Delhi : Ministry of External Affairs, Publication Division, 1989).

.........................., Indira Gandhi's speech on India's view on the New International Economic Order (New Delhi: Publication Division, 1982).

.........................., The Nation Prepares (New Delhi : Ministry of Information and Broadcasting, Publication Division, 1963).

.........................., The Gazetter of India, vol.IV (New Delhi: Ministry of Education and Social Welfare, Department of Culture, 1978).

.........................., Foreign policy of India (New Delhi : Govern ment of India, Publication Division, 1987).

.........................., Foreign Policy of India : Texts of Documents (New Delhi:Government of India, Publication Division, 1958).

.........................., Import and Export Policy (April 1984 to March 1985) vol.2 (New Delhi : Ministry of Commerce, Controller of publication, 1984).

........................, Report 1971-72 and 1981-87(New Delhi : Ministry of External Affairs, Publication Division, 1987).

........................, Paradox of India-Pakistan Relations (New Delhi: Ministry of Information and Broadcasting, Publication Division, 1971).

........................, Note of Dissent on Report of the Committee on Export Strategy (New Delhi: Government of India Publication, 1981).

........................, Selected speeches of Jawaharlal Nehru (1949- 53) (Delhi: Government of India, Publication Division, 1954).

........................, Selected Speeches of Lal Bahadur Shastri (New Delhi, Publication Division, 1974).

........................, Selected Speeches of Indira Gandhi : The year of Challenge (New Delhi : Ministry of Information and Broadcasting , Government of India, Publication Division, 1973).

........................, Selected Speeches of Indira Gandhi : The Years of Endeavour (New Delhi ; Ministry of Information and Broadcasting, Government of India, Publication Division, 1974).

........................, Selected Speeches of Indira Gandhi, vol.III (1972-77) (New Delhi : Ministry of Information and Broadcasting, Government of India, Publication Division, 1978).

........................, Selected Speeches and Writings of Indira Gandhi, vol.IV (New Delhi : Ministry of Information and Broadcasting, Publication Division, 1985).

........................, Selected Speeches and Writings of Indira Gandhi, vol.V (New Delhi : Ministry of Information and Broadcasting, Publication Division, 1986).

........................, Statement of Foreign Policy, Prime Minister Rajiv Gandhi (May-August 1985) (New Delhi : Ministry of External Affairs, 1985).

........................, Statement on Foreign Policy, Prime Minister Rajiv Gandhi (New Delhi : Ministry of External Affairs, Publication Division, November 1986).

........................, Statement on Foreign Policy, Prime Minister Rajiv Gandhi (New Delhi : Ministry of External Affairs, Publication Division, June 1987).

........................, Statement on Foreign Policy, Prime Minister Rajiv Gandhi (New Delhi : Ministry of External Affairs , Publication Division, September 1987).

.........................., Statement on Foreign Policy, Prime Minister Rajiv Gandhi (New Delhi : Ministry of External Affairs, Publication Division, December 1987).

.........................., Statement on Foreign Policy, Prime Minister Rajiv Gandhi (New Delhi: Ministry of External Affairs, Publication Division, April 1988).

.........................., Statement on Foreign Policy, Prime Minister Rajiv Gandhi (New Delhi : Ministry of External Affairs, Publication Division, May 1988).

.........................., Statement on Foreign Policy, Prime Minister Rajiv Gandhi (New Delhi : Ministry of External Affairs, Publication Division, September 1988).

.........................., Statement on Foreign Policy, : Prime Minister Rajiv Gandhi (New Delhi : Ministry of External Affairs, Publication Division, December 1988).

.........................., Lok Sabha Secretariat, Indian Ocean as a zone of peace (New Delhi : Publication Division, 1987).

.........................., India's view on the Indian Ocean (January 1980-October 1981) (New Delhi : Ministry of External Affairs, External Publicity Division, 1982).

.........................., Reports, Data Sources and unpublished theses and other materials : Draft Five Year Plan (1978-83) (New Delhi: Planning Commission, 1984).

.........................., Reports, Data Sources and unpublished theses and other materials : Draft Sixth Five Year Plan (New Delhi : Planning Commission, 1989).

India, Lok Sabha Secretariat, Parliament and Foreign Policy : A study (New Delhi : 1972).

Embassy of the USSR, Prime Minister Indira Gandhi visits USSR (New Delhi : Information Department of the USSR Embassy, 1982).

.........................., USSR-India Summit (November 18-20, 1988) (New Delhi: USSR Embassy, 1988).

United States Information Service, Indo-US Cooperation in education and culture (New Delhi : The Embassy of United States of America, 1990).

.........................., Congress and the Nation : A Review of Government and politics, vol.VII(1985-89) (Washington D.C. : Congressional Quarterly Inc., 1990).

.........................., Congress and the Nation: A Review of Government and politics, vol.VI (1981-84) (Washington D.C. : Congressional Quarterly lnc., 1985).

.........................., Essay in Understanding : Prime Minister Rajiv Gandhi made his first official visit to the United States (New Delhi : USIS, American Centre, 1985).

.........................., India and the United States (New Delhi : USIS, 1987).

.........................., A Common Faith : 40 years of Indo-US coop- eration (1947-87) (New Delhi : American Centre, 1988).

Lok Sabha Debates : vol.VI(23), 9 July 1980 vol.XII(4) 19 February 1981; vol.XII(7), February 24, 1981; vol.XII(9), 26 February 1981; vol.XIII(19), 12 March 1981; vol.XIV(24), 19 March 1981; vol.XIV(29), 26 March 1981; vol.XV(33), 1 April 1981; vol.XV(34), 2 April 1981: vol.XV(33), 8 April 1981; vol.XV(35), 8 April 1981; vol,XVI(50), 29 April 1981; vol.XVII(55), 7 May 1981; vol,XVIII(2), 18 August 1981; vol.XVIII(4), 20 August 1981; vol.XVIII(9), 27 August 1981; vol.XXV(16), 12 March 1982; vol.XXVI(29), 30 March 1982; vol.XXXV(19) 22 March 1983; vol XXXVI(21), 24 March 1983; vol.XXXVII(40), 28 April 1983; vol.XLII(10), 6 December 1983; vol.XLIII(19), 19 December 1983; vol.XLIII(22), 22 December 1983; vol,XLIV(6), 1 March 1984; Vol.XLIV(10), 6 March 1984; vol. XLV(13), 9 March 1984; vol.XLVIII(52), 9 May 1984; vol.XLX(15), 10 August 1984; vol.II(9),22 March 1985; vol III(11), 25 March 1985; vol.III(19), 9 April 1985; vol III(20), 10 April 1985; vol.IV(22), 12 April 1985; vol.IV(22), 16 April 1985; vol.IV(26), 18 April 1985; vol.V(32), 26 April 1985; vol.V(33), 29 April 1985; vol.VI(44), 15 May 1985; vol.VI(46), 17 May 1985; vol. VII(1), 23 July 1985; vol. VII(2), 24 July 1985; vol VII(5), 29 JUly 1985; vol. VIII(11), 6 August 1985; vol. VIII(12), 7 August 1985; vol.XI(15), 9 December 1985; vol. XII(22), 18 December 1985; vol.XIV(20), 20 March 1986; vol.XV(24), 31 March 1986; vol. XV(25), 1 April 1986; vol.XV(27), 2 April 1986; vol.XV(29), 7 April 1986; vol.XVI(32), 10 April 1986; vol.XVI(34), 15 April 1986; vol.XVII(41), 28 April 1986; vol.XVIII(5), 23 July 1986; vol.XXI(3), 6 November 1986; vol.XXI(8), 13 November 1986; vol.XXI(3), 6 December 1986; vol. XLV(21), 13 December 1988.

Rajya Sabha Debates: vol.CXV(11), 6 August 1980; vol.CXVI(19), 12 December 1980; vol. CXVII(2), 17 February 1981; vol.CXVII(4), 19 February 1981; vol. CXVII(5), 20 February 1981; vol.CXVII(18), 11 March 1981; vol. CXVIII(2), 21 April 1981; vol.CXVIII(5), 24 April 1981; vol. CXVIII(14), 8 May 1981; vol.XXIII(29), 5 May 1983; vol.CXXVII(15), 12 August 1983; vol.CXVIII(10), 6 December 1983; vol.CXVIII(11) 7 December 1983; vol.CXX(12), 8 May 1984; vol.CXXXI(16), 13 August 1984; vol.CXXXII(3), 21 January 1985; vol.CXXXII(8),30 January 1985; vol.CXXXIII(8), 21 March 1985; vol.CXXXIII(9), 21 March 1985; vol.CXXXIII(9), 22 March 1985; vol. CXXXVI(16) 10 December 1985; col.CXXXVIII(9), 5 May 1986; vol.CXL(4), 7 November 1986; vol, CXLII(9), 27 April 1987.

Books

Adiseshiah, Malcolm S., *Role of Foreign Trade in Indian Economy* (Delhi : Lancer International, 1986).

............, (ed.), *India's International Economic Relation : The Present and the Perspective* (New Delhi : Lancer Publishers, 1990).

Aggarwal, Ashok Kumar, *India's Trade and Economic Coopera-tion with Developing and Socialist Countries* (New Delhi : Commonwealth Publishers, 1989).

Akbar, M.J., *Nehru : The Making of India* (London: Viking, 1988).

............, *India : The Siege within* (Middlesex: Penguin, 1985).

Akhtar, Majeed (ed.), *Indian Ocean : Conflict and Regional Cooperation* (New Delhi : ABC Publishing House, 1986).

Alam, Mohammed B., *India's Nuclear Policy* (Delhi: Mittal Publication, 1988).

Anand, R.P., *South Asia : In Search of a Regional Identity* (New Delhi: Banyan Publications, 1991).

Appadorai, A. and M.S. Rajan, *India's Foreign Policy and Relations* (New Delhi : South Asian Publications, 1985).

Athawale, Sanhita, *India's Indian Ocean Islands : A Study— Political and Strategic importance* (New Delhi: ABC Publishing House, 1991).

Attar Chand, *International Relations* (Delhi : Anmol Publishers, 1992).

Azam, Kousar J., *India's Defence Policy for the 1990s* (New Delhi : Sterling, 1992).

Bajpai U.S. and A.K. Damodaran (ed.), *Indian Foreign Policy (The Indira Gandhi Years)* (New Delhi : Radiant Publishers, 1990).

Ballard, G.A., *Rulers of the Indian Ocean* (Delhi : Neeraj Publication House, 1984).

Bandopadhyay, Jayantanuja, *Making of India's Foreign Policy : Determinants, institutions, processes and personalities* (2nd) (New Delhi : Allied, 1980).

........................, (ed.), *Dimensions of Strategy : Some Indian Perspectives* (Calcutta : Minerva, 1989).

Banerjee, B.N., *Indian Ocean : A whirlpool of unrest* (New Delhi : Paribus Publishers, 1984).

.........................., *Peace, Friendship and Cooperation* (Delhi : B.R. Publishing Corporation, 1987).

Bhambhri, C.P., *World Bank and India* (New Delhi : Vikas, 1980)

.........................., *The Foreign Policy of India* (New Delhi : Sterling, 1987).

.........................., *Politics in India : 1947-1987* (New Delhi : Vikas, 1988).

Bhargava, M.L., *Indian Ocean Strategies through the ages*(New Delhi : Reliance, 1990).

Bhasin, V.K., *Super Power rivalry in the Indian Ocean* (New Delhi : S. Chand and Co., 1991).

Bhatia, Vinod (ed.), *Indo-Soviet Relations: problem and prospects* (New Delhi : Panchsheel Publishers, 1984).

.........................., *Indian National Congress and Soviet Union* (New Delhi: Panchasheel Publishers, 1985).

.........................., (ed.), *The October Revolution and 70 years of Indo-Soviet Relations* (New Delhi : Panchasheel Publishers, 1987).

.........................., *Indira Gandhi and Indo-Soviet Relation* (New Delhi: Panchasheel Publishers, 1987).

.........................., *Jawaharlal Nehru : A Study in Indo-Soviet Relations* (New Delhi : Panchasheel, 1989).

Bhatt, G.D., *Indo-Soviet Relations and Indian Public Opinion* (Delhi : Pacifier Publications, 1989).

Borsa, Giorgio (ed.), T*rade and Politics in the Indian Ocean: Historical and Contemporary Perspective* (New Delhi : Manohar Publications, 1990).

Bose, Nemai Sadhan, *India and the United States : Reflec ions and Relationships* (Calcutta : Firma KLM Ltd., 1982).

Bradnock, Robert W., *India's Foreign Policy Since 1971* (London : Royal Institute of International Affairs, 1990).

Brands, H.W., *India and the United States* : The Cold Peace (Boston : Twayne Publishers, 1990).

Braun, Dieter, *Indian Ocean : Region of conflict or Peace Zone?* (Delhi: Oxford University Press, 1983).

Brown, Norman W., *The United States and India and Pakistan* (Cambridge : Harvard University Press, 1963).

Chaturshreni, Ved Vati, *Indo-US Relations* (New Delhi: National Publishing house, 1980).

Chaudhary, K.C., *Non-Aligned Summitry* (Delhi: Capital Publishing House, 1985).

Chawla, Vijay, *India and the Superpowers* (Jaipur: Panchasheel, 1973).

Chopra, Maharaja K. *India and the Indian Ocean : New Horizons* (New Delhi : Sterling, 1982).

Chopra, P.N., Ram Gopal and M.L. Bhargava, *A Century of Indian National Congress (1885-1985)* (Delhi : Agam Prakashan, 1986).

Chopra, V.D., *India and the Socialist World* (New Delhi, Allied, 1983).

........................., *Pentagon shadow over India* (New Delhi, Patriot, 1985).

........................., (ed.), *NAM Summit : New Delhi to Harare* (New Delhi Patriot, 1986).

Christman, Henry M., *Indira Gandhi Speaks* (New York: Taplinger Publishing co., 1975).

Coates , Ken, *The Most dangerous decade : World Militarism and the New Non-aligned Peace Movement* (Nottingham : Spokesman, 1984).

Crunden Robert M.(ed.), *Traffic of Ideas between India and America* (Delhi : Chanakya Publications , 1985).

Damodaran A.K. and U.S. Bajpai(ed). Indian Foreign Policy : the Indira Gandhi Years (New Delhi : Radiant Publication, 1990).

Dillon, Teresa Lynn, *India and the United States : A need for improved relations* (Washington : Information Service, U.S. Department of Commerce, 1985).

Dowdy, William M. and Trood, Russell B.(ed.), *Indian Ocean : Perspective on a Strategic* area (Durham : Duke University Press, 1985).

Ducan, Peter J.S., *The Soviet Union and India* (London : Routledge, 1989).

Dutt, V.P., *India's Foreign Policy* (New Delhi : Vikas Publishing House Pvt. Ltd., 1984).

........................., *India's Foreign Policy* (New Delhi : Vikas, 1987).

........................., *India and the World* (New Delhi : Sanchar Publishing House, 1991).

Etinger, Y.(ed.), *NAM History and Reality : A Study* (Delhi : Allied Publishers, 1987).

Fartyal, H.S., *Role of opposition in the Indian Parliament* (Allahabad : Chaitanya Publishing House, 1971).

Gaikwad, Sanjay, *Dynamics of Indo-Soviet Relations: The era of Indira Gandhi.* (New Delhi : Deep and Deep Publications, 1990).

Gandhi, Rajiv, Gaurav Chinh (New Delhi : Bharatiya Rashtriaya Congress, 1985).

Ganju, M., India's Foreign Policy (Bombay : The New Book Company, 1951).

George, Timothy, *India and the Great Powers* (Hampshine : Gower for international Institute for Strategic Studies, 1984).

Ghosh, Ramesh Chandra, *India and the World* (Calcutta : World Press, 1970).

Glazer, Sulochana Raghavan and Nathan Glazer (ed.), *Conflicting Images : India and the United States* (Glenale Dale, Maryland : Riverdale Co. Publishers 1990).

Gopal, S. *Jawaharlal Nehru : A biography* (Vol.1) (London : Jonathan Cape, 1975).

.........................., *Jawaharlal Nehru : A biography* (vol.3) (Bombay : Oxford University Press, 1976).

........................., (ed.), *Jawaharlal Nehru : An anthology* (Delhi : Oxford University Press, 1980).

.........................., (ed.), *Jawaharlal Nehru : Selected Works* (Vol. 1-15) (New Delhi : Orient Longman, 1972).

Goswami, P.K., *U.P.S. and Downs of Indo-US relations (1947-1983)* (Calcutta : Firma KLM, 1983).

Gould, Harold A. and Sumit Ganguly (ed.), The Hope and the Reality (San Francisco : West View Press, 1992).

Grover, Verinder (ed.) (vol.6), *International Relations and foreign policy of India* (New Delhi :Deep and Deep, 1992).

.........................., (vol.7), *International Relations and Foreign Policy of India* (Delhi: Deep and Deep , 1992).

Guha, Ashok (ed.). *Economic Liberalization, Industrial Structure and Growth in India* (Delhi : Oxford University Press, 1990).

Gupta, Karunakar, *Indian Foreign Policy (In defence of national interest) (Calcutta :* The World Press Pvt. Ltd., 1956).

Gupta, M.G., *Indian Foreign Policy (Theory and Practice* (Agra : Y.K. Publishers, 1985).

........................., *Foreign Policies of Major World Powers* (Agra : Y.K. Publishers, 1986).

........................., *Rajiv Gandhi's Foreign Policy : A Study in Continuity and Change* (Agra : M.G. Publishers, 1987).

Gupta, Rakesh (ed.), *India's Security Problem in the Nineties* (New Delhi : Patriot, 1989).

Hagelberg, Gerhard, *What Path for India* (New York : For East Reporter, 1989).

Haksar, P.N., *India's Foreign Policy and its problems* (New Delhi : Patriot Publishers, 1989).

........................., *India's Foreign Policy and its problems* (New Delhi : Patriot Publishers, 1989).

Haksar, P.N., et.al., *Studies in Indo-Soviet Relations* (New Delhi : Patriot publishers, 1986).

Harrison, Selig, S. and Subramaniam, K.(ed.), *Superpower rivalry in the Indian Ocean : Indian and American Perspectives.* (Oxford: Oxford University Press, 1989).

Hingorani, R.C., *Nehru's Foreign Policy* (New Delhi: IBH Publishing Co. Pvt. Ltd., 1989).

Iyer, Nandhini, *India and the Indian Ocean ; Groping for a policy* (1949-70) (New Delhi: ABC Pub. House, 1985).

Jain, B.M., *South Asia, India and United States* (Jaipur : RBSA Publishers, 1987).

........................., (ed.) *Reflections on India's Foreign Policy* (Jaipur : RBSA Publishers, 1990).

Jain, R.K., *US-South Asia Relations (1947-82): A documentary Study (Vol.1 and 3)* (New Delhi : \Radiant Publishers, 1983).

Jaisingh , Hari, *India and the Non-Aligned world : Search For a New Order* (New Delhi: Vikas, 1983).

Jha, Nalini Kant, *Internal crisis and Mrs. Gandhi's Foreign policy* (Patna : Janaki Prakashan, 1985).

Josh, Harcharan Singh, *India's Foreign Policy* (New Delhi : Surjeet Publications, 1989).

Kakkar, A.N., *Indian Ocean* (Allahabad : New Book House, 1987).

Kamath, P.M.(ed.) *Indo-US relations: Dynamics of Changes* (New Delhi : South Asian Publishers, 1987).

Kapur, Ashok, *Indian Ocean : Regional and International power Politics* (New York : Praeger, 1982).

Kaul, B.N., *India and Superpowers* (New Delhi: Pulse Pub- lishers, 1989).

Kaul, T.N., *Some aspects of India's foreign policy* (New Delhi : Lancer International, 1988).

Kaul, T.N. et.al., *Indo-Soviet Relations : Prospects and problems* (New Delhi : Patriot Publishers, 1991).

Kaushik, Devendra, *Indian Ocean : A Strategic dimension* (New Delhi : Vikas Pub. House, 1983).

........................., *Perspectives on Security in Indian Ocean region* (New Delhi : Allied , 1887).

Khilani, Niranjan M., *Realities of Indian Foreign Policy* (New Delhi : ABC Publishing House, 1984).

Kidwai, M. Saleem, *Indo-Soviet Relations* (New Delhi: Rima Pub. House,1985).

Kishore, M.A., *Jana Sangh and India's foreign policy* (New Delhi : Associated Publication House, 1969).

Kovalenko, Ivan and Rais Tuzmukhamedov, *The Non-Aligned Movement : The Soviet view* (Delhi : Sterling, 1987).

Krasa, Milostav(ed.), *Jawaharlal Nehru and the foreign policy of India* (Prague: Oriental Institute of the Czchoslovak Academy of Sciences, 1990).

Kunzru, H.N. et. al., *For a democratic Foreign Policy* (Bombay : Democratic Research, Service, 1985).

Kuznetsov, Felix et.al.,(ed.), *Sahayatra : Bharat tatha Soviet Sangha ko Jornewali Sanskriti, itihas aur Sahitya ki kariya——Lekhakan, kaviyan aur kalakaron ki kalam se* (Delhi : Rajpal, 1987).

Limaye , Madhu, *Problems of India's foreign policy* (Delhi : Atma Ram & Sons, 1984).

Longer, V., *The Defence and Foreign Policies of India* (New Delhi : Sterling Publishers, 1988).

Luciani, Giacomo (ed.) *Mediterranean region : Economic interdependence and the future of society* (London : Croom Helm, 1984).

Madan Gopal, India as a world power : *Aspects of foreign policy (ed. 2)* (New Delhi : Sagar Publications, 1974).

Malik, Yogendra K. and Vajpeyi, Dhirendra K., *India The Years of Indira Gandhi* (New York : E.J.Brill, 1988).

Mansingh, Surjeet, *India's Search for Power (Indira Gandhi's Foreign Policy, 1966-82)* (New Delhi : Sage Publications, 1984).

Masaidan, P.N., *Jawaharlal Nehru's Foreign Policy : Determinants, principles and conduct* (Nagpur : Nagpur University, 1977).

Mathur, Girish (ed.), *Sinews of self reliance* (New Delhi : Allied, 1987).

Mellor, John W. (ed.), *India : A Rising Middle Power* (Boulder, Colorado : West View Press, 1979).

Menon, Gopinath, P., *Results and Prospects of Soviet-Indian Economic Cooperation* (New Delhi : USSR Embassy, 1986).

Mikhin, V., *Indo-Soviet Treaty : Fifteen Years* (New Delhi : Sterling Publishers, 1986).

Mishra, B.B., *Congress Party and government : Policy and performance* (New Delhi : Concept Publishing, 1988).

Misra, K.P., *Foreign Policy of India* (New Delhi : Thomson Press (India) Ltd., 1977).

.........................., *Non-aligned Movement and India's Chairmanship* (New Delhi : Lancer Books, 1987).

Misra, R.N., *Indian Ocean and India's Security* (Delhi: Mittal, 1986).

Mukherjee, Neela and Amitav Mukherjee, *India's Foreign Trade by Regions (1950-1986)* (New Delhi : Indus Publishing Company, 1988).

Muravyov, Andrei, *Soviet Indian economic Relations : Trends and Prospects* (New Delhi : Panchasheel, 1988).

Murthy, K. Satchidananda, *Indian Foreign Policy* (Calcutta : Scientific Book Agency, 1964).

Murthy P.A.N. and B.K. Srivastava (eds.), *Neutrality and Non- Alignment in the 1990s* (New Delhi : Radiant, 1991).

Nagar, K.S., *India's Security : Superpower threat* (New Delhi : Reliance Publishing House, 1987).

Nagar, K.S. and Gautam Sharma (eds.), *India's Security: Super Power Threat* (Delhi : Reliance Publishing House, 1990).

Naik, J.A. (ed.), *Indian Politics : Documents, Events and Figures* (1980) (Kolhapur : Avinash Reference Publications, 1983).

.........................., *India and the West Documents* : 1980 (Kolhapur : Avinash Reference Publications, 1983).

.........................., *India and the West Documents* : 1981 (Kolhapur : Avinash Reference Publications, 1987).

Namboodiri, P.K.S. et.al., *Intervention in the Indian Ocean* (New Delhi : ABC Publishing House, 1982).

Namboodiripad, E.M.S., *BJP- RSS : In the Service of right reaction* (Delhi : Communist Party of India (Marxist), 1988).

Nanda, B.R. (ed.), *Indian Foreign policy* (The Nehru Years) (Delhi : Radiant, 1990).

Nanda, Ravi, *Evolution of National Strategy of India* (New Delhi : Lacer Books, 1987).

.........................., *National Security : Perspective, Policy and Planning* (New Delhi : Lancer Books, 1991).

Narayanan, K.R., *India and America : Essays in understanding* (New Delhi : Dialogue Publication, 1984).

Nawaz, Shamsa, *India's Nuclear Weapons Programme* (Lahore : Progressive Publication, 1985).

Nayar, Balder Raj, *Superpower dominance and Military Aid : A Study of Military Aid to Pakistan* (Delhi : Manohar, 1991).

Nihal Singh, S., *The Yogi and The Bear (Story of Indo- Soviet Relation)* (New Delhi : Allied Publishers, 1986).

Noorani, A.G., *India, the Superpowers and the Neighbours : Essays in Foreign Policy* (New Delhi : South Asian Publishers, 1985).

Ojha, G.P., *Mrs. Gandhi's Foreign Policy Choice* (Meerut : Mrinal Books, 1982).

Oldenburg, Philip and Marshall M. Bouton (eds.), *India Briefings, 1990* (San Francisco : Westview Press, 1990).

Palaniandi, M., *Bharat Soviet Maitri: Akhand aur atoot* (New Delhi : New Literature, 1985).

Palmer, Norman D., *The United States and India : The Dimensions of Influence* (New York : Praeger, 1984).

Pant, Har Govind, *India's Foreign Policy* (Jaipur : Panchsheel Prakashan, 1971).

Paranjpe, Shrikant, *US Non Proliferation Policy Action : South Asia* (New Delhi : Sterling Publishers, 1987).

Patel, Satyavrata Ramdas, *Foreign Policy of India : An inquiry and* Criticism (Bombay : Princess Street, 1958).

Punia, Narendra Kumar, *The dynamics of Indo-Soviet economic relations* (1953-90) (Meerut : Anu Books, 1990).

Rai S.S., *Red Star and the Lotus : The Political Dynamics of Indo-Soviet relations* (Delhi : Konark Publishers, 1990).

Rais, Rasul, B., *Indian Ocean and the Superpowers : Economic, political and Strategic Perspectives* (London : Croom Helm, 1986).

Rajan, M.S., *The future of Non-alignment and the Non aligned Movement* (Delhi : Konark Publishers, 1990).

........................., (ed.), *India's Foreign Relations during the Nehru era : Some studies* (Bombay : Asia, 1976).

Ramamurthy, K. and G.N. Srivastava, *NAM Today* (New Delhi : Indian Institute for Non-aligned Studies, 1985).

Ranga, N.G., *Quintessence of Non-Aligned Movement (Half a Century of India's Contribution)* (New Delhi : Milind Publications Private Ltd., 1983).

Rao, Kilaru Ram Chandra, *India, United states and Pakistan : A triangular Relationship* (Bombay : Himalaya Publishing House, 1985).

Rao, Mopidevi Sundara, *Trends and Determinants of India's Foreign Trade* (Allahabad : Chugh Publication, 1991).

Rasgotra, Maharajakrishna, *Rajiv Gandhi's World View* (Delhi : Vikas Publishing House, 1991).

Rasgotra, M. et. al.(eds), *India's Foreign Policy in the 1990s* (N.Delhi : Patriot publishers, 1990).

Ray, Hemen, *The enduring friendship* (Soviet-Indian relations in Mrs. Gandhi's days) (New Delhi : Abhinav Publications, 1989).

........................., (ed.), *Indo-Soviet Relations* (New Delhi : Jaico Publishing House, 1973).

Reddy, Padmanava B., *The Economics of Non-aligned Movement* (Delhi : Discovery Publishing House, 1989).

Rikhye, Ravi, *Militarization of Mother India* (Delhi : Chanakya Publications, 1990).

Salvi, P.G., *India in world Affairs* (Delhi : B.R. Publication, 1985).

Satish Chandra (ed.), *Indian Ocean : Explorations in history, commerce and politics* (New Delhi : Sage 1987).

Satish Kumar (ed.), *Yearbook on India's Foreign Policy, 1981-82* (New Delhi : Sage, 1984).

Satish Kumar(ed.), *Yearbook on India's Foreign Policy, 1982-83* (New Delhi : Sage, 1985).

Satish Kumar (ed.), *Yearbook on India's Foreign Policy, 1983-84* (New Delhi : Sage, 1986).

Satish Kumar (ed.). *Yearbook on India's Foreign policy,1984-85* (New Delhi : Sage, 1987).

Satish Kumar (ed.), *Yearbook on India's Foreign Policy, 1985-86* (New Delhi : Sage, 1988).

Satish Kumar (ed.), *Yearbook on India's Foreign Policy, 1986-87* (New Delhi : Sage , 1988).

Satish Kumar (ed.), *Yearbook on India's Foreign Policy, 1987-88* (New Delhi : Sage Publications, 1988).

Satish Kumar (ed.), *Yearbook on India's Foreign Policy, 1989* (New Delhi: Sage, 1990).

Satish Kumar(ed.), *Yearbook on India's Foreign Policy, 1990-91* (New Delhi : Tata McGraw-Hill Publiscation Co., 1991).

Sen, Gautam (ed.), *India's Security Considerations in Nuclear Age* (New Delhi : Atlantic Publishers, 1986).

Shanmugam, A., *Indian Parliament and the United States* (Anna Malai nagar: Annamalai University, 1989).

Sharma, P.L., *India and the Fourth World* (New Delhi : Pankaj Publications, 1985).

Sharma, Shankar Dayal, *Reading in Indo-Soviet Friendship and Cooperation* (Bombay : Central Press, 1987).

Sharma, Shri Ram, *Indian Foreign Policy Annual Survey,* 1981 (New Delhi : Sterling, 1985).

Sindhu, K.S., *Indian Ocean, a Zone of Peace : A Study of Indian View Point* (New Delhi : Harnam Publications, 1983).

Singh, Baljeet, *Indian Foreign Policy: An Analysis* (New Delhi : Asia Publishing House, 1985).

Singh, Darshan (ed.), *Soviet Foreign Policy Documents, 1980* (New Delhi : Sterling, 1981).

Soviet Foreign Policy Documents, 1982 (New Delhi : Sterling, 1984).

........................., *Soviet Foreign Policy Documents. 1984* (New Delhi : Sterling Publishers Pvt. Ltd., 1986).

........................., *Soviet Foreign Policy Documents, 1985* (New Delhi : Sterling, 1986).

........................., *Soviet Foreign Policy Documents, 1986* (New Delhi : Sterling, 1988).

........................., *Soviet Foreign Policy Documents, 1987* (New Delhi : Sterling, 1988).

........................., *Soviet Foreign Policy Documents, 1988* (New Delhi : Sterling, 1989).

Singh, Jasjit (ed.), *Asian Security : Old paradigms and New Challenges* (New Delhi : Lancer International, 1991).

........................., *Indo-US Relations in a Changing World.* (New Delhi: Lancer International, 1992).

Singh, K.R. et. al., *Indian Ocean and U.S. Soviet Detente* (New Delhi : Patriot, 1991).

Singh, Rajvir, *U.S. Pakistan and India : Strategic relations* (Allahbad : Chugh Publications, 1985).

Singh, Satinder, *A Strategy for Indian Defence* (New Delhi : Lancer International, 1986).

Singh, S.P., *Political Dimensions of India-USSR Relations* (New Delhi : Allied Publishers, 1987).

Singham, A.W. and Shirley Hune, *Non-alignment in an age of Alignments* (Westport : Lawrence and Hill Co., 1986).

Sisodia, S.S., *Foreign Policy of India : Indira Gandhi Era* (With Special Reference to Non-Alignment) (New Delhi : Inter-India Publications, 1985).

Sondhi, M.L., *Non-Appeasement : A new direction for Indian Foreign Policy* (New Delhi : Abhinav Publications, 1972).

........................., *Foreign Policy and legislatures : An analysis of Seven Parliaments* (New Delhi : Abhinav Publications, 1988).

Srivastava, G.N.(ed.), *Non-Alignment and Nuclear Disarmament* (New Delhi : Indian Institute for Non-aligned Studies, 1985).

Subramaniam, K., Zuberi, M. and R. Ramanna, *Problems of living in Nuclear Age* (Chandigarh : Center for Research in rural and Industrial Development, 1985).

Sudarshan Kumar, *Forty years of Foreign Policy : Tension Free India* (New Delhi : Archives Publishers, 1989).

Tandon, Rameswar, *Some Perspectives on India's Trade Policy* (Allahabad: Chug Publications, 1983).

Tanver Sultan, *Indo-US relations* (New Delhi : Deep and Deep Publications, 1982).

Tharoor, Shashi, *Reasons of State : Political development and India's Foreign Policy under Indira Gandhi (1966-1977)* (Delhi : Vikas Publishing, 1982).

Thayer, Carlyle A. and Ramesh Thakur, *Soviet Relations with India and Vietnam* (Londonon : MacMillan, 1992).

Theil, H., *Introduction to Econometrics* (New Delhi : Prentice- Hall of India, 1981).

Tiwari, H.D., *India and the Problem of Nuclear Proliferation* (Delhi : R.K. Publishers, 1988).

Vajpayee, Atal Behari, *Continuity and change in India's Foreign Policy* (New Delhi : Ministry of External Affairs, 1978).

.........................., *New Dimensions of India's Foreign Policy* (New Delhi : Vision Books, 1979).

Vas, E.A., *The Search for Security : Controlling Conflict and Terrorism* (Dehra Dun : Natraj Publishers, 1989).

Verma, Shrikant (ed.), *Seven Hundred Days* (An Appraisal (Delhi: AICC(I) Publication, 1982).

Victor, Cecil, *India : the security dilemma* (New Delhi : Patriot, 1990).

Vinod, M.J., *United States Foreign Policy Towards India : A diagnosis of the American approach* (New Delhi : Lancers Books, 1991).

Vladimirov, Leonid P. (ed.), *The Soviet Indian Phenomenon* (New Delhi : Allied, 1989).

Wimmel, Kenneth, *Soviet and American naval forces in the Indian Ocean : Arms race, Military balance Zone of Peace* (New Port : U.S. Naval War College, NTIS, 1976).

Wizimirska, Barbara (ed.), Jawaharlal Nehru : *The influence of Ideas and Actions on the formation of International Relations* (Warszawa : Polski Instytut Spraw Miedzynarodowych, 1991).

Zaidi, A.M., *The Story of Congress Pilgrimage : Report of the General Secretaries, vol. 7 (1970-1985)* (New Delhi : Indian Institute of Applied Political Research, 1990).

........................., (ed.), *Immutable Policy of friendship and Cooperation : The Foreign Policy of the Indian National Congress during the last hundred years* (New Delhi : Indian Institute of Applied Political Research, 1985).

Articles

Alekseyev, Aleksandr, "USSR-India : Cooperation for the benefit of the peoples", International Affairs, vol.5 , May 1987, pp.46-52.

Anand, J.P., "India's Indian Ocean neighbours", Strategic Analysis, vol.12(2), May 1989, pp.147-64.

Ashok Raj, "US hi-tech diplomacy and the Indian Super computer deal", Strategic Analysis, vol.12(6), September 1987, pp. 735-37.

Ayoob, Mohammad, "India in South Asia : The quest for re gional predominance", World Policy Journal, vol.7(1), Winter 1989-90, pp.107-34.

Bandopadhyaya, J., "Problems of Peace and Development in the Indian Ocean Area", Asian Studies, vol.6(1), January- March 1988. pp. 3-5.

Banerjee, Jyotirmoy, "Moscow's Strategic link with New Delhi : An interim assessment", China Report, vol.19(1) January-February 1983, pp,7-20.

.........................., " Moscow's Indian alliance", Problems of Communism, vol,36(1), January-February 1987, pp.1-12.

Beriendranath, Dewan, "Mrs. Gandhi's visit to USA : An adventure into understanding", Indian Foreign Review, vol. 19(21), 15 August 1982, pp. 7-10.

Bhambhri, C.P., "Ideology and Political Parties in India", Economic and Political weekly, vol.3(16), 20 April 1968, pp.643-46.

.........................., "Lok Sabha elections, January, 1980 : Ideas on foreign policy in the election manifestoes", International studies, vol.19(2), : April-June 1980, pp.243-52.

.........................., "USA and India : conflict and convergence", Mainstream, vol.20(46),: 17 July 1982 pp.7-10.

.........................., "Relevance of the Summit", Link, vol.25(8), 3 October 1982, pp. 10-11.

........................., "Whither national parties?", Link, vol.25(9), 10 October 1982, pp.7-8.

........................., "India's Foreign Policy", Social Scientist, 113, October 1982, pp.51-55.

........................., "India : self-reliance, the safeguard", World Focus, 5(8) (56), August 1984, pp.33-36.

........................., "Imperialism in India", Social Scientist, vol.13(2), February 1985, pp.38-45.

........................., "Perspective on Indo-American relations", Mainstream, vol.24(20), 18 January 1986, pp. 13-15.

........................., "United States and India", World Focus,vol.12(3), March 1991, pp.9-11.

Bhargav, G.S., "Soviet Connection", Janata (Annual Number), vol.42(1) : January 1987, pp.29-30.

Bhattacharya, S.S., "Geo-Political importance of the Indian Ocean", Strategic Analysis, vol.14(7), October 1991, pp.803-24.

"BIG help towards self-reliance", Link, vol.23(17), 7 December 1980, p.27.

Bipan Chandra, "BJP-RSS and Nationalism", Link, vol,34(9), 13 October 1991, pp.8-9.

Bogdanov, Yuri, "New landmarks in USSR-India relations", Socialism : Principles, practice, prospects, (1), January 1989, pp.35-36.

Bose, Deb Kumar, "India's options in nuclear world", Econom ic and Political Weekly, vol.20(38), September 21, 1985, pp. 1594-96.

Chadda, Maya, "India and the United States : Why detente won't happen", Asian Survey, vol.26(10), October 1986, pp.1118-36.

Chakravarthy, Nikhil, "Indo-US perspective : A historical overview", Man and Development, vol.7(3), September 1985, pp.56-67.

........................., "Evolution of foreign policy", Word Focus, vol.8 (11-12), November-December 1987, pp.49-51.

........................., " Evolution of Indian Foreign Policy", World Focus, vol.9(8), August 1988, pp.12-14.

Chakravarty, Sumit, "Indo-Soviet relations : Rethinking old assumptions", Mainstream, vol.29(27), 27 April 1991, pp.33-35.

Chatterji, Rakhahari, "Democracy and the opposition in India", Economic and Political Weekly, vol.23(17), April 23, 1988, pp. 843-47.

Chopra, Pran, "New politics and the US" Monthly Commentary, vol.31(11), June 1990, pp. 9-10.

Choudhary, Sukhbir, "Can India maintain equidistance from the Super Powers?" India Quarterly, vol.37(4), October-December 1981, pp. 583-89.

Clemmons, Byard Q., "Military justice in India and the United States : A comparison", Strategic Analysis, vol.12(2), May 1989, pp.205-30.

Cohen, Stephen Phillip, "Right for the right reasons? The Reagan administration and India", India International Centre Quarterly. vol. 15(2), Summer 1988. pp.31-41.

.........................., "India and America : Towards a realistic relationship"? Asian Affairs, vol.15(4), Winter 1988-89, pp.197-93.

Damodaran, A.K., "Non-Alignment and India's Foreign Policy", Indian and Foreign Review, vol.20(15), 15 May 1983, pp.7-9.

.........................., "Indo-US relations : Perceptions and dilem mas", Man and Development, vol.8(2), June 1986, pp. 9-20.

Dhanjal, Gursharan Singh, "Security factor in Indo US relations", Mainstream, vol.27(26), 25 March 1989, pp.15-18.

Dias, Jessica Theresa, "Indo-Soviet relations : Changing trends and their regional impact", Pakistan Horizon, vol.42 (3-4), October 1989, pp.68-80.

Dixit, Aabha, "India and her neighbours : Mixed success", Link, vol.33(1), 12 August 1990, pp.6-10.

Dixit, J.N., "India's Foreign Policy", Strategic Analysis, vol, 13(12), March 1991, pp.1387-1410.

Doctor, Adi H., "India's Indian Ocean Policy", Indian Journal of Political Science, vol.51(3), July-September 1990, pp. 36079.

Dutt, R.C., "Soviet Union and India", Mainstream, vol.26(22), 12 March 1988, p.6.

"Principled foreign policy", Mainstream, vol.29(32), 1 June 1991, p.6.

"Economic Cooperation with United States," Southern Econo mist, vol.20(5), 1 July 1981, pp.4-5.

"Economic frictions, conflicts", Link, vol.23(23), 18 January 1981, pp.10-12.

Elkin, Jerrold F. and Ritezel W. Andrew, "Debate on restruc turing

India's higher defence organisation", Asian Survey, vol.24(10), October 1984, pp.1069-85.

Flalkovsky, Andrei, "USSR-India : Together into the third millennium", International Affairs, (12), December 1988, pp.3-7.

Frankel, Francine R., "Play the India card", Foreign Policy, vol.(62), Spring 1986, pp.148-66.

Gandhi, Rajiv, "Address to UNSSOD III", Strategic Digest vol.18(8), August 1988, pp.1033-39.

Ganguly, Shivaji, "India's foreign Policy initiatives, "India Quarterly, vol.41(3-4), July-December 1985, pp.390-400.

Garner, John W., "Indian factor in recent Sino-Soviet relations", China Quarterly, (125), March 1991, pp. 55-85.

Gehlot, N.S., "Opposition in Indian Political System : Problem of role perception", Indian Journal of Political Science, vol. 46(93), July-September 1985, pp.330-52.

Georgeiv, V., "Soviet-Indian Cooperation : Tangible results and broad prospects", International Affairs, (8), August 1985, pp.23-29.

........................., "Event of historic significance", International Affairs, (1), January 1987, pp.20-27.

Ghosh, Partha S., "Non alignment and India", Third World vol.1, January-February 1984, pp.4-7.

Glebov, Ivan, "USSR and India : cooperation in the interests of progress and peace", International Affairs, (2), February 1988, pp. 26-32.

Ganslaves, Eric, "Changing international order : Foreign Policy dimensions", Mainstream , vol.27(18), January 28, 1989, pp. 47-50.

Gorbachev, Mikhail, Speeches (extracts), Foreign Affairs Report, vol.37(9-10-11), September-November 1988, pp.124-40.

Gorbachev-Rajiv Gandhi quest for world peace", Foreign Affairs Report, vol.37(9-10), September-November 1988, pp.65-156.

Goyal, D.R., "RSS attempt to Hinduise politics", Secular Democracy, November 1983, pp.3-10.

........................., "Confluence of Volga Ganga", Secular Democ racy, vol.19(11), November 1986, pp. 6-9.

Gupta, Amit, "Indian arms industry: a Lumbering giant?", Asian Survey, 30(9), September 1990, pp.46-61.

Gupta , Anirudha, "Living with neighbours : Which way?", Economic and Political Weekly, vol.25(7-8), February 17-24, 1990, pp. 371-72.

Gupta, N.L., "BJP vision of India", Link, vol.34(8), 6 October 1991, pp.4-8.

Haksar, P.N., "New dimensions of Indo-Soviet relations", Mainstream, vol.25(11), 22 November 1986, pp.16-18.

Hardgrave, Robert L., "Why India matters : The challenge to American Policy in South Asia", Asian Affairs, vol.11(1), Spring 1984, pp.45-56.

Hari Kumar K.N., "Trading Non-alignment for high tech Rajiv's record US visit", Economic and Political Weekly, vol.23(17), 23 April 1988, pp.848-53.

.........................., "Rajiv and the US : Trading non-alignment for hi-tech?" Mainstream, vol.26(29), 30 April 1988, pp.17-26.

Harison Selig S., "India and United States : Opportunities and dangers", Mainstream, vol.23(31), 30 March 1985, pp.17-22.

Horn, R.C. "Afghanistan and the Soviet-Indian Influence Friendship", Asian Survey, vol.23(3), March 1983, pp.244-60.

"India and The Super Powers" India International Centre Quarterly, vol.12(1), March 1985, pp.43-64.

"India and the World : Towards the Year 2000", World Focus, vol.7(11-12), November-December 1986, pp.3-88.

"India'S role in shaping international relations", Reprint From the Soviet Press, vol.37(1), 30 November 1983, pp.36-42.

Indian Institute of Foreign Trade, "Import and Export Policy of India (April 1985-March 1988) : Salient Features", Foreign Trade Review, vol.XIX, No.4, January-March 1985, pp.595-614.

"Indira Gandhi's Keynote address at commemorative session of twentieth anniversary of Non-aligned countries in New Delhi on February 11, 1981", Forign Affairs Record, vol.27(2), February 1981, pp.63-65.

"Indira's US visit : some reflections", Mainstream, vol.20(51), 21 August 1982, pp.4-5.

"Indo-Soviet Relations : Towards a better future", Foreign Affairs Report, vol.35(11-12), November-December 1986, pp.1-67.

"Indo-Soviet relations : A saga of friendship", World Focus, vol.8(4), April 1987, pp.3-32.

Jaya Ramu, P.S., "Trends in world politics and the challenges to Indian Foreign Policy", Indian Journal of Political Science, vol.52(2), April-June 1991, pp.185-94.

Jha, L.K., "Indo-US relations : Changing Perspective", Man and Development, vol.7(3), September 1985, pp.39-45.

.........................., "Indo-US Relations Changing perspectives", Man and Development, vol.7(3) September 1985, pp.39-45.

Jha, S.K., "Ties with India", World Focus, vol.11(9), September 1990, pp.15-18.

Josh, Harcharan Singh, "India, Soviet Union and world peace", Foreign Affairs Report, vol.37(9-10-11), September-November 1988, pp.65-69.

Kamath, P.M., "Politics and National Security : American influence on Indian thinking', Indian Defence and Strategic Analysis, vol.16(3), January-March 1984, pp.273-85.

Kanjilal, Tanmoy, "Outside interference in South Asia and the perception of India, Pakistan and Nepal", Asian Studies, vol.7(4), October-December 1989, pp.15-40.

Kapur, Ashok, "Indian Foreign Policy : Perspectives and Present Predicaments, Round Table, (295), July 1985, pp.230-39.

Kapur, Harish, "India's Foreign Policy under Rajiv Gandhi", Round Table, (304), October 1987, pp.469-80.

Kaul, P.K., "Widening and consolidating Indo-US relations", Economic Times (supplement), 4 July 1987, pp.1 and 4-5.

Kaul, T.N. "Indo-US relations", Man and Development, vol.7(3), September 1985, pp.46-55.

.........................., "INF agreement, nuclear disarmament and India",Man and development, vol.10(1), March 1988, pp.12-26.

.........................., Personal view of the Soviet Union through forty years",International Affairs, vol.(7), July 1988, pp.117-24.

Khan, A., "Dragon's teeth of BJP", Mainstream, vol.29(25); 13 April 1991, pp.19-20.

Khan, R., "Fall out in India : US-Pak-China axis", World Focus, vol.4, No.20, August 1983, pp.30-36.

.........................., "Peace and Security in nuclear age", Secular Democracy, vol.19(11), November 1986, pp.11- 14.

Khanam, I., "Indo-Soviet relations", Indian Journal of Politics, vol.18 (3&4), September-December 1984, pp.117-28.

Kidwai, M.S., "Kashmir as a factor in Indo-Soviet relations", Indian Journal of Politics, vol.18(3&4), September-December 1984, pp.39-46.

Corneev, Victor L., "Indo-Soviet relations : Expanding economic ties", Commerce, vol.143(3665), 12 September 1981, pp.459-62.

Korovikov, V. "USSR-India : Landmarks of friendship", Reprints from the Soviet Press, vol.38(7), April 15, 1984, pp.48-50.

Kothari, M.K., "Pressures on India's Foreign Policy", Marxist, vol.6(3-4), July-December 1988, pp.67-73.

Kreisberg P.H., "India after Indira", Foreign Affairs, vol.63(4), Spring 1985, pp.873-91.

Krish nan, N., "Positive Contributions at the UN", World Focus, vol.8 (11-12), November-December 1987, pp.56-60.

Lall, John S., "Foreign Policy in Focus", Mainstream, vol.22(33), April 14, 1984, pp.21-23.

Leonidov, M., "New aspects of the USA's Policy towards India", International Affairs,(8), August 1986, pp.112-15.

Malhotra, Inder, "India and the Non-aligned movement", World Focus, vol.6(9), September 1985, pp.,29-31.

Mansingh, Surjit, "Reluctant duo : What India expected of America", Asian Affairs, vol.15(4), Winter 1988-89, pp.204-11.

Mathew, George, "Should India go nuclear?", Radical Human ist, vol.49(5), August 1985; pp.31-35.

Mehta, Jagat S., "Revitalising India's foreign policy", Monthly Commentary on Indian Economic Conditions, vol.26(5), December 1984, pp.47-50.

........................., "United or divided by their democracies?" Mainstream , vol.23(41), 8 June 1985, pp.4-5 and 29-31.

Milhollin, Gary, "Dateline New Delhi : India's nuclear Cover-up", Foreign Policy, (64), Fall 1986, pp.161-75.

........................., "Stopping the Indian bomb", American Jour nal of International Law, vol.81(3), July 1987, pp.593-609.

Mishra, B.N., "US Strategy in the Indian Ocean : India's perception and response", Asia Pacific Community, (18), Fall 1982, pp.64-79.

Misra, K.P., "India's non-alignment and the Indo-Soviet Treaty", Biiss Journal, vol.4(2), April 1983, pp.39-47.

.........................., "Indo_American relations divergences out weigh convergences", Man and Devel, vol.7(3), September 1985, pp.68-78.

.........................., "Strengthening non-alignment", World Focus, vol.8(11-12), November-December 1987, pp.53-55.

Mithaltin, Gary, "Stopping the Indian bomb", American journal of International Law, vol.81(3), July 1987, pp.593-609.

Mittal, L.S., "Indo-American relations: Recent trends", Journal of Political Studies, vol.16(1), February 1983, pp.1-16.

Mukherjee, Dillip, "Indo-Soviet economic ties", Problems of Communism, vol. 36(1), January-February 1987, pp.13- 24.

.........................., "Challenge to Foreign Policy", Seminar., (377), January 1991 (Annual), pp. 52-54.

Muni, S.D., "Indo-US relations : The Pakistan factor", Man and Development, vol.8(3), September 1986, pp.9-27.

Murthy, C.S.R., "India and the dead-locked zone of peace in the Indian Ocean", Indian Defence and Strategic Analysis, vol.17(1), July-September 1984, pp.87-100.

Narasimha Rao, P.V., "Threat to India real", I ink, vol.24(24), 26 January 1982, pp.7-8.

Nayar, Kuldip, "Russia wrong or right", Seminar (265), September 1981, pp.34-38.

Nehru, B.K., Indian-American relationship", Man and Develop ment, vol.7(3), September 1985, pp.25-38.

"New Delhi-Moscow-Washington : Indicators for Indian foreign policy",world Focus, (67), July 1985, pp.3-24.

Noorani, A.G., "History of the BJP (1989-1990)", Mainstream, vol.29(23), 30 March 1991, pp.7-11.

Oldenburg, Philip, "India and the United States : Accidental or Inevitable antagonists?", Asian Affairs, vol. 15(4), winter 1988-89, pp.220-29.

Paranjpee, Shrikant, "India's nuclear status: A Policy note", Asian Affairs, vol. 13(2), Summer 1986, pp.56-60.

Parasher, S.C. "Gorbachev visit to India : A historical perspective", India Quarterly, vol.42(4), October- December 1986, pp. 447-58.

.........................., "Indo-Soviet relations : Historical per spectives", Foreign Affairs Reports, vol.37(9-11), September-November 1988, pp.70-80.

Parthasarathy, G., "India and non-alignment", Mainstream, (22), Annual Number, 1984, pp. 15-18.

Parthasarathy, M., "Prospects of new neighbourhood Policy", Mainstream, vol.28(16), 10 Feb 1990, pp.5-6.

Pareecha, R.S., "India's role as regional coordinator", Link, vol.33(27), 10 February 1991, pp.10-11.

Pasricha, P.M., "India's current strategic environment", Strategic Analysis, vol.8(8), November 1984, pp.711-15.

Patel, J.K., "India and regional cooperation", Review of International Affairs, vol.41(963), 20 May 1990, pp.19-21.

Poulose, T.T., :India and the Indian Ocean : changing strategic perspectives", Asia Pacific Community, (29), Summer 1985, pp. 131-39.

Puri, Balraj, "Growth and decline of party system in India", Radical Humanist, 51(5) (221), August 1988, pp.43-46.

Raja Mohan, C., "India's nuclear diplomacy : The need for clarity", Strategic Analysis, vol.9(11), February 1986, pp.1076-87.

.........................., "US-Pakistan strategic consensus and India", Strategic Analysis, vol. 11(12), March 1987, pp.1375-90.

"Indo-Soviet efforts to restructure world order", Mainstream, vol.27(8), 19 November 1988, pp.15-19.

Rajan, M.S., and Joshi, N., "Soviet Union and India's nuclear policy", Mainstream, vol.28(40), 28 July 1990, pp.15-17.

Ramchandran, K.N., "India, China and the Superpowers", India Defence and Strategic Analysis, vol.19(1), July- September 1986, pp.140-52.

Ramesh Babu, B., "Mutual carping to reciprocal restraint and beyond : Speculations on the future of Indo-US rela tions", Indian journal of American Studies, vol.13(1), January 1983. pp.107-18.

Razvi, Mujtaba S.M., "India and the Security of Indian Ocean/South Asian States", Round Table (311), July 1989, pp.317-22.

Reshma, "Indo-Soviet relations and the Pakistan factor", Indian journal of Politics, vol.21(1-2), March-June 1987, pp.72-77.

Rodionov, N., "Brezhnev's package : The details", Eastern Economy, vol. 76(7), 13 February 1981, pp.459-60.

Rothermund, Indira, "Gandhi and the Reflective foreign policy of Nehru". Gandhi Marg, vol.11(4), January- March 1990, pp.421-29.

Rubinoff, Arthur G., "Multilateral imperative in India's foreign policy", Round Table, (319), July 1991, pp.313-34.

Sahay, Vikant, "Is India a Big Brother?", Mainstream, vol.28(17), 17 February 1990, pp.29-30.

Samaddar, Ranabir, "India's Foreign Policy : A hiertherto ignored aspect", Asian Studies, vol.7(4), October- December 1989, pp.1-14.

Sardesai, S.G., "Some thoughts on the BJP", Mainstream, vol.28(38), 14 July 1990, p.7.

........................., "Dialogue with the BJP", Mainstream, vol. 28(43), 18 August 1990, p.10 and p.34.

Sarma, Amarendra, "Role of Opposition in the Indira legislature", Journal of Parliamentary Information, vol.31(4), December 1985, 566-70.

Sen, Abhimanyu, "India's foreign policy", Marxist, vol.5(2-3), April-September 1987, pp. 82-114.

Sen Gupta, Bhabani, "Supplying with neighbours", Economic and Political Weekly, vol.25(10), 10 March 1990, pp.475-78.

Sethi, J.D., "Challenge before the Opposition", Mainstream vol.XXVI (40), 16 July 1988, pp.7-11.

Shah, Rajiv, "Beginning of a change", LINK, vol.32(51), 29 July 1990, pp.4-8.

Sharma, M.L., "BJP to BHP : Old wine new bottle", Third Concept, vol.4(50-51), April-May 1991, pp.59-62.

Sharma, Narendra, "Whither BJP?" Mainstream, vol.29(17), 16 February 1991, pp.4-5.

Sharma, Pushpa, "Paradoxical nature of Indo-US relations", Mainstream, vol.24(11), 14 June 1986, pp.29-34.

Sharma, Ritu, "India's Soviet Connection : A Changing para dign of Eco-strategic dimension", Strategic Analy sis, vol.13(6), September 1990, pp.675-686.

Sharma, S.K., "Indo-American relations : why non chalance?" Journal of Political Studies, vol.18(1), February 1985; pp.36-44.

.........................., "Indo-American relations in the 1980's : A theoretical perspective", Asian Profile, vol.13(6), December 1985, pp.11-22.

Sharma, T.R. "Estimating political parties' Strength : A plea for an alternative ", Political Science Review, vol.21(2-3), April-September 1982, pp.225-42.

Shaumian, Tatiana, "Stability of Indo-Soviet relation", Mainstream, vol.25(11), 22 November 1986, pp.32-33.

.........................., "India's foreign policy : Interaction of global and regional aspects", Asian Survey, vol.28(11), November 1988, pp.1160-69.

Shrivastava, B.K., "Indo-US relations : Search for mature and constructive ties", India Quarterly, vol. VII(1), January-March 1985, pp.1-5.

Singh, Kuldip, "Politics of Soviet arms supplies to India, 1955-72", Journal of Political Studies, vol.21(1), February 1988, pp.84-91.

Singh, Jasjit, "External threats to Security", World Focus, vol.8(11-12), November-December 1987, pp, 39-42.

.........................., "Indian Security : A framework for national strategy", Strategic Analysis, vol. 12(8), November 1987, pp.885-90.

.........................., "External threats to Security", World Focus, vol.8(11-12), November-December 1987, pp.39-42.

...., "India's strategic and security perspec tives", Strategic Analysis, vol.13(5), August 1990, pp.475-501.

.........................., "Managing nuclear challenge", Strategic Analysis, vol.14(6), September 1991, pp.633-44.

Singh, R.M., "25 years of Indo-Soviet economic cooperation", Indian economic Almanac, vol.1(1), December 1980, pp.48-51.

Singh, Ravinder Pal, "Indo-Soviet military cooperation : Experiences, trends and opportunities", Strategic Analysis, vol.13(9), December 1990, pp.1081-99.

Singh, Satyavir, "Nuclear threat to India : The Indian Ocean front", Foreign Affairs Report, vol.39(6), June 1990, pp.75-84.

Singh, S. Nihal, "Why India goes to Moscow for arms", Asian Survey, vol.24(7), July 1984, pp.707-20.

.........................., "Can the US and India be real friends?" Asian Survey, vol.23(9), September 1983, pp.1011-24'.

Sinha, S.K., "Our Nuclear Compulsions", Radical Humanist, vol.49(5), August 1985, pp.23-25.

Sisson, Richard and Vanderbok, William, " Mapping the Indian electorate-II : Patterns of weakness in the Indian party system", Asian Survey, vol.24(10), October 1984, pp.1086-97.

"Soviet-Indian Summit statement", Strategic Digest, vol.19(1), January 1989, pp.1-4.

Subramaniam, K., "India's Security : present and future", Strategic Analysis, vol.8(7), October 1984, pp.634-39.

.........................., "Security issue in South Asia", Strategic Analysis, vol.9(9), December 1985, pp.827-39.

.........................., "India's security challenges and responses : Evolving a security doctrine", Strategic Analysis, vol.12(1), April 1987, pp.1-12.

.........................., "Indian Security Perspectives". Strategic Analysis, vol.21(5), August 1987, pp.511-24.

.........................., "Indian security environment", World Focus (Annual Number), vol.10(11-12), November-December 1990, pp.33-36.

Subramaniam, R.R., "Indo-US security relations during the decade 1979-89", Strategic Analysis, vol.14(2), May 1991, pp.163-72.

"Text of Indo-Soviet joint declaration", Economic Times, 27 September 1982, pp.925-8.

"Text of Indo-Soviet Joint statement", Monthly Public Opin ion Surveys, 34(3)(399), December 1988, pp.5-8.

Thomas, Raju G.C., "Prospects for Indo-US security ties", Orbis, vol.27(2), Summer 1983, pp.371-92.

.........................., India's nuclear and space programs : De fence or development?", World Politics, vol.38(2), January 1986, pp. 315-42.

Thornton, Thomas R., "Gorbachev's courtship of India : India and the Soviet Union", Round Table,(304), October 1987, pp.457-68.

Trakru, Manohar, "Indo-US relations : An assessment", Indian Foreign Review, vol.19(20), 1 August 1982, pp.9-10.

Travis, Thorn A., "United States -India relations : Obstacles and opportunities", India Quarterly, vol.42(4), October-December 1986, pp.381-90.

Tripathi, Deepak, "India's foreign policy : The Rajiv factor", World Today, vol.44(7), July 1988, pp.112-14.

"USSR-India : New Frontiers Cooperation", Socialism: Theory and Practice, (2) (151), February 1986, pp.99-104.

Vajpayee, Anil Kumar, "Emergence of the BJP : Confusion regarding causes", Indian Journal of Political studies, vol.51(4), October-December 1990, pp.491-506.

Varilov, V., "Solid foundations of Soviet-Indian relations", Secular Democracy, vol.19(11), November 1986, pp.35-42.

Varma, S.P., "Domestic roots of India's foreign policy", International studies, vol.24(2), April-June 1987. pp..145-50.

Vasudevan, Parvathi, "Prospects for non-alignment : India's role", India Quarterly, vol.39(1), January-March 1983, pp.50-62.

Vinod, M.J., "Images of India in the United States : Retro spect and prospect", Indian Journal of Political Science, vol.50(3), July-September 1989, pp.376-88.

.........................., "Attitudes towards India: contrasting approaches of the United States and the Soviet Union", India Quarterly, vol.46(1), January-March 1990, pp.17-46.

Viswam, S., "Indo-US Relations: Assertion of pragmatism", Mainstream, vol.20(47), 24 July 1982, pp.6-8.

.........................., ''Confusion in Opposition politics", Main stream, vol.22(35), 28 April 1984, pp.5-6 & 33.

.........................., ''No high expectations", Mainstream, vol.23(41), 8 June 1985, pp.8-14.

Vyas, P.S. "Indian Foreign Policy : An Overview", Strategic Analysis, vol.10(1), April 1986, pp.23-29.

Wariavawalla, Bharat, "Stagnant Indo-Soviet relation", Strategic Analysis vol.9(4), July 1985, pp.310-13.

Wirsing, Robert G., "Soviet relations with Pakistan and India Prospects for change", Strategic Studies, vol.13(2), Winter 1989, pp.52-71.

Wood, Glynn L. and Vaagenes, Daniel, "Indian defence policy A new phase", Asian Survey, vol.24(7), July 1984, pp.721-35.

Yadav, R.S., "Future of Indo-Soviet treaty in changing environment", Mainstream, vol. 29(42), 10 August 1991, p.25.

News Papers

Amrit Bazar Patrika (Calcutta).

Blitz (Bombay).

Deccan Herald(Banglaore).

Economic Times (New Delhi).

Financial Express (Bombay).

Hindu (Madras).

Hindusatan Times (New Delhi).

Holiday (Dacca).

Indian Express (New Delhi).

International Herald Tribune (Paris).

Izvestia (Moscow).

Los Angeles Times (Los Angeles).

Muslim (Lahore).

National Herald (New Delhi).

News Time (Hyderabad).

New York Times (New York).

Novosti (Moscow).

Patriot (New Delhi).

Pravda (Moscow).

Soviet Land (Moscow).

Soviet News (Moscow).

Statesman (New Delhi).

Telegraph (Calcutta).

Tribune (Chandigarh).

The Times (London).

Times of India (New Delhi).

Washington Post (Washington).

Journals

American Journal of International Law (Washington).

Asian Affairs (London).

Asia Pacific Community(Tokyo).

Asian Recorder (New Delhi).

Asian Studies (Calcutta).

Asian Survey (California).

Biiss Journal (Dhaka).

China Report (New Delhi).

Commerce (Bombay).

Conflict Studies (London).

Economic and Political Weekly (Bombay).

Foreign Affairs (New York).

Foreign Affairs Record (New Delhi).

Foreign Policy (Washington).

Foreign Trade Review (New Delhi).

Indian Quarterly (New Delhi).

Indian Defence and strategic Studies (New Delhi). Indian and Foreign Review (New Delhi).

Indian Economic Review (New Delhi).

Indian Journal of Political Science (New Delhi). International Affairs (Moscow).

International Studies Quarterly (Colombia).

International Studies (New Delhi).

Link (New Delhi).

Mainstream (New Delhi).

Man and Development (Chandigarh).

Marxist (New Delhi).

Monthly Commentary on Indian Economic Conditions (New Delhi).
Monthly Public Opinion Surveys (New Delhi).
Orbis (Philadelphia).
Organiser (New Delhi).
Problems of Communism (Washington).
Radical Humanist (New Delhi).
Round Table (London).
Secular Democracy (New Delhi).
Seminar (New Delhi).
Social Scientist (New Delhi).
Socialism : Theory and Practice (Moscow).
Southern Economist (Banglarore).
Soviet Review (New Delhi).
Span (USIS, New Delhi).
Strategic Analysis (New Delhi).
Strategic Studies (New Delhi).
World Affairs (Washington).
World Development (Washington).
World Focus (New Delhi).
World Literature Today (Oklahoma, Norman).
World Marxist Review (London).
World Meetings (New York).
World Policy Journal (New York).
World Politics (Princeton).
World Review (Queensland, Australia).
World Today (London).

Index